Beyond Hierarchy:
Gender, Sexuality and the
Social Economy

Sarah Oerton

Taylor & Francis
Publishers since 1798

UK	Taylor & Francis Ltd, 1 Gunpowder Square, London EC4A 3DE
USA	Taylor & Francis Inc., 1900 Frost Road, Suite 101, Bristol, PA 19007

First published 1996

A Catalogue Record for this book is available from the British Library

ISBN 0 7484 0352 3 (cloth)
ISBN 0 7484 0353 1 (paper)

Library of Congress Cataloging-in-Publication Data are available on request

Typeset in 10/12 pt Times Roman
by Best-set Typesetter Ltd, Hong Kong

Printed in Great Britain by SRP Ltd, Exeter

Gender, Change & Society: 4

Beyond Hierarchy

For my parents,
Ena and Peter Oerton

Acknowledgments

I am indebted to many friends and colleagues for their support at various stages of the research for and writing of this book. I should like to thank Helen Brown, Margaret Greico, Mary Mellor, Roger Spear and Alan Thomas for their helpful comments on earlier rough drafts of my work. The support and advice received from my doctoral supervisor, Chris Cornforth and others in the School of Management, at the Open University, have gone a long way to helping me complete this research. I would like to thank Chris in particular for his comments, interest and encouragement. I was also supported financially by the Open University, which has provided me with a stimulating environment in which to work over the years. For a woman researcher working in a pre-dominantly male-dominated university department, feminist support was indispensable. Jo Phoenix and Sasha Roseneil provided me with sympathetic intellectual and political responses to the research and Gill Kirkup and Sylvia Walby offered some constructive input into the process of reworking some of my ideas, particularly in the final stages.

The writing of this book has been a long, involved process and as acknowledgments conventionally contain mention of the writer's family, I should like to thank Janet Oerton, Erin Oerton and Meryl Gaskill who have inevitably engaged in my pattern of work over the last few years. Several other friends and colleagues have also sustained and distracted me through the most trying periods involved in the writing of the book, and I should like to thank AlisonTindall, Jane Gardner, Karen Atkinson and Gill Plain for their friendship and various forms of hospitality. Other women friends have been there for me since the early days of my research and writing, in particular Sue Wright, Laura O'Mahony, Yasmin Mahmud and Gaynor Harper. Karin Richards also helped with the typing and checking of the References section, and I should like to thank her for her careful and detailed work. Finally, I would like to thank all the co-operative and collective workers interviewed for this research – for their time, patience, humour and willingness to assist in the research. To preserve their anonymity, all the names of the workers, their co-workers and the organizations for which they worked at the time of interview have been altered to protect them. Having said that, these are still their stories and I trust I have represented them fairly.

Sarah Oerton
July 1996

Contents

Part I

Chapter 1

Introduction

For some time now there has been a growing interest in the social economy, largely understood as a non-profit or third sector distinct from both the public (statutory) and the private (business) sectors of the economy and comprising, amongst other things, co-operative businesses, campaigning and social movement organizations, mutual aid societies and non-profit, voluntarily-managed associations and groups (Cornforth and Hooker, 1989; Paton, 1991; Taylor 1986; Thomas and Thomas, 1989). This interest in the social economy has been relatively recent however, and there is still much scope for research, particularly in terms of identifying both the distinctiveness and diversity of the sector, as well as looking at how it is constituted in organizational terms. To date, this is a contested project largely because there is no single definition of the social economy that translates easily from location to location. For some, the social economy is often collapsed or elided with the voluntary sector, which itself has been described as a 'rag-bag', containing every type of organization not included in either the public or private sectors of the economy and having no one internal defining feature of its own (Hatch, 1980). However, in general terms the social economy is usually understood to comprise value-based organizations orientated towards the provision of some kind of common benefit or public good, rather than the generation of (private) profit. For example, Paton argues that value-based organizations 'whose members share a strong commitment to a common cause, be it organic gardening, scouting, assisting those with AIDS or feminism' are the '*heartland*' of the social economy (Paton, 1991: 6, emphasis added).

Although the organizational principles and practices of the social economy may not always be as clearly developed or articulated as those of the public and private sectors, much of what legitimately constitutes the social economy includes large, bureaucratized organizations, with leaders who exercise power and control over subordinates. However, at the same time as there has been a growth of academic interest in the social economy, there has also been much more acknowledgment in the mainstream literature on work and organizations of the need to 'de-layer', to encourage *flatter*, *less* or *non-hierarchical* ways of organizing in all sectors of the economy, and particularly in cases where enterprises are small to medium-sized.[1] In short, it is recognized that there is much value in seeking to reduce power

differentials between members/workers within organizational settings in order
to reduce or eliminate unnecessary hierarchy. This has involved promoting
working practices in many organizations which emphasize collaboration,
flexibility and networking. As Ashbridge Management Research Group
(1988) claim:

> Organizations in future will be ... 'flatter' and more fluid in struc-
> ture, and more fast-moving ... The need to manage issues
> across ... the organization will lead to the growing importance of
> 'horizontal' management [i.e. the management of lateral relation-
> ships] as opposed to 'vertical' management [i.e. the management of
> hierarchical relationships] (Ashbridge, 1988: 37).

One of the central platforms for flatter organization is the devolution of power
and control, so that instead of a small number of full-time managers planning
and controlling the activities of many workers, organizations now require the
collaboration of many specialists who have a significant managerial component to their work and have to be involved in decisions. Hence modern firms
are conceived of as necessarily becoming more participative in terms of sharing power and as having to rely increasingly on a common culture to ensure
integration and commitment.

Whereas flatter, less or non-hierarchical organization cannot be used as a
defining feature of the social economy since in some cases performing the
organization's task may be controlled through bureaucratic procedures and
hierarchical structures not dissimilar from those of conventional public or
private sector organizations, nevertheless participative, consultative and
democratic forms of management have special importance for organizations in
the social economy, because of their origins as associations with socially
beneficial goals. This means that having a flatter, less or non-hierarchical
organizational structure may be integral to the way tasks are carried out in
order to ensure that the social goals of the organization are realized. In short,
there is a necessary overlap between *how* they organize and *what* they are
trying to achieve.[2] If social goals or values include some commitment to
participation and democracy, an organization is more or less bound to intro-
duce co-operative and collective ideals into its working practices. It is these
organizations that are of central concern in this book.

Across a range of non-profit businesses and voluntarily-managed, grant-
aided organizations in the social economy, workers have sought to organize in
ways which reflect their beliefs about private ownership, returns on capital,
and the efficacy of traditional management hierarchies. Such workers are to be
found in flatter, less or non-hierarchical organizations which, in principle, at
least, allow them to have greater power and control over their work than might
be the case in more hierarchical organizations. For the most part this has
meant adopting a co-operative or collective structure, and, in the case of some

women, working in women-only organizations.[3] It is remarkable that flatter organizations have attracted so little academic interest until recently, even though they have been central to the political project of feminism for some considerable time (Brown, 1990; Fried, 1994; Martin, 1990; Rothschild, 1990). In order to explore this neglect it is necessary to briefly review some of the background to the emergence of co-operative and collective forms of organization in the period of second-wave feminism.

Feminism and Flatter Organizations

Historically there have been many attempts by women to promote flatter forms of organization, including worker co-operatives, social movement organizations and some collective voluntary sector projects, where differences between members can be overcome so as to reduce or eliminate hierarchy (Gould, 1980; Kanter, 1975; Rothschild-Whitt, 1979). Such organizations may be seen as archetypes for the democratic, participatory groups characteristic of second-wave feminism, where values of autonomy, flexibility, collaboration and equality are stressed. Furthermore, in the 1970s and early 1980s, many feminists believed that collective and co-operative working was not just the way to organize politically, but was also the solution to hierarchy and class, race and gender inequalities in waged and unwaged work.

Both co-operatives and collectives therefore have been informed by and inform feminist politics. For example, Thornley (1981) noted the influence of feminism among the 'new co-operators' in Britain from the 1960s onwards and Jackall and Crain (1984) found that over 60 per cent of co-operators in small co-operatives in the United States were women. Furthermore, almost half the co-operatives sampled in their study were in traditionally feminine sectors of employment (for instance, food-related businesses) and members were mostly young, college-educated and white. Thomas (1990) reports from findings of a 1988 survey of worker co-operatives in the UK that 14 per cent of those co-operatives responding defined themselves as women-only, but his findings do not indicate whether women-only co-operatives differed in terms of the average size of their workforce from mixed-sex co-operatives, or what the proportion of men to women in mixed-sex co-operatives was, so it is difficult to estimate the proportion of women currently employed in the UK worker co-operatives sector. However, it is possible to be fairly confident on the basis of such research, that co-operatives have widespread appeal and support amongst politicized women generally and amongst feminists in particular.

In the early days of second-wave feminism, many women were also attracted to collective working, arguing that it was a desirable and radical way to end (male) power and hierarchy. Women-only collectives, often following in the traditions of women's action and consciousness-raising groups, saw themselves as accountable in terms of feminist principles and politics. In the 1990s, women-only collectives continue to exist and thrive to a greater or lesser degree; there are still a number of collectively-run women's centres in the UK, including black women's centres, rape crisis centres, women's aid centres/offices/refuges, and well-women or women's health centres. There are also a handful of centres for counselling and therapy, women's workshops and lesbian centres. As Trevithick (1987) has stated: 'The existence of these Centres and Helplines highlight how much practical and emotional support women give to each other and the degree to which more and more women are choosing to join or form women-only groups and organizations' (Trevithick, 1987: 1). Efforts by feminists to organize without hierarchy and without leaders is informed by an often clear and coherent *political* analysis therefore, such that the adoption of values of equality and empowerment are seen to arise directly from a feminist analysis of the social order. As Brown argues: 'Organising within the women's movement is thus a conscious political act' (1992: 9).

Flatter organizations may set out as or end up as all-women or women-only. They may be all-women in that no men are available or eligible as prospective workers due to forms of occupational segregation by gender in the labour market, or they may be women-only in that they do not recruit or employ men as part of their overall social and political policies. This book will use the term *women's co-operative* or *women's collective* to encompass both all-women and women-only organizations, and where it is important to distinguish between the two, this will be made explicit. There is a tendency to assume that because of the attempt to flatten the hierarchical structure of these particular organizations, women workers in both women's and mixed-sex co-operatives and collectives will enjoy parity and equality with their men counterparts. This book will demonstrate that this does not necessarily follow and that there is a need to address this explicitly in the literature on the structuring of gender and sexuality in work and in organizations. This is something which has been largely neglected in such research until recently, a point that will be developed more fully in Chapter 2.

This book thus seeks to analyse the experiences of waged workers in flatter organizations, with specific reference to gender and sexuality. Given that one of the characteristics of some of the organizations in the social economy is their flatter, less or non-hierarchical structure, it has been all too easily assumed that such organizations will allow workers to realize goals of equity and empowerment, and that gender and sexuality will make little difference to the experiences of workers within such organizations. Where there is an absence of formal hierarchy, so the argument goes, there is likely to be an absence of gendered and sexualized inequalities, since hierarchy is premised upon divisions which are to an extent constituted by gendering and sexualizing processes and practices. As a result, flatter, less or non-hierarchical organizations such as worker co-operatives and grant-aided or voluntary sector collective organizations, perhaps more than other, larger and more bureaucratized organizations in the social economy (or the public or private sectors for that matter), are seen as places in which it is possible for workers, and women workers in particular, to overcome some of the obstacles associated with inequalities of gender and sexuality in more complex, hierarchical organizations in particular and in the labour market more generally. Whether this is the case or not remains to be seen, and the central concern of this book is to explore the extent to which women and men workers in co-operative and collective organizations do achieve goals of equity and empowerment, or whether they are highly constrained by the environment in which they are located.

This book sets out to explore these assumptions on the basis of collecting and analysing fieldwork data on the experiences of both women and men workers in a cross-section of different co-operative and collective organizations. To some extent the literature on worker co-operatives and collectively-run organizations in the voluntary sector reflects this expectation that gender is not a problem for workers in these organizations. Such organizations have been studied, both theoretically and empirically, by focusing upon a number of social, political, organizational and economic concerns. Issues of gender and sexuality have not been paramount amongst these concerns. As a result, these dimensions of workers' experiences in flatter organizations have been seen as, at worst, totally irrelevant or at best as secondary to their experiences of waged work. Where gender has been explicitly addressed, as in studies of women's co-operatives and women-only collectives (Brown, 1992; Wajcman, 1983), the focus has been upon single-sex organizations, and there has been little research which systematically *compares* men's and women's experiences of waged work in such organizations, and how it informs and is informed by the gender of workers and the gender composition of the organization. This book sets out to remedy this neglect.

The Focus of the Research

The focus of the research undertaken here is to theorize various dimensions of waged work in flatter organizations by means of comparing women's experiences of such settings with that of their men counterparts. The paucity of comparative studies of women's and men's work is largely the result of the high degree of gender segregation by occupation in the labour market (Martin and Roberts, 1984; Rees, 1992). By taking the organization in which workers are situated as the site for analysis, and by approaching the research undertaking with a critical feminist awareness, this book attempts to avoid both the 'gender-blindness' of many organizational studies, and the single-sex concentration of much of the research on gender and work. By focusing upon both women and men workers in flatter organizations, both groups can be studied independently of their occupations, since what this research does is group workers according to their organizational location and not their occupational position.

The scope of the research is thus wide-ranging, since it includes focusing upon a range of occupations, including workers in professional, semi-professional, administrative, technical and creative occupations, as well as workers in skilled and semi-skilled manual occupations. It should be noted that this project is therefore one of a few pieces of research which explicitly set out to analyse experiences of waged work in other than a primarily occupationally-differentiated context. It thus seeks to avoid the single-occupation concentration of much of the theoretical and empirical research upon gender and work. This has important ramifications for the arguments developed in this book, in that the analysis seeks to provide insights into the experiences of a range of men and women workers in widely different occupational categories, but whose commonality lies in their location in flatter organizations, with all that that entails.

The book thus focuses upon specific dimensions of the experience of waged work in flatter organizations, including that of being a *gendered and sexualized* worker as well as that of being a *co-operative or collective* worker, and how the two are conceptually intertwined. The aim is in part, to explore the extent to which flatter organizations reflect and reinforce gendering and sexualizing processes and practices, and the extent to which such organizations can allow workers to overcome inequalities of gender and sexuality. For if such inequalities are to be countered in any organizational or work setting, it might be reasonable to assume that the flatter the hierarchy, the more equality between women and men workers will prevail. By studying women and men workers in these specific social economy organizations, it is not the intention here to confine the analysis to organizational or economic factors alone, but to consider the structural and discursive processes which constitute and inform women and men workers' experiences, their identities and value-orientations. In approaching their experiences in this way, the emphasis is upon the ways in which waged work in flatter, less or non-hierarchical organizations both *constrains* and *empowers* women and men workers in radically different ways.

From the point of view of theory, this approach to the analysis of waged work and the labour market is valuable because it focuses upon both women and men workers in settings where it has been assumed that gender inequalities have less significance. By using flatter organizations as a critical site for analysis, existing theories of gender and sexuality in work, organizational life and the labour market more generally can be critiqued and developed. In summary, in such specific contexts as worker co-operatives or collectively-run project organizations, traditional theories of the relations between gender, sexuality, power, organizations and the labour market may be considered to have less purchase. But it is precisely because such organizations have been viewed unproblematically as settings in which gendering and sexualizing processes and practices are likely to be absent, that there is an urgent need to make them the prime focus here.

The Theoretical Framework

The book develops a number of lines of argument which seek to contribute to the current state of theory on gender, sexuality, work, organizations and the labour market. To begin with, much of this existing theory recognizes that gender inequalities relegate women to an inferior and subordinate position in both waged and unwaged work. There is a wealth of literature on women's experiences of paid employment and household or domestic labour which support this view. As a result, this book addresses as one of its main lines of argument, the proposition that the extent to which workers in flatter organizations can overcome gender inequalities is necessarily constrained and limited. In short, it can be argued that working in a flatter organization does not mean that women workers' experiences will correspond to those of their men counterparts.

This first line of argument draws upon and critiques theories of gender, sexuality and work which are socio-structural in emphasis. Socio-structural theories of women's work, inasmuch as they tend to homogenize women and downplay differences between women, can lead to an expectation that *all* women will be subject to socio-structural gender power relations, even single, middle-class and well-educated women of the kind assumed to predominate in flatter organizations (Goffee and Scase, 1985; Jackall and Crain, 1984). Despite attempts by flatter organizations to enable both women and men workers to create and sustain their waged work on equal terms, it is reasonable to suggest that workers in these organizations will largely have failed to overcome structural and discursive processes and practices which position women and men in unequal economic, social and political power relations to one another. These over-arching structural and discursive constraints will necessarily shape the differential experiences of women and men workers in flatter organizations in ways which reflect and reinforce men's power positions *vis-à-vis* women.

Much of the socio-structural theorizing of gender, sexuality and work has focused upon the extent to which women's waged and unwaged work can be explained in terms of wider socio-structural power relations. Women's work is seen to be characterized by discernible patterns which arise, some have argued, from the structural demands of capitalism. The matter goes deeper than this, however, and some feminists have argued that patterns of women's waged and unwaged work are explicable more in terms of patriarchal power relations and women's subordination to men in the family and elsewhere, than in terms of capital-labour relations of exploitation and appropriation. Some theorists, notably, dual systems theorists, have favoured explanations which incorporate both capitalist and patriarchal power relations. Nevertheless, whatever the emphasis, most socio-structural theories of women's work rest on the premise that women's employment cannot be adequately understood without reference to their domestic or family positions, and this is held by some to be the central pivot upon which women's working lives need to be theorized.

Socio-structural theories suggest that women workers in flatter organizations experience forms of discrimination and disadvantage which do not characterize the experiences of their men counterparts. These inequalities reflect the position that women workers occupy in the wider society *vis-à-vis* men, and it is argued that the extent to which they can be overcome by workers in co-operative and collective organizations is necessarily limited. In other words, the experiences of women and men workers in flatter organizations reflect and even constitute wider gender power relations. Whereas flatter organizations are characterized by an absence of formal hierarchy, they are not independent of nor unaffected by socio-structural and discursive gender power relations, and as a result, it is argued that the extent to which women and men workers in such organizations can overcome these constraints is likely to be highly circumscribed.

On the other hand, it has been suggested that when workers have some degree of power and control, they have greater scope to challenge or negotiate aspects of their working lives. There is some scope for worker's *agency*, allowing for greater resistance and manoeuvre on the part of workers in flatter organizations compared with those working in more complex, hierarchical organizations. But since gendering and sexualizing processes take different forms for women than for men, the extent and form of resistance and manoeuvre is necessarily gender-specific. This second line of argument developed in this book rests on the proposition that working in flatter organizations allows room for manoeuvre and resistance in both women's and men's working lives. Socio-structural and discursive power relations are neither static nor fixed; workers can adopt strategies which can be both challenging and subversive and which bring them tangible benefits. It can be argued that rather than simply reflect and reinforce dominant power relations, women and men workers in flatter organizations destabilize and undermine the socio-structural and discursive constraints which surround them, but since women occupy a different position in the labour market and in the family than men, resistance and manoeuvre for women workers necessarily takes on a different meaning and emphasis than for their men counterparts.

This second line of argument draws upon theories of gender, sexuality and work which focus upon strategy and agency. Socio-structural theories tend to be all-embracing and are sometimes insufficiently grounded in empirical substantiation of their theoretical claims. Workers are not simply passive victims of socio-structural inequalities, it is argued; they can and do develop strategies to overcome the constraints they face in waged and unwaged work. These strategies can be multi-faceted but one such strategy for the feminist project has involved the founding and running of flatter, less or non-hierarchical organizations within which women may find themselves working on equal terms with their men counterparts, or working independently of men altogether. In many cases, women workers have, as committed feminists, created autonomous or separatist women-only organizations which enable them to avoid the more obvious forms of men's power and control over their work. This, it is argued, needs to be examined in terms of the contribution made by such women and by their organizations to a radical agenda for equity and empowerment, and not merely as unworkable, amateur and/or marginalized alternatives to conventional power relations in work and organizational life.

Agency-orientated theories of gender, sexuality and work have dealt with the minutiae of women's working lives, charting, for example, the various work profiles of different groups of women workers, their life-cycles and career expectations. Rather than assuming the primacy of women's subordination in waged work, attention has been given to the commitment and motivation that women show towards their jobs. The detailed nuances of women's workplace cultures have been analysed and women's contradictory positioning within such cultures explored. Sexism and heterosexism within waged work is now firmly on the theoretical and empirical agenda, too. This is largely the result of studies of hidden areas of work, such as the incidence of sexual harassment or the disclosure of lesbian or gay sexuality at work. The consequences for those workers who do not conform to a socially approved heterosexual identity in the workplace have been explored by feminists and others. In recent years, the diffuse rather than top-down forms that power and resistance can take have been considered with particular reference to sexuality, since organizations are now considered to be saturated with the sexual, and for flatter organizations, sexuality may be as much a contested site for the contestation of power and control relations as gender. These are arguments that this book seeks to address alongside considerations of the gendering of worker's experiences of waged work in flatter organizations.

Plan of the Book

The book is divided into two parts; in the first five chapters the theoretical background to the research is set out. Following on from this introduction, the aim of the next four chapters is to locate the main concerns of the book as outlined in this introduction within their theoretical contexts. The review of the literature which follows in Chapters 2, 3, 4, and 5 aims to provide an overview of research on gender and sexuality in organizations and the labour market with two purposes in mind. First, the intention is to examine research which throws light, however indirectly, upon some of the concerns already specified. Second, the intention is to look in particular at any shortcomings that existing research may exhibit and to identify directional pointers as a result, which, it is hoped, will act to set the scene for the analysis of the empirical data presented in Part II.

Part II details the empirical findings of the research; Chapter 6 provides a summary of the methods used to obtain the empirical data, and outlines the sample of workers and the sample of organizations which comprise the study. Chapter 7 presents the findings related to the material and discursive constraints experienced by women and men workers in flatter organizations, Chapter 8 examines how both workers and their organizations are marginalized, albeit in ways which are differentially informed by gender and sexuality, and Chapter 9 highlights some of the ways in which it is possible for workers to resist and challenge wider material and discursive constraints, and in so doing achieve tangible benefits for themselves and their organizations. Finally, Chapter 10 presents the conclusions to the research.

Summary

It should be clear from the arguments presented so far, that the adoption of gender and sexuality as constructs around which to organize an analysis of women and men workers' experiences of waged work in flatter organizations is likely to be extremely fruitful. It is suggested that by means of a comparative study of women and men workers in such organizations, it is possible to focus upon the ways in which gendered and sexualized power relations manifest themselves in that most unlikely of settings – the co-operative or collective organization. Such an approach will be able to highlight those facets of women and men workers' experiences which reflect and confirm inequalities of gender and sexuality and to point to the ways in which women workers are relegated to a subordinate position *vis-à-vis* their male counterparts. It is also able to highlight the ways in which women and men workers in flatter organizations actively engage with such subordination and attempt to challenge and resist gendered and sexualized power relations.

In terms of the importance of this analysis for existing theories of gender, sexuality and work, it is clear that some of the socio-structural arguments advanced to point to the wider economic, social and political power relations which circumscribe women workers as women, are both useful and problematic. In adopting a socio-structural approach alone, difference and diversity may be lost. It is therefore important to pay some attention to the forms of resistance and manoeuvre that women and men workers in flatter organizations engage in, when faced with the constraints imposed upon them by wider gender power relations. This means analysing the data with a fine tooth comb, as it were, to identify the extent to which women and men workers are able to effect fissures in the structures and discourses of power and to move beyond hierarchy as it were, in order to address some of the meaning of hierarchical power and control relations constituted not only by gender and sexuality, but, as will be seen, by familialism too.

These are arguments which will be uncovered and explored in the course of this book, but in addition the aim is also to move beyond debates based around socio-structural versus agency-orientated theories of gender, sexuality and work, since neither are sufficient by themselves to explain the different and unequal experiences of women and men workers in flatter organizations. It is also mistaken to see the two lines of argument identified so far as located at contrasting ends of the economic/material versus cultural/discursive, since there will be explicit attempts throughout the analysis which follows to specify the ways in which the economic/material and cultural/discursive are linked. The cultural and discursive, like the economic and material, are sometimes conceptualized as external forces which are thought to act at the macro-level, exerting power at a great distance over the individual agent/ subject. However, they can also be seen in terms of constituting resources upon which individuals draw in defining and redefining their subjective experiences. Where there are a number of competing discourses within a social arena, then workers may be provided with choices, indicating to them a variety of strategies for action. The creative tensions within the discourses of gender, sexuality and familial power relations may provide women and men workers in flatter organizations with just such choices, and this should not be overlooked.

Finally, it must be acknowledged that the analysis contained in this book builds upon a rich feminist tradition of research, since without a critical feminist approach to the data, little headway could have been made. This book is thus informed throughout by a critical feminist position, an issue that is implicit throughout. Rather than embark upon a discussion of the difficult issues raised by the claim to being feminist research, what follows next is a review and critique of some of the existing literature on worker co-operatives and collectives in the voluntary sector, with specific reference to gender, sexuality and power. It is to this review that Chapter 2 is directed, and the extent to which the research ultimately provides feminist insights and analysis will be left to the reader to judge.

Notes

1 *Flatter*, *less* or *non-hierarchical* ways of working, is a convenient short-hand for what others have referred to as *collectivist-democracy* or *participatory-democracy* (Rothschild and Whitt, 1986). However, since these terms borrow from more conventional discourses of political organizational activity, rather than engage more directly with the issue of structured inequalities, the use of the terms *flatter*, *less* or *non-hierarchical* is preferable.
2 Thomas and Thornley (1989) give an example of this necessary overlap in terms of Women's Aid. They argue: 'the effectiveness of the services being offered depends very much on the ability of the organisation to empower women and children who use refuges. It would be totally *ineffective* in such a case to organise in a hierarchical, nonparticipative way; in other words, power-sharing and participative working are essential to the effective running of the organisation', (1989: 5, original emphasis).

Introduction

3 As both Thomas (1990) and Trevithick (1987) have noted, both worker co-operatives and collectives in the voluntary sector have a large proportion of women working in them, both on a voluntary and political basis, and as waged workers depending upon the survival and success of such organizations as the source of their livelihoods.

Chapter 2

Gender Issues in Flatter Organizations

This chapter seeks to examine the existing research on worker co-operatives and non-profit or grant-aided collective organizations, with specific reference to research which has raised gender issues as problematic or has focused upon differences between women's and men's experiences of waged work in such organizations. Before doing that however, it is necessary to discuss the various interpretations that surround the usage of the terms *co-operative* and *collective*.

Specifying what is meant by a co-operative or collective is not a simple or uncontested matter. Working co-operatively or collectively has been variously described as team, joint or democratic working; in each case there is an emphasis upon the less or non-hierarchical structure of the enterprise or project, and the attempt to create and foster 'participatory-democracy' in such settings (Mansbridge, 1980; Rothschild and Whitt, 1986; Stanton, 1989). Rothschild and Whitt have defined a collective or co-operative as 'any enterprise in which control rests ultimately and overwhelmingly with the member-employees-owners, regardless of the particular legal framework through which this is achieved' (1986: 2). Much of the contemporary support for flatter organizations is based upon the belief that they can provide a high quality, more satisfying work environment or that there is practical (economic) value in promoting less or non-hierarchical forms of organization which emphasize flexibility, autonomy and collaboration. However, with the exception of infamous critiques such as those of Freeman (1974) and Landry et al. (1985), these assumptions have not tended to come in for much critical scrutiny and the literature on the successes and failures of both worker co-operatives and voluntary sector collectives is relatively scant (Cornforth, 1983).

A Framework for Co-operatives and Collectives?

Discussion of what constitutes flatter forms of organization will begin by examining the research on collective organizations. Although collectives are not structureless, specifying what constitutes a collective is problematic and there have been few systematic attempts to undertake this task. Difficulties in defining a collective arise because there are many different kinds of collective organization; some collectives are political and voluntary, whereas others are the source of people's livelihoods. Some attempt to give all workers the same responsibilities for all tasks (impossible if the work is very complex) whereas others attempt to give workers their own areas of responsibility. Collective organizations also have different histories and different reasons for coming into being. One of the most influential analyses of what they term the collectivist–democratic organization comes from the US and is offered by Rothschild and Whitt (1986) who characterize such organizations in terms of power and authority residing in the collectivity as a whole with delegation, if any, only operating temporarily and being subject to recall. Compliance, which is conceived of as fluid and open to negotiation, is always to the collective as a whole and not any single leader or manager. Regulations are only minimally stipulated; most rules are *ad hoc* and individual. Organizational controls are primarily based upon personalistic or moralistic appeals and work relations are considered to be holistic and of value in themselves. Normative incentives are primary and instrumental incentives secondary. Employment is based on friendship networks, shared socio-political values and informally assessed knowledge and skills so that reward differentials, if any, are strictly limited by the collectivity. There is an elimination or reduction of hierarchical positions in the collectivist–democratic organization and as a result, the concept of career advancement is considered to be meaningless. Finally, there is a minimal division of labour, particularly in relation to intellectual (high status) tasks and manual (low status) tasks such that overall, there is a demystification of expertise and a general combination/rotation of specialist jobs and functions to the benefit of all (Rothschild and Whitt, 1986: 62–3).

Organizations in the social economy, as has been seen, are characterized by the pursuit of social and political goals. Stanton (1989) in his analysis of collective working or what he terms 'self-management' in a small UK social work agency, argues that the commitment to working collectively in this particular organization arose not as an end in itself but as a consequence of the aim underlying all the unit's work, that aim being the participation and empowerment of clients as well as staff (1989: 10). According to Stanton, collectives are collaborative, responsive and open; both lines of communication and of accountability tend to be lateral rather than deferential. There is an acknowledgment of physical space in collectives as a common resource rather than something to be allocated according to rank. There is an acceptance in collectives of the open exercise of both group and individual power, so that criticism and support can be seen as inextricably linked and understood as constructive rather than destuctive. There is extensive delegation in collective organizations; authority rests with the group which reviews its own and individuals' work. Hence the authority of the whole, rather than that of the management, is paramount (Stanton 1989: 328).

Notwithstanding these positive features, collectives have also been seen as failing in certain ways; as being *temporary hang-outs* for certain kinds of people (mostly young, white, middle-class and well-educated) and as *idealistic* (composed of utopian, philanthropic and self-help enthusiasts). They are also viewed as small, weak, unbusinesslike/unprofessional, unable to recognize and reward expertise, and unable to deal effectively with differences between oldtimers and newcomers (Freeman, 1974; Landry et al., 1985). Landry et al. (1985) argue that the many failures of radical organization can be attributed to an excessive emphasis on power-sharing and the process of working collectively, to the detriment of the organization in terms of effectiveness, financial control, marketing and so on. Freeman has argued that in collectives, informal elites emerge and may be difficult to subject to democratic control because they are not explicitly acknowledged. She refers to this process as the 'tyranny of structurelessness (1974: 151).

There is less difficulty clarifying what is meant by a worker co-operative and certainly more attention has traditionally been given to doing so (Bradley and Gelb, 1983; Coates, 1976; Eccles, 1981; Lockett, 1978; Oakeshott, 1978). Put simply, worker co-operatives are businesses wholly or substantially owned by the people working democratically in them. This means that membership is open and voluntary; there is democratic control, usually on the basis of one member, one vote; and there is equitable distribution of any surplus (some equally amongst members, some reinvested and some allocated to community services). There may also be a degree of job rotation and a commitment to equal opportunities and equal pay policies. In the UK, the majority of worker co-operatives are now *common ownerships*; there is no share capital, and any reserves or retained profits that build up are shared in common (Industrial Common Ownership Movement, 1983). Neither can the business be sold for the proceeds to be shared amongst the workforce. Workers have the right to membership of the co-operative, possibly after a probationary period, and the ultimate authority is the general meeting of all members, although authority can be delegated on a day-to-day basis to waged workers.

Worker co-operatives tend to be concentrated in certain sectors of the economy, such as catering, cleaning, printing and publishing, theatre and media/film production, wholefood retailing and book selling. Most worker co-operatives are in the service sector, although certain areas of manufacturing, particularly in engineering, building, property maintenance, house renovation, and textiles are increasingly well represented, as are technologically-orientated co-operatives concerned with environmental protection (Cornforth et al., 1988; Thomas and Thornley, 1989). Some of the discussion around worker co-operatives has centred on the difficulties inherent in developing various typologies to classify them. The most common approach has been to base such attempts on the circumstances surrounding a co-operative's origins. According to Cornforth et al. (1988), it is possible to categorize worker co-operatives according to the social and economic conditions in which the organization was founded, and according to the dominant motivations and commitments of founder members. Thus the origins of a worker co-operative may lie in the failure of all or part of an existing business, or in the conversion from a viable existing business or community project, or in the formation of a completely *new-start* business. The dominant form of motivation behind the founding of a co-operative may be philanthropic, as in the case of altruistic, new-start entrepreneurs or *endowments* where the original owners hand the business over to the workforce. Other motivations may be radical or idealistic, and would include so-called *alternative* co-operatives based upon a commitment to workplace democracy, equality and production for need rather than profit. Finally, founders may be motivated by the desire to create or save jobs, as in the case of job-creation, new-start co-operatives, known as *rescue* or *phoenix* co-operatives, which are designed to save jobs on the closure of all or part of a failing business (Cornforth et al., 1988: 8–10).

Like collectives, worker co-operatives have been subject to criticisms; they have been characterized as places where workers will learn little but the harsh reality of the (largely hostile) marketplace and will struggle to survive (Rothschild and Whitt, 1986; Thornley, 1981). Thornley talks of the 'hotch-potch of ideas and ideals . . . the internecine strife and moral judgements' that characterize co-operative enterprises (1981: 172). She claims that '[the sector] will be dominated by the "small is beautiful" doctrine of the libertarians, and receive no more than a sidelong glance from the trade union movement' (1981: 172). There are also criticisms levelled at both co-operatives and collectives with regard to workload; it is often said that workers become over-stretched and 'burnt out', worrying about too many areas of the work at too great a level of detail. More pervasively, flatter organizations are often characterized as radical alternatives to conventional (hierarchical) organizations, and this alternative image is bound up with discourses of co-operative and collective organizations which position them as left-wing, radical and hippy as well as being unworkable, plagued by hidden hierarchies and inefficient.

Inadequate start-up and pump-priming capital, small asset bases and difficulties in financing growth are also seen as near-intractable problems for worker co-operatives (Jeffries and Thomas, 1987). Co-operatives are thought to be doomed to degeneration such that they will become, if they survive and over time, indistinguishable from conventional businesses. As Mellor, Hannah and Stirling (1988) express it: 'The room for manoeuvre for co-operatives under capitalism is severely circumscribed' (1988 or 9. xi). Like collective organizations, co-operatives are often considered to be inept at confronting and handling conflict in a constructive manner, so that debate and dissent are seen as ever-present, time-consuming and potentially destructive (Martin, 1989). Finally, co-operatives and collectives have traditionally been informed by 'essentializing' discourses which posit the desire for collectivism or co-operation as spontaneous, natural and innate; as bringing out the best social instincts amongst a (homogenized) group of like-minded people (Brown, 1992) and/or as the outcome of long-held dreams, visions and desires deeply embedded within individuals (Thornley, 1981: 178). As a result, some writers have presented co-operatives and collectives as highly desirable but totally impracticable; as fragile, short-lived structures which will eventually come

under the control of one or a few leaders, thus losing their defining characteristics. Handy for example, has coined the term the 'collectivist dream', captur-
ing a sense of both the strong attraction of the ideal and the difficulties of
attempting to put it into practice (1988: 134).[1] Notwithstanding all these problems, flatter organizations are still a critical site for analysis for some of the
most pressing concerns raised by hierarchical power and control relations.

Gender Issues in Voluntary Sector Organizations and in Small Businesses

Having attempted to clarify what is meant when referring to collective and co-
operative organizations, it is time to turn our attention to the extent to which
such organizations are informed by gendering processes and practices, and
how this impacts upon the experiences of the women and men working in
them. Before doing this however, it is worth examining what research on
voluntary sector organizations and small businesses generally has concluded
with respect to gender and sexuality. It is noteworthy that very little of the
research on voluntary sector organizations explicitly foregrounds gender issues, although there are some hints that in working collectively, an organization may be meeting the specific needs of women, some of which are thought
to be lacking in more conventional employment (ICOM Women's Link-Up,
1991; Undercurrents, 1981).

Most mainstream research on voluntary sector organizations and small
businesses has simply ignored gender issues. Johnson (1981) and Lane (1981),
for example, have examined what motivates people to become employees in
the voluntary sector rather than enter business, commerce or the public sector.
It is generally supposed, they argue, that workers' commitment to voluntary
sector organizations arises because there is a scarcity of employment, or that
the jobs available in the private or public sectors are unsatisfactory or even
meaningless in comparison. They suggests that the main need is for *self-
actualization*, a need which employees appear to be prepared to put before
good pay, status or other material rewards. Lane's contention is that employees' needs for self-actualization may be best met by the introduction of
participative management structures and collective decision-making systems
in voluntary sector organizations. But although this is his *main* recommenda-
tion, he fails to problematize this with relation to gender (or sexuality for that
matter). It is thus clear that social economy organizations as a whole deserve
greater attention in terms of gauging workers' motives and commitments, and
whether they differ according to gender. Stanton (1983, 1989) in his analysis of
collective teamworking in the personal social services, suggests that exploration of gender issues in such settings is long overdue. For example, one of the
issues he identifies as important is the finding that men are frequently excluded
from collectives on the assumption that they are unable to share power. But
the extent to which this holds true for *all* mixed-sex collective organizations is

yet to be established. In terms of how commitment, motivation, flatter organization and gender overlap and intersect, there is a need to explore this with reference to the experiences of both women and men, since there has been a paucity of comparative research in this area, as there has been of comparative research on women and men workers generally.

In contrast, the subject of *female entrepreneurs* – women who found and run their own small businesses – has attracted considerable academic attention in the UK in the last decade (Cromie and Hayes, 1988; Goffee and Scase, 1985). Goffee and Scase (1985) have shown that despite the growth in women's self-employment, women's small business ownership still tends to reflect traditional female areas of employment, such as hotels and catering, handicrafts, hairdressing and floristry, and most small businesses owned and run by women are located in the service sector. They argue that this is largely accounted for because choice of a business idea is affected by previous work experiences, but there are other (gendered) constraints which affect women's start-up and survival in business. According to Goffee and Scase, the greatest barriers to women's success in business are financial discrimination and lack of training and knowledge, with women in non-traditional areas of employment experiencing the greatest problems. Given these obstacles, it is not surprising that women entrepreneurs often choose a business where there is ease of entry, namely where there are low capital requirements and where managerial and business training is not essential. Similarly, women founding and running worker co-operatives might do so in order to minimize some of these problems too, although Howarth (1988) has highlighted the difficulties that women still face in setting up worker co-operatives, which she cites as the problems women face in raising finance and acquiring training, women's child-care and domestic responsibilities and their lack of self-confidence.

There are some similarities but also some differences in the analysis presented by Goffee and Scase of the experiences of female entrepreneurs and my own analysis of women workers in flatter organizations, which needs detailing. Goffee and Scase argue that four types of female proprietor can be identified, each dependent upon the degree (high/low) to which they are influenced by two factors; first, their commitment to entrepreneurial ideals, and second, the extent to which they are prepared to accept conventional gender-role relations (high/low). One type, which Goffee and Scase term *radical proprietors*, figure as low on both counts, and it is this group of women who exhibit similarities with some of the women workers in this research undertaking. Whereas it should be noted that Goffee and Scase focused only upon women *founders* or *co-founders* of small businesses, nevertheless, amongst the radical proprietors that Goffee and Scase identified, there was an overlap with the women workers who are the subject of this book in a number of respects. For example, radical proprietors were all founders or co-founders of businesses in which the pattern of ownership was typically based upon 'jointly owned partnerships and co-operatives' (Goffee and Scase, 1985: 57). It was also claimed that such women 'usually see themselves as members of the feminist movement' (1985: 99). Direct experience of 'male-imposed career blockage' within hierarchical organizations had served to motivate these radical proprietors. Such women tended to come from white, middle-class backgrounds and had taken advantage of inherited wealth for business purposes. They also directed their businesses towards altruistic goals and were 'providing self-financing services for women and using accumulated assets to further the long-term interests of women' (1985: 57). Finally, Goffee and Scase characterized jointly-owned partnerships and co-operatives as offering 'a context in which feminists can form personal identities and life-styles free from the contaminating influences of men. Such enterprises therefore are often regarded as *an alternative to marriage and the family* (1985: 57, emphasis added).

Their analysis raises a number of important theoretical issues concerning relations of gender, sexuality and power which need discussing. There are three main problems with Goffee and Scase's account. First, they treat all single, divorced and lesbian women as a homogeneous group and assume that by virtue of eschewing marriage, and devoting themselves to business enterprise, such women somehow escape from the subordination which other (married) women experience within the nexus of home/family and the labour market. In short, all single women without children are seen as sharing the privileged positions of men, in that it is assumed that they do not have to deal with the constraints of being a (married) woman (with children) in the labour market, and are not subordinated within familial power relations. However, it is likely that even single women without children are more highly constrained at work than men, since most single women do not tend to find that their work experiences parallel those of their men colleagues and co-workers. For example, they are still subject to sexist and heterosexist workplace cultures, sexual harassment and discrimination, and suffer worse pay and promotion prospects than both their single and married men counterparts (Spencer and Podmore, 1987).

Second, Goffee and Scase's analysis is predicated upon a construction of women's lives in which marriage and the family are conjoined and posited as *alternatives* to careers and business enterprise. In other words, they confirm rather than contest a traditional 'career versus marriage/motherhood' model of women's lives, setting them out as either/or choices for women. They present attachments to conventional gender roles as central to the construction of their typology, and link childbearing and childrearing, if not strictly with marriage then at least with heterosexuality. Their model then presents marriage, childrearing and childbearing as the antithesis to paid employment, careers and proprietorship. This dichotomy is not very helpful for theorizing the experiences of women and men workers in flatter organizations. In a model of this type, the variety and complexity of the experiences which women workers in particular have tend to go unrecognized. For example, there are no longer (if there ever were) clear career paths for women to pursue. The structuring of full-time, part-time and job-share positions for women and the high incidence of job insecurity that women face in the labour market, tends to mitigate against them making a long-term investment in careers. But at the same time, more women are moving in and out of the labour market with a view to establishing working histories with a recognizable career profile. Although this clearly involves contesting the meaning given to careers as traditionally constructed (with linear, full-time employment in mind), Goffee and Scase seem to underestimate the importance of these reconfigurations. In any case, the somewhat simplistic career versus marriage/motherhood dichotomy which they adopt is in need of revision in terms of its application to women workers in flatter organizations, as elsewhere.

Third, Goffee and Scase conflate feminism and separatism, assuming that all feminists are separatists, which is not the case. They also fail to highlight the significance of sexuality to feminism, and issues of lesbianism are buried in the subtext of their discussion of radical proprietors, without ever being explicitly confronted and addressed. They present radical proprietors as somehow outside marital and familial relations, simply by virtue of their low commitment to traditional gender role relations. But it is unclear whether this conflation of *feminist* with *separatist* is a coding for *lesbian*, since it is pivoted upon a rejection of traditional gender roles of wife and mother in particular. This academic negation of lesbianism serves to maintain the link between heterosexuality and reproduction, and preserves assumptions about women's economic dependence upon men. Few lesbians are supported by men nor are they likely, if and when they have children, to bring them up with male partners. The typology is therefore something of a misnomer as far as its application to lesbians is concerned, but this is never clearly explicated in Goffee and Scase's analysis.

To dichotomize women's lives in terms of 'career versus marriage/motherhood' is problematic, as Cromie and Hayes (1988) have shown.[2] Cromie and Hayes argue that it is not marriage but motherhood, and specifically women's responsibilities at the stage of family formation, that is the key to understanding women's entry into business. On the basis of interviews with 34 recent and aspiring women proprietors, Cromie and Hayes argue that: 'first impressions suggest that married women had different reasons compared to single women for creating businesses. After some time however, it emerged that it was the possession of children, not marriage, that was the principal distinguishing feature' (1988: 99). This led them to construct a three-fold typology based on the extent to which women entrepreneurs had managed to combine small business proprietorship with their domestic commitments, particularly during the critical childrearing period of their lives.

The typologies constructed by both Goffee and Scase (1985) and Cromie and Hayes (1988) hinge upon similar and traditional criteria, such as the acceptance by women proprietors of conventional gender role relations, and the difficulties that married women face in combining childcare with the running of a business. Both studies therefore conclude that women's experiences of setting up and running a small business, as in the labour market generally, cannot be understood without reference to women's marital and familial roles, which go deep to the heart of their waged work experiences. Both studies are also concerned with the extent to which female entrepreneurship constitutes an attempt by women to overcome their 'subordination' (Cromie and Hayes, 1988: 111). They view the overall impact of female proprietorship as likely to be small, although Goffee and Scase do conclude that their radical proprietors are likely to be *both* empowered and constrained by their 'need to trade in a capitalist economy' (1985: 140). In this way, women's difficulties in founding and running small businesses are explained not in terms of gendering processes and practices *per se*, but in terms of capital–labour relations. This leaves the issue of why women *as women* experience specific difficulties, unacknowledged and unexplained.

On the whole, therefore, the literature on gender inequalities in voluntary sector organizations and small businesses is patchy and incomplete, and does not offer very much that is useful for theorizing the ways in which gender and sexuality inform the experiences of women and men workers in co-operative and collective organizations. However, there is some (scant) literature which explicitly addresses this area, and it is to that literature that the next section is directed.

Gender Issues in Co-operatives and Collectives

Research upon the significance of gender as a determinant of worker's experiences in flatter organizations is, like that on voluntary sector organizations and small businesses generally, relatively scant, even when the research has been carried out by women (Rigge and Young, 1983; Thornley, 1981). Some research on worker co-operatives simply assumes an ungendered worker (Coates, 1976; Oakeshott, 1978; O'Connor and Kelly, 1980). In worker co-operatives in particular, gender has not been seen as significant since what is considered crucial are attempts to avoid the exploitation involved in capital–labour relations, so that ultimately ownership and control is conceived of as resting with the workforce/members of the co-operative, irrespective of whether such members/workers are women or men. In short, gender inequalities are seen as secondary if not irrelevant in most of the literature on worker co-operatives. Because they have been seen traditionally as alternatives to share-holding businesses, perhaps it is not surprising that the research should reflect that more traditional preoccupation with the divisions between capital and labour, not ones based on gender, or for that matter sexuality. For example, the structures and practices of worker co-operatives themselves are held to make them less able to raise capital both internally and from outside; all sorts of devices are then instituted to overcome financial difficulties. Some co-operatives encourage loans and shares from their members/workers, some buy second-hand plant and machinery and some pay very low wages, sometimes employing outworkers and using the same tactics as other small enterprises, such as short time and wage cuts, to stay in business. But this is not thought to be an effect of or informed by gender.

Some research on worker co-operatives *does* allude to the significance of gendering processes and practices, but has tended to collapse gender inequalities onto those of class. For example, Mellor, Hannah and Stirling (1988) recognize the divisions generated by *both* capitalist and patriarchal relations of production, but tend to view the latter as secondary in their analysis. Other research on collectivist-democratic organizations has also viewed class inequalities as more significant than those of gender, in terms of affecting both levels of participation and attempts to exercise power in a democratic way in the collective (Mansbridge, 1980: 191). Gender is clearly not a central focus of these studies, and whereas some consideration is given to the ideas and practices of feminism, this is not grounded, especially in the case of Mellor, Hannah and Stirling's work, in any empirical substantiation of their theoretical claims for gender. Specifically, they do not provide any detailed evidence for their claim that there was a widespread feeling amongst female co-operators, that women were less well-equipped than men to work co-operatively, although it could be surmised that they were talking more about women's *perceived* lack of business skills and confidence. However, even this theoretical claim appears on the face of it, to be at variance with other feminist research on women's 'co-operation' in the broad sense of the term. For example, Spender (1982) has argued that women enter into and promote discourses of *fair shares* and *co-operation* as opposed to men's entry into and promotion of discourses of *competition* and *winning*. Spender claims that the flatter organizations developed by women are: 'merely an extension of the co-operative, turn-taking talk that women normally engage in' (1982: 136). However, as pointed out earlier, there is a danger here of falling into a form of essentialism which positions women as somehow *naturally* better suited to flatter rather than hierarchical working, and as *naturally* unable to compete effectively (with business*men*) to secure the successful survival of their enterprises.

Nevertheless, the difficulties that women workers in flatter organizations face in terms of being taken seriously *as women* do have specific and damaging economic consequences that often go unrecognized and unanalysed. Bowman and Norton (1986) argue that in the voluntary or non-profit sector, women generally have less influence than men in deciding how capital, in the form of direct and indirect grants and loans, should be spent. They argue that the opportunities for obtaining funding for paid staff in (all-women and women-only) voluntary organizations, or for accessing suitable accommodation and acquiring management expertise is bound up with issues of women's position in society: 'The very fact that women do join together in [women-only] groups and organizations has often been regarded as a threat. Starving women of finances and resources like meeting places is only one of the responses that women have had from their opponents. Ridicule and suppression are also familiar tactics' (1986: 11). There is a need therefore to specify and analyse the gendering processes and practices involved in raising finance, securing accommodation, paying staff and so forth in those flatter organizations that are dominated in numerical or status terms by women, or are all-women or women-only. The extent to which the difficulties faced by certain flatter organizations are bound up with structures and discourses of gender and sexuality may then become clearer.

The difficulties which arise from the positioning of flatter organizations on the margins or periphery of the 'real' (namely, serious, conventional, hard-nosed) world of business and economics have already been established in the literature on flatter organizations, but not the extent to which such positioning is gendered (Munroe, 1989; Paton, 1980). Thomas and Thornley claim that alternative co-operatives, although they may include many commercially and politically successful enterprises, are likely to: 'remain in several senses, marginal. They appeal only to an idealistic minority, they are more or less restricted to certain sectors ... and they must remain fairly small to retain anything of their collectivist ideals' (1989: 8). Wallsgrove argues that: 'Collectives are more than averagely precarious, on the economic margins, because they are usually aiming to do something more radical than be unhierarchical IBMs' (1990: 20). Other feminists have drawn attention to the ways in which the marginal, peripheral position occupied by flatter organizations may be compounded by the positioning of women's experiences as insignificant and trivial, so that when women not only found and run women-only business enterprises, but do so on a co-operative or collective basis, they are seen as 'beyond the pale' (Cadman, Chester and Pivot, 1981). In short, it would appear that women in such organizations are viewed and treated differentially from their men counterparts, due to the operation of these 'marginalizing' discursive practices. This issue warrants further exploration and will be discussed in more detail in relation to the empirical findings discussed in Part II of the book.

This marginalization of co-operative and collective workers, and in particular of *women* co-operative and collective workers, is borne out by ethnographic and case-study research on women workers in flatter organizations. For example, the idea that such women and their enterprises are not taken seriously is discussed by Wajcman (1983) in her ethnographic study of a women's footwear manufacturing co-operative, based in Norfolk, which traded between 1973–1979. Wajcman argues that there was a growing belief amongst some of the women working in the co-operative that they needed a male boss because he would command the respect of the women members and the male suppliers and customers they dealt with. Some of the women in the co-operative saw the male suppliers and customers as the crux of the problem; as women, they felt they were vulnerable to such men, who believed that women could not run a business and did not know what they were doing. Mellor, Hannah and Stirling reinforce this point about women workers' marginalization when they refer to the attitudes prevalent in one of the women's clothing co-operatives that they studied. The deterioration in the co-operative's financial position and internal relationships were accompanied by references (by the women workers) to traditional notions of men as figures of authority and respect. As one woman interviewed in their study commented: 'I sometimes think that we could do with a man here to tell them what is what. They would listen to a man.' (1988: 145).

The literature on co-operatives and collectives generally, and on women's co-operatives and collectives in particular, has therefore been characterized by analyses which tend to point to flatter organizations as marginal, small-scale, utopian and/or bound to fail. In many cases, these characteristics are often presented as a consequence of the economic failings of *workers* attempting to create alternative forms of organization, irrespective of whether these workers are women or men, or whether the organization is mixed-sex or all-women/women-only. For example, Wajcman, in her study of a women's co-operative that ceased trading in 1977, argues that it was the fact of being *workers in a co-operative*, not that of being *women workers* that explained their 'self-sacrifice' (1983: 186). In this way, she views women workers as 'not unusual' (thus no different from men workers) in terms of what is entailed in working in a co-operative and she argues that 'few co-operatives have been financially viable and that most survive through the *collective efforts of the workforce* who tolerate low pay, unpaid overtime, and poor working conditions' (1983: 186, emphasis added). The fact that all the workers in the co-operative she studied were *women* thus appears incidental in her analysis, when weighed against their position as *workers in a co-operative* business.

On the whole then, gender-related issues and any analysis of gendering processes and practices have tended to remain buried in much of the literature on co-operatives and collectives. For example, there is little research on whether people's reasons for staying in or leaving flatter organizations differs according to gender, or why women and men seek to work in such organizations in the first place and whether their reasons differ.[3] Once women and men are working in such organizations, it tends to be assumed that their difficulties (in staying afloat, in being taken seriously and so on) are the result of their being *workers in a co-operative or collective organization*, not because they are *women or men*. It is clear therefore that there is a need for more detailed research on the gendering of workers' experiences in flatter organizations in order to find a way through this theoretical and empirical impasse. Some of this may be provided by ethnographic and case-study work, of which there has been a relatively large amount (Cornforth, 1981; Emerson 1983; MacFarlane, 1987; Oliver, 1987; Paton, 1979; Plumpton, 1988; Rhoades, 1980; Thomas, 1985; Tynan, 1980a, 1980b, 1980c; Tynan and Thomas, 1984; Woolham, 1987). It is to such research that the next section is directed.

Case Study Research on Co-operatives and Collectives

Despite this rash of empirical case-study research on worker co-operatives in the UK over the last 10 years and more, few of these studies explicitly address issues of gender in flatter organizations either. In fact, gender tends to surface in a muted form in many of the case studies and is often conceptualized in ways which are not just uncritical, but which tend to 'naturalize' gender power relations. For example, Tynan in her case study on an all-women's retail grocery co-operative based in Sunderland between 1976 and 1979, claims that: 'Where a job (such as washing the bacon slicer or cleaning the floor) appeared, *the women did it spontaneously, much as they would at home*' (1980b: 10, emphasis added). Tynan assumes that there is nothing problematic about making this connection between waged and unwaged work in relation to women, since it is often assumed that women are *naturally* involved in domestic chores both in their homes and (paid) workplaces.

However, not all case-study research fails to problematize gender power relations. MacFarlane (1987) in his research on Suma Wholefoods, a mixed-sex worker co-operative based in Leeds, argues that although both women and men were attracted to the co-operative because it appeared to represent an alternative to working in (male-dominated) hierarchies, in practice these expectations were not fully met, and that this was, to a large extent, contingent upon gender. He argues that it was felt by workers that an informal and hidden hierarchy existed in the co-operative, partly based upon gender and partly based upon length of experience. But because this informal hierarchy was not acknowledged, it was very difficult to tackle. The male domination of the co-operative however, is presented by MacFarlane in fairly individualistic terms related to men's personality and men's stronger position as 'oldtimer' or veteran members of the co-operative. MacFarlane does contend that male domination was resolved by changing the co-operative's formal structures; concerted efforts ot equalize the ratio of men to women in the co-operative, the formation of subgroups and a women's group meant that by 1985 'male domination had been broken' (1987: 81).[4]

MacFarlane further recognizes that what he refers to as the 'institutionalised sexism' operating at Suma Wholefoods reflected and reinscribed specific tensions and contradictions around gender and sexuality. Several factors operated to exclude women who had a commitment to co-operatives and a knowledge of wholefoods from the co-operative, but who were constrained by child-care commitments and by their 'unwillingness to take on physically hard and culturally male work' (1987: 83). The way that the co-operative was organized meant that all member/workers had to call upon large reserves of energy over and above normal work commitments. In short, in terms of making an after-hours commitment to the co-operative, all workers were expected to be available to work long hours in peak periods. At Suma, what this meant was that workers not only had to be flexible in terms of the hours they put in but also had to be prepared to enter non-traditional areas of work, so that women drove lorries and fork-lift trucks (and presumably, men cleaned the toilets?). This meant that the co-operative had recruited increasing numbers of women who were active feminists and/or lesbians, since such women: 'have a strong political commitment to equal working practices and are more likely to have established shared child-care arrangements where appropriate' (1987: 83).

But herein lay some of the gendered tensions and contradictions within the co-operative. Women workers who draw upon feminist political analyses, MacFarlane argues, are less likely to subscribe to the convention that waged work should be prioritized over everything else, and are likely to maintain that women in particular should not fall into the trap of working long hours for low pay since this merely reinforces women's inferior position in the labour market. Feminist co-operators are thus less likely to respond to collective pressures to work long hours for low pay, despite the assumption that all co-operative workers will do this. Not suprisingly, tensions around these gendered contradictions eventually had quite dramatic consequences in that post-1985, long-serving men tended to withdraw from active participation in the new management structures at Suma and several men left the co-operative at this time.

MacFarlane's case-study research is useful because it identifies several facets of worker's experiences in flatter organizations which are well-established in the more substantive theoretical literature (Cornforth et al., 1988). For example, on the subjects of the rewards of co-operative working, MacFarlane found that the benefits most often cited by workers were 'having control over your own work' and 'getting on with people', which referred to 'the relative ease of making relationships and the helpful attitude of one worker to another' (1987: 75). There are problems with MacFarlane's analysis however. He does not problematize these benefits with reference to the gender of workers, despite analysing the contradictions that surrounded gendering practices and processes regarding women's and men's experiences of work in the co-operative. Neither is the pattern of high turnover, or what is known as 'burn-out' in worker co-operatives, to which MacFarlane draws attention, analysed as gender-specific in any way. Without detailed cross-gender comparisons with workers in other co-operative organizations however, some of MacFarlane's conclusions have to be taken as tentative, since a single case study, if it is not informed by a highly critical feminist awareness, may result in some gendering processes and practices simply being unacknowledged.

There are still further problems with MacFarlane's analysis. The erratic and uncertain careers of workers in the co-operative are discussed in a gender-empty (and for that matter class, age and race-empty) manner. He uses quite crude rationales based upon individual preferences for explaining why workers at Suma lacked a career or more specifically, failed to develop a career after graduating. He unproblematically attributes their leaving conventional employment to the idea that they were simply: '*bored* by the career structure, hierarchy and exploitation' (1987: 69, emphasis added). There is no analysis of whether this rejection of conventional employment operated differently for men than for women, nor whether it was contingent upon experiences of sex discrimination. MacFarlane simply argues that workers were: 'disenchanted with the work environment in conventional organizations and had done something about this' (1987: 71). Whether this disenchantment manifested itself differently for women and men is not touched upon. Furthermore, whereas it is important to acknowledge that an individual's preferences can operate to guide them in certain directions, a wholly individualistic explanation of the different career profiles of women and men in flatter organizations is difficult to sustain, empirically and theoretically. MacFarlane further fails to problematize his contention that since the majority of workers at Suma wholefoods were graduates, they could have 'obtained well-paid jobs *if they chose*' (1987: 72). He makes no reference to the subtle forms of discrimination which tend to exclude women, minority ethnic groups, people with disabilities, the elderly, lesbians and gay men, from having access to well-paid and senior positions within the labour market, and assumes that all graduates enjoy equal opportunities by virtue of their higher qualifications.[5]

The issue of careers in flatter organizations is an interesting one because it is often assumed that there is no possibility of creating a formal (pyramidal) career structure in flatter organizations (Brown, 1992; Paton, 1991). Much of the literature on flatter organizations as a whole tends to conceive of careers in such organizations in terms of a gender-neutral process of maturation (Cornforth et al., 1988). It has been argued that workers are prepared to withstand a period of self-exploitation in the early days of their involvement, while they acquire skills and experience, but as they grow older and assume more financial commitments, they will be less likely to tolerate working long hours for low pay, and will be looking for better material rewards. Cornforth et al. (1988) distinguish between co-operatives in which a mixture of instrumental and social orientations predominate, and co-operatives in which moral and political commitments are found. They point out that even in the latter case, more instrumental orientations are found as 'co-operators grow older and typically acquire dependants' (1988: 111). That this may be so is not in question, but the different ways in which this may operate for men and women does need exploring. For example, Mansbridge has argued that there are differences between the career aspirations of women and men in collective organizations. She argues that 'women at Helpline seemed less likely than men to think of their work as part of a career. Only 15 per cent of the women interviewed intended to stay at Helpline for more than a year, compared to 53 per cent of the men' (1980: 192–3). But whereas intentions regarding their length of stay amongst the workers in the collective differed according to gender, this may not have translated quite so obviously into security of tenure or turnover rates, given the differential opportunities for employment in other (more hierarchical) organizations that men and women experience. In order to assess the implications of Mansbridge's findings, it would be necessary to know more about the types and levels of employment that women from Helpline went on to. It would also be useful to know the extent to which work experience gained in the collective acted as a grounds for other (better paid, higher status) forms of employment, and whether this differed by gender. Clearly however, the extent to which workers in flatter organizations have careers at all in the conventional sense, is problematic.

All of these themes will be returned to in the course of this book. Before that, it is necessary to consider some of the issues related to women and the labour market and to review the research on gender, work and organization. This is the subject of the review and critique of the literature contained in Chapter 3.

Notes

1 Notwithstanding these criticisms however, there has been what many have referred to as a resurgence of flatter organizations in the 1980s and 1990s. For a time, co-operative organizations were being hailed as panaceas for unemployment, alienation, inner city decay and industrial strife (Thornley, 1981). It is not surprising that co-operatives continue to have strong appeal to a wide cross-section of people seeking to set up and work in democratically-owned and controlled businesses. From a low point of about 35 co-operatives in the early 1970s, UK numbers have grown rapidly. According to Thomas (1990) there were an estimated 1400 worker co-operatives trading during the mid to end of 1988. The average number of full and part-time workers per co-operative was 4.5 and 1.6 respectively. Thus it was estimated that the 1400 co-operatives employed approximately 6300 full-time and 2400 part-time workers between them – a total of 8540 workers, which, it was predicted, would rise to reach the 10,000 mark by the beginning of the 1990s.
2 While Goffee and Scase have produced a four-fold typology consisting of *conventional, innovative, domestic* and *radical proprietors,* Cromie and Hayes present a three-fold model of *innovators, dualists* and *returners.* Whereas there is no neat degree of fit between the two models, the absent fourth category in Cromie and Hayes' model is that of the *radical proprietors*; there were no women in their sample who sought to found co-operative businesses embodying the value commitments of what Cromie and Hayes rather disparagingly refer to as 'feminists and the like' (1988: 94).
3 Leaving aside the somewhat incomplete analysis provided by Tynan and Thomas (1981), it is fair to say that the research into the motivations and commitments of workers in the social economy is not simply deficient with relation to gender. Hadley and Hatch (1980) for example, have commented that in relation to the voluntary sector, the motivations of *volunteers* have been studied and debated, but *employed staff* have received very little attention, even in terms of class and age, let alone gender and sexuality.
4 It is interesting to note that male dominance was denied by a significant number of men (and some of the women) in the co-operative and that the formation of the women's group was seen as 'divisive and sexist' (MacFarlane 1987: 81) by some of the men. MacFarlane claims that it is

possible to interpret this by arguing that men fail to recognize the informal and subtle forms of sexism experienced by women. But he also argues that men and women in the co-operative had different attitudes towards work, with men seeing careers in the co-operative in hierarchical terms: '[so that] a person starts in the warehouse and progresses eventually to the specialist office functions like buying and marketing and accounts. On the other hand, women viewed careers in the co-op as circular so that moving from buying to order-picking or front office was perfectly acceptable' (1987: 82). This gendering of career aspirations does reflect the different value-orientations of men and women towards work in flatter organizations, but it also acts to position men as more powerful in terms of status, skills and responsibilities.

5 Carter (1987) also makes similar assumptions in respect to his doctoral research on consciousness and control in worker co-operatives when he states: 'I was not interested in "alternative" co-operatives because they were dominated by middle class idealists. I was concerned with the impact of co-operatives on the broader working classes who did not possess the education and background to escape to a middle class career when it suited them' (1987: 143).

Chapter 3

Gender, Work and the Labour Market

In order to expose and analyse the gender dynamics of women's and men's differential positions in flatter organizations, it is necessary to examine issues of women's employment. One of the major changes in the UK labour market during the twentieth century has been the increased economic activity rate of women. The percentage of women defined as economically active has risen from 11 per cent prior to the First World War to just over 40 per cent in 1971 to more than 50 per cent in the late 1980s (Department of Employment, 1988; Labour Force Survey, 1990 and 1991). Since the Second World War in particular, the increase in the number of women in employment has far outstripped the increase in the number of men. For example, from 1951 to 1976, the number of women in employment rose by three million while in the same period, the number of men in work rose by only 300,000. More than 10 million women now do some kind of paid work outside the home. During the decade from 1990–2000, the labour force is likely to increase by 675,000. Almost all of the increase in jobs is expected to occur amongst women, who will make up 45 per cent of the labour force by 2001 (Department of Employment, 1991).

It has been noted that economic activity rates are highly dependent upon marital status, with a significant trend in women's employment being the increase in the percentage of married women who now do some kind of paid work outside the home (Glendinning and Millar, 1987). Even this trend is not without complications. Martin and Roberts (1984) reveal patterns of women's activity over their lifecycles, involving movement into and out of full-time and part-time employment, and illuminate the complexity of the major shifts in the post-war period. They show that women have a rich variety of patterns of participation in the labour market and demonstrate a clear commitment to paid work. The picture is not wholly positive, however; Dex (1988) has argued that women, both with and without children, experience downward occupational mobility over their working lives, mainly as the indirect result of women's concentration into part-time jobs.

Despite the increase in women's economic activity rates and the positive results for women that are thought to follow from it, much of the research upon women's employment has held that when women enter the workforce, they do so on terms that are less favourable to them than men (Beechey, 1983; Cockburn, 1988; Dex, 1988; Knights and Willmott, 1986). This is often attributed to the differential roles husbands and wives play in the family, and their differing responsibilities for child-care and domestic labour. Married women's activity rates are highly dependent upon their family commitments; in particular, the number and ages of their dependent children (1991 Census Report of Great Britain, 1993). These trends inevitably have consequences for women's employment experiences since the extent to which women can combine paid work with their domestic commitments will differ according to the number and ages of their children and the constitution of their family households. However, family commitments are not the only consideration when analysing women's employment, and the labour market, as constituted by capitalist and patriarchal power relations, plays a significant part in shaping women's work experiences.

Occupational Segregation By Gender

Despite the optimism about the growth of women's employment, the majority of women workers in the UK today are still in traditional female occupations (Jensen, Hagen and Reddy, 1988). Segregation by type of work and gender is a fundamental feature of the UK labour market. Whereas men are engaged in a wide range of activities, with few from which they are absent, women are grouped into a handful of occupations. The 1981 Census showed that two-thirds of women in paid work belong to only three out of 27 occupational groupings and the 1991 Census, which reduced the groupings to 18, confirmed this concentration. These groupings are clerical jobs (33 per cent), service sector jobs (23 per cent) and professional jobs (14 per cent). Furthermore, this pattern of occupational segregation by gender is taken to be a relatively stable feature of employment distribution in the UK over the twentieth century (Hakim, 1979, 1981). Not only do women experience horizontal segregation, but they also tend to be crowded into the subordinate ranks within occupations. This feature of women's employment, known as vertical segregation by gender, is held to be diminishing, however, particularly in recent years (Bagguley and Walby, 1988).

Occupational segregation is viewed as the main way in which differential wage levels have been reinforced and is a direct cause of poverty for many women (Glendinning and Millar, 1987). In 1986 more than 50 per cent of women earned less than half of the average male wage (Lewis and Piachard, 1987). By the end of the 1980s, women's average wages were running at 76.6 per cent of men's and their hourly rate was even lower at 68.2 per cent (Equal Opportunities Commission, 1988). Other effects of women's reduced earning capacity are fewer fringe benefits such as pension schemes and company cars and in the long term, increased poverty in old age. Occupational segregation by gender is therefore held to be the most significant cause of gender inequality in paid work and it is often held that the removal of occupational segregation will substantially reduce gender inequalities in work.[1] The centrality of occupational segregation as the major source of gender inequality in paid work is problematized when dealing with workers in flatter organizations, since they may not have specified job titles and the duties they undertake may range from the managerial to the administrative to the manual. In some flatter organizations there are deliberate attempts to blur job demarcations, and women workers may find themselves undertaking a similar range of tasks and responsibilities to their men co-workers. It is therefore crucial to focus upon the extent to which factors other than occupational segregation reflect and reinforce gender inequalities in the experiences of workers in flatter organizations, not because such segregation is supposedly less marked in co-operatives and collectives (although it might be), but because of the consequence these other factors have for how theorizations of the relationship between gender and the labour market are couched.

Women and Part-Time Jobs

Within paid work there are other forms of segregation apart from that of occupation and one important area of gender inequality is that of employment status, in particular whether a job is full or part-time. One feature of the expansion of women's employment is the growth in the numbers of women employed part-time. According to the Labour Force Survey (1992), 41.9 per cent of economically active women are employed on a part-time basis, compared to 2.2 per cent of economically active men and, according to the 1991 Census, over 90 per cent of part-time jobs are done by women. The UK has one of the highest proportions of part-time employees of any OECD country (European Foundation for the Improvement of Living and Working Conditions 1991). It is a particular subset of the female population however which has moved into part-time employment. The most common pattern is for women re-entering the labour force after a break for child-rearing to return to part-time employment (McRae, 1991).

Part-time jobs are characterized by a number of features which distinguish them from full-time jobs. Part-time jobs are highly segregated from full-time jobs and particularly from men's full-time jobs. In the main, part-time jobs are manual jobs in the service sector and they are usually located at the bottom of the occupational hierarchy. Even those women who work part-time in higher-level jobs, for example, in administration or the nursing, teaching or social work professions, are almost always in the lower grades. Part-time employment is clearly related to downward occupational mobility. Martin and Roberts (1984) found that of those women who were in clerical work prior to family formation, the majority returned to the workforce as part-time employees, 44 per cent to clerical work and 56 per cent to lower level occupations in retail and service industries.

People working in part-time jobs also lack many of the advantages that accrue to people in full-time employment. Most of the protection offered to full-time workers does not generally apply to those working 30 hours or less a week. According to Dale and Glover (1990), 49 per cent of permanent part-timers do not fall within most employment legislation (taking casual or non-permanent to refer to contracts of less than three years). Full-time employees, especially men, are considerably better paid than part-time employees because they are usually in higher graded jobs and they benefit more often from overtime pay, shift premiums and bonus payments. Part-time workers are frequently excluded from benefits such as sick pay, paid holidays and occupational pension schemes. According to Martin and Roberts (1984), and with reference to women only, 53 per cent of full-time employees but only 9 per cent of part-time employees belonged to an occupational pension scheme; 81 per cent of full-time employees received sick pay compared with only 51 per cent of part-time employees.

The opportunity to enrich skills is also substantially lower in part-time jobs and part-time workers are often employed for the absolute minimum number of hours deemed necessary to do a specific job. It is much less likely that there will be any slack time in their working day. The intensity of much part-time employment is often commented upon and it is somewhat ironic therefore that part-time workers are often talked about as if they were somehow not quite real or proper workers. The distinction between women in full-time and part-time employment is, however, more complex than it appears at first sight. Hakim (1991) argues that most women do not set their sights on a career and are not committed to full-time work. She distinguishes between two approaches to work evident amongst women in Western industrial societies. She argues that a minority – possibly one in five – are career-orientated; they want full-time employment, promotion, job security and financial rewards from their work. For these women, child-rearing is a temporary interruption to their working lives. For the others, the large majority, child-rearing is an alternative to work. For them, work tends to have a lower priority than home life, and has to fit in around domestic commitments. This generally pushes them towards accepting part-time work. These women, Hakim argues, are prepared to accept lower paid, lower status, insecure employment as a price for jobs which are convenient and close to home. More importance, in other words, is attached to things like flexible hours, a friendly work environment and a short journey to work. In Hakim's words: 'This explains women's high satisfaction with the casualised and low paid jobs of the periphery – such as homeworking – a research finding that feminists and trade unionists have difficulty accepting' (Hakim 1991: 113).

Hakim's point is that women collude in the processes which ensure that the majority of them are working in lower paid, lower status jobs. This focuses attention upon the element of choice open to women in their selection of jobs rather than seeing women's position in the labour market as determined entirely by external socio-structural and economic forces. As Hakim puts it: 'the unstated assumption among sociologists is always that job segregation is *imposed* on women, unfairly and against their will' (Hakim 1991: 102, original emphasis). The evidence, however, suggests the need for 'replacing the all too common view of women as downtrodden and even grateful slaves with a perspective [of women workers] as self-determining actors' (1991: 115). It should be noted that this tension between socio-structural forces and the agency of workers themselves fits with the theoretical propositions concerning the gendering of worker's experiences in flatter organizations discussed in Chapter 1. To some extent, it can be argued that women and men workers in flatter organizations are choosing to commit themselves to work in such organizations, and may even have the power and control to decide whether those jobs should be structured on a full-time, part-time or job-share basis, as well as how different jobs are to be rewarded and what status accrues to them. The extent to which women and men workers in flatter organizations are offered the opportunity of becoming 'self-determining actors' in these structures and processes therefore needs exploring in the light of Hakim's contentions concerning part-time employment.

Traditional Sociological Approaches to Women's Work

Having briefly outlined patterns of women's employment, their concentration into the lower ranks of low paid, low status occupations and their predominance in part-time employment, it is now necessary to review the theoretical arguments that have emerged in sociological research on the gendering of work. Within industrial sociology there has been a tradition of research that has neglected to study women workers at all, has treated male and female workers as unisex, or has treated women workers as a problem (Dex, 1985). It has also been assumed that only work which is remunerated through the cash nexus as part of labour market transactions is 'real work'. This delineation of work to paid employment, or even more narrowly, to full-time paid employment, lies behind much of the traditional research on gender and work. Furthermore, industrial society is held to be typified not only by the centrality of full-time, paid employment but also by impersonal, bureaucratic norms and the differentiation of the material and economic from the ideological and cultural. The sociology of work has traditionally reflected this division.

This does not mean to say that nothing has changed; it is true that sociological interest in women's work has expanded rapidly in recent years and it can be argued that it has become the subject of extensive theorizing and empirical study. In many ways this reflects the success of feminists in focusing attention upon gender divisions in the spheres of production and reproduction, as well as women's increased participation in paid work. As Crompton and Sanderson argue:

the rate of women's employment has been increasing within a social context that has included the growth of 'neo' or 'second wave' feminism and the extension of legal citizenship rights for women, and an academic context that has included a sustained, self-consciously feminist critique of 'malestream' sociology. (1990: 1)

Academic approaches to the analysis of women's work outside formal employment, and women's participation in the informal and hidden economies, have also developed in part because neither traditional job structures nor full employment can be taken for granted as far as women workers are concerned. But even where women's employment is the central focus of the enquiry, women are usually studied as employees within hierarchical organizations. With few exceptions (Brown, 1992; Cadman, Chester and Pivot, 1981; Fried, 1994; Wajcman, 1983) there has hardly been any discussion at all of women creating and running flatter organizations. This is in spite of a history of politicized women pursuing strategies which enable them to combat gender-related disadvantages in paid work by channelling their energies into collective project organizations and co-operative businesses (Gould, 1980; Martin, 1990; Rothschild, 1990).

A traditional view of women as domestic creatures with different skills and natures has underlain much of the thinking, and certainly many rationalizations, about women's role in the labour market over the last few decades (Myrdal and Klein, 1956). In the early days of research on gender and work, there were two conflicting views as to whether the movement of women into paid work would drastically alter women's lives. One view was that paid work changes very little; women are exploited at home and paid work is merely another form of enslavement. More women are spending more of their lives in paid employment outside the home and yet most women still see their main role as caring for husbands and children in the family home (Martin and Roberts, 1984). Coyle (1984) for example, suggests that women have acquired a 'dual role' or 'double burden' in which they combine paid employment with the unpaid domestic labour of the family. Coyle has argued that this modification of the sexual division of labour, rather than its transformation, is the crux of the matter, since the subordination of women in the family allowed for the specific exploitation of women at work. The other view was that paid work changes women's lives a great deal; it gives them a theoretical equality with men, financial independence and broader horizons (Hertz, 1986). In spite of the low status of much of women's employment, a 'work identity' as well as the identity of being a wife and mother, is clearly important to women (Sharpe, 1984). In this view, it is no wonder that women are reluctant to give up paid work, no matter how ill-paid or unrewarding such work may appear to be.

The Gender/Job Model

One of the main theoretical frameworks within which the literature on gender and work has developed is that of the *gender/job* model of women's work and men's work (Fledberg and Glenn, 1979). This model emphasizes the links between women's work or productive roles and their domestic or reproductive roles, and the ways in which work roles complement or co-exist with domestic roles. As Fledberg and Glenn express it:

> While analyses of men's relationship to employment concentrate on job-related features, most analyses of women's relationship to employment (which are rare by comparison) virtually ignore type of job and working conditions. Where it is studied at all, women's relationship to employment is treated as *derivative* of personal characteristics and relationships to family situations. (1979: 526, emphasis added).

According to the gender/job model, women's roles in the family are seen as integral to their experiences of work outside it. Much of the early research on women and work was couched in terms of this model. For example, early feminist research was concerned to account for the rising rate of economic activity amongst married women, and to assess the impact of this trend upon familial relationships (Musgrove and Wheeler Bennett, 1972; Myrdal and Klein, 1956).

The work of a number of early sociologists, from Mincer (1960, 1966) to Parsons and Bales (1956), also rests upon the view that women's employment experiences are largely determined by their domestic or family positions. The common feature of most of these accounts is that they tend to view women as being at a disadvantage in the labour market *because* of their domestic responsibilities. Seen in this way, women's restricted employment opportunities are theorized as being caused by their 'deficient' experiences in the home.[2] In other words, it is argued that in order to participate in the world of paid work on the same terms as their male counterparts, women have to liberate themselves from the patriarchal nuclear family. The adoption of a gender/job model is only of limited use in studying women workers in co-operative and collective organizations, however. All that the model suggests is that issues concerning domestic labour and child-care commitments must be considered when studying women workers, but not when studying men workers. It is also of limited usefulness in terms of exploring the divisions between work and home, public and private life, production and reproduction. Broadly speaking, the model highlights how the first of each of these pairs (work, public life and production) have been associated with men and accorded greater cultural worth, whereas the second of each of these pairs (home, private life and reproduction) have been associated with women and have a more shadowy and inferior existence. But this fails to explain why men and women were allocated to these spheres in the first place, nor how certain processes and practices operate to either confine women and men in this way or allow for their resistance. In short, all that can be argued is that to ignore women's domestic roles when considering their lives of paid employment is to omit a defining feature of women's work.[3]

But this is almost a truism and as a result the model is thus not without serious shortcomings.

There are further problems with the gender/job model. This way of ordering the spheres of paid and unpaid work as a series of opposites may not fit the lives of women workers in flatter organizations for whom there may be more blurring of work and home than would appear to be suggested by this simple binarism. As was suggested in the last chapter, research has indicated that the experiences of workers in co-operative and collective organizations may spill over between work and family (Cornforth et al., 1988). In other words, both women and men in flatter organizations may see their commitment to co-operative and collective ways of working as embedded in both dimensions, as reflecting hopes and aspirations for more democratic, participatory ways of working in both paid and unpaid contexts. It can be argued therefore that dualistic models of the gender/job type may be too simplistic for theorizing the experiences of men and women workers in flatter organizations.

Subsequent contributions to the debate have been concerned with looking at whether women's experiences of paid work can best be explained not by reference to the nuclear family but by reference to the workings of the labour market (Cockburn, 1983, 1985; Hartmann, 1979, 1981; Walby, 1988, 1990). In short, whether socio-structural and ideological determinants of women's employment positions lie outside the family, and in the labour market itself. Walby (1988) argues that women's entry into lower status, poorly paid jobs is not solely explicable in terms of the lack of assets (in terms of skills and experiences) that they bring with them due to their position in the patriarchal nuclear family. Walby claims that the patriarchal strategies and activities of the labour market itself constrain women's experiences of employment, and in particular, it is occupational segregation by gender that emerges as the critical explanation of gender inequalities in waged work.

While not denying that occupational segregation by gender acts as an explanation for women's poorer pay and promotion prospects, it can operate to disguise some of the more subtle forms of discrimination and exclusion that relegate women to an inferior position in the labour market. This book focuses upon women and men workers in specific *organizations*, and thus occupation is not a primary factor in terms of theorizing the differential experiences of work for such women and men workers. To focus upon workers in specific organizations is thus to promote analyses of work and the labour market that do not necessarily follow those theories that rest upon occupational segregation as a key feature in explaining women's experiences of waged work. The significance of socio-structural and discursive forces in the shaping of worker's experiences is a further theme in the literature on gender and work. Sociological approaches which examine the ways in which women's labour is of benefit to both capitalism and patriarchy need to be reviewed in terms of how they apply to the experiences of women and men workers in flatter organizations, and it is to these approaches that the next section is directed.

Marxist Feminist Approaches

Dispute continues over what socio-structural theory best explains women's position in the labour market, their lower average pay, status, promotion prospects and their concentration in a limited range of occupations. Analyses of women's position in the wider social structures of capitalism and patriarchy have been seen as crucially important in understanding women's experiences of paid work and the discursive underpinning of their gendered positions. Unlike the gender/job model, these theories do not tend to take as their starting point women's roles as wives and mothers in family households. A number of socio-structural theories which place capitalism and patriarchy at the centre of the frame have been offered as explanations for women's disadvantaged position *vis-à-vis* men in the labour market. In addition, there is a wealth of criticism which is both addressed to and which develops these socio-structural theoretical approaches.

As a starting point for looking at socio-structural theories of gender and work, marxist feminist theories will be drawn upon. Such analyses are concerned primarily with the sexual division of labour in paid and unpaid work and with the spheres of production and reproduction. It is still ideas from marxist writings which form the basis of much theoretical analysis of women's paid and unpaid work, although feminists have tried to combine this with analyses which draw upon the concept of patriarchy. The debate about the relative power of capitalism and patriarchy as tools for explaining gender inequalities in paid and unpaid work, and about the precise nature of the link between the two, have been going on since the early 1970s. In brief, marxists argue that women's work is critically structured by the relationship between capital and labour and not by men's ability to appropriate women's labour as such, which is a dimension to which feminists give more emphasis.

Women's involvement in paid and unpaid work was conceptualized in the early days of marxist feminist analysis by means of what has become known as the *domestic labour* debate. The search for what Himmelweit calls the 'material basis of sexism' (1983: 107) led to critiques examining the role of household work in the production process. Of particular importance to the debate was the argument that housewives, through their unpaid labour, reproduce the labour force on a daily and generational basis and thus indirectly contribute to surplus value and capital accumulation (Dalla Costa and James, 1972; Gardiner, 1976; Seccombe, 1974). As such, unpaid work in the family home was a source of profit to the capitalist class. Housework, it was argued, is real work but is disguised because it is discursively constructed as a normal and natural part of women's lives, undertaken not under any contract of employment and with undefined, unremitting tasks and responsibilities. The domestic labour debate however saw the position of housewives solely in terms of the needs of capital and there was insufficient recognition that men as a social group might also profit from the inferior position of women in employment or their assignment to domestic duties.

Another marxist feminist theory which attempted to explain women's position in paid work was that predicated on the idea of the dual labour market (Piore, 1975). This theory suggested that the existence of different kinds of employment arises because the labour market is divided into two or more separate sectors between which it is very difficult for workers to pass; the primary labour market where employees are seen as more skilled, jobs are secure and there are higher rates of pay and better conditions, and the secondary labour market, where employees are seen as less skilled, jobs are casual or prone to insecurity and the pay is low and conditions poor.[4] The two sectors are seen to have developed as the result of the increasingly technical nature of the labour process, however, and not as the result of the different capacities brought to work by men and women. Barron and Norris (1976) took up dual labour market theory to argue that it is women who are primarily to be found in those jobs which make up the secondary labour market and that this is the explanation of women's poorer pay and job opportunities. They suggest that women are an ideal source of supply because employers perceive them as having characteristics of dispensability, low economism, lack of interest in acquiring training, low levels of trade union organization and so on. Their clearly visible social difference also makes them easier to recruit. Barron and Norris (1976) do not see the creation of a dual labour market as the result of men's and women's different labour market experiences – for example, as the result of women's greater involvement in domestic labour – but as a response to the needs of employers for two types of labour. A primary workforce consisting of a stable core of committed, skilled workers is valuable to an employer and is attracted and retained by better pay and conditions, while marginal groups can be taken on and laid off as the economy expands and contracts. At the same time collective action by all workers is made much less likely since, whereas benefits accrue largely to those in the primary labour market, concerted industrial action and class solidarity are inhibited.

On the face of it, this does seem a reasonable explanation of women's labour market position as many women do work in jobs which display secondary characteristics. But not all do; many characteristic women's jobs, such as teaching and nursing, are not of the secondary kind. They require training, experience and skill and many women do have careers within them, some working for years for a single employer and taking a primary role. Moreover, some casualized secondary jobs, for example in agriculture and construction, are largely filled by men. Problems arise with the theory because it is insufficiently related to the occupational structure and because it is ahistorical and static. It assumes that women are an undifferentiated mass, located within a single sector. The theory is also confined to an analysis of capitalist employer's normative beliefs and values and does not see capitalist or patriarchal structures in terms of organized opposition. It also presents the labour market as non-specific or immaterial in terms of being implicated in processes of gendering; according to the theory, the sexual division of labour is largely predetermined *outside* the labour market. Although the theory illuminates some aspects of woman's work, it does not go very far in explaining gender segregation, especially of the vertical kind. Theories couched in terms of capitalist interests also ignore the problem of how gender segregation comes to predate capitalism. Dual labour market theory cannot explain why it was socially acceptable to allocate women to secondary jobs in the first place or why male workers seized hold of the primary jobs for themselves.

Marxist feminists have perhaps more commonly turned to a third explanation of women's position in the labour force, that of the reserve army of labour (Beechey, 1977, 1978; Benston, 1969; Bruegal, 1979). The concept of the industrial reserve army is of central importance in Marx's analysis of the capitalist mode of production. He argues that its role is two-fold; to act as a flexible pool of labour to meet certain labour market requirements as and when they arise, and to act as a competitive force whose presence tends to undermine the material position of other workers. Not only does the reserve army act as a lever which promotes capital accumulation, but its growth is said to be an inevitable consequence of capital expansion, particularly when this entails a change in the composition of capitalist industry itself towards more labour-saving methods of production. Beechey (1977) maintains that married women in particular have become a reserve army of labour for low paid, unskilled and semi-skilled work in particular centres of industry because they offer certain advantages to capital; married women can be paid wages at a cost which is below the value of their labour power, and they constitute a flexible working population which can be brought into use and dispensed with as the conditions of production change. Bland et al. (1978) have also described in detail the ways in which they consider that women can fulfil the criteria for the categories of Marx's reserve army of labour; namely that they are floating, latent, stagnant and pauperized. Women constitute a reserve army of labour in this classical marxist sense in that they are easily drawn in and out of the labour market according to the expansion or contraction of the economy and a need for a corresponding change in the size of the workforce. They argue that women are particularly suited to the reserve army in that they are likely to be less skilled, less unionized and working more often in small firms and businesses. In addition the organization of redundancy on a 'first in, last out' basis means that women, who move in and out of employment more often than men, as the result of family responsibilities, are more likely to be made redundant in times of cut-backs in the workforce. Thus women's subordinate position in the labour market can be directly related to their function as a reserve army.

The difficulties with the reserve army theory derive from the attempts to apply pre-existing marxist categories to the feminist analysis of women's paid work. Barrett (1980) has pointed out first, that women cannot be both a cheap and flexible labour force *and* a reserve army, since their low pay should result in their being kept on and not discharged during periods of recession. Second, the fact that women make up almost the entire workforce in certain occupations such as nursing and clerical work means that they would be impossible to displace in periods of recession in the way that the theory suggests. Empirical evidence suggests that certain groups of women have indeed been protected from unemployment by the degree of horizontal segregation which character-izes their job (Martin and Wallace, 1984; West, 1982). Furthermore, whereas women have been segregated into low-paid clerical and service jobs, there is no indication that such work is predominantly casualized.

All of these marxist-inspired feminist analyses are problematic because in focusing upon the socio-structural imperatives of capitalism, they present capitalism as a disembodied and reified structure.[5] Employers and managers are presented as omnipotent and the labour force as submissive. There is no analysis of employers, managers and workers as active agents within the labour market and the resistance to managerial control by worker agency is disregarded. As a consequence, employers and managers are treated as the unproblematic agents of capital and their practices are 'read off' as the out-come of the capitalist imperative to secure surplus value. Power tends to be reduced to questions of class, and women are added on in a mechanical way. In the absence of a theory of men's domination both in the labour market and the family, crucial questions concerning the dynamics of gender inequalities in paid and unpaid work tend to be neglected. These difficulties are partly offset by feminist theories which have focused upon the exclusionary power of organized male workers within a system of patriarchal power relations, and it is to these theories that we now turn.

Feminist Approaches

Feminist theories, which focus primarily upon patriarchal structures, dis-courses and strategies, are perhaps more useful in terms of gaining a fuller understanding of gender inequalities in paid and unpaid work. Whereas it is sometimes difficult for feminists to build upon marxist accounts of class and gender, it is nonetheless helpful to return to the theme of the relations of production and reproduction, albeit in a critical capacity, in attempts to theo-rize women's employment experiences within a feminist framework. Few feminists take the classical marxist view that the position of women in contem-porary society can be explained solely in terms of the relationship of capital and labour (Zaretsky, 1976). Most feminists have come to the conclusion that classical marxist theory is *gender-empty*, providing a theory of places within class structuration without explaining who fills those empty places nor why (Hartmann, 1981). On the basis of historical and empirical evidence, some feminists have argued that analyses of patriarchal power structures and ideo-logies are crucially necessary for understanding gender inequalities in the labour market, and in particular for explaining why men and women are constituted in different and specific ways as *gendered and sexualized* workers (Adkins, 1995).

By focusing upon patriarchal structures and ideologies, feminist theorists have highlighted the way that groups of organized men workers and men employers have been able to oppose the entry of women workers into specific sectors of the labour market, and in particular those jobs that command higher wages and higher status. For example, it has been argued by feminist theorists that women's marginalization in the workforce is underpinned and maintained through the ideology of women's economic dependence and through the operation of the family or living wage (Humphries, 1977; Land, 1982; Rubery, 1980). Barrett and McIntosh (1980) in tracing the history of the family wage, argue that organizations of the working class colluded with pressure from the bourgeoisie in the nineteenth century to structure the working population along gender lines and that women (as potential competitors with working-class men) were excluded from certain sectors of production. The campaign for the family wage, which was espoused by many trade unions from the 1840s onwards, has been linked to moves to exclude women from heavy agricultural and manufacturing work and either confine them to the home or channel them into work seen as fitting for women, such as domestic service or laundering and sewing. Such a movement found enthusiastic support amongst middle-class reformers and philanthropists, and working-class men trade unionists. It is less clear how working women responded, although Lewis (1984) suggests that by the end of the nineteenth century, they had come to share the view that it was better for wives to stay at home. However, this did not stop most working-class women from working or from having to work.

The notion of the family or living wage helps to sustain the idea that men are breadwinners and women dependent housewives, an idea which has been particularly influential in the past in framing state welfare provision and social policy. For the most part however, the family wage remains an ideal rather than an actuality, and helps to perpetuate the association between women and domesticity. Only a minority of working-class men (the labour aristocrats) in the nineteenth and early twentieth centuries have ever really earned enough to support a family without contributions from other family members, and in the 1990s even middle-class couples find it necessary that both go out to work to maintain the standard of living thought proper to their class. While the family wage therefore remains linked to an ideal vision of a breadwinning man supporting a non-earning dependent wife and children, it can be seen as underpinning gender inequality and the definition of women's work as secondary.

One of the earliest feminist analyses of patriarchal power relations in paid and unpaid work was provided by Delphy (1980a, 1980b), who views gender as the primary form of inequality and rejects the classical marxist concentration upon capitalism and class. Delphy stresses the importance of the patriarchal nuclear family in understanding women's position in paid and unpaid work and sees all women as occupiers of another mode of production, which she variously refers to as the family, domestic or patriarchal mode of production. It should be noted that this is not the same as seeing women as necessarily part of the family proper, although the patriarchal nuclear family is seen as important in Delphy's analysis. For Delphy, this family or domestic mode of production is the site of patriarchal exploitation and she argues that patriarchal oppression is the common, specific and main oppression of all women. In short, male dominance is rooted in the family or domestic mode of production, which is patriarchal in form and is perpetuated by the institution of monogamous marriage and heterosexuality. Delphy supports her arguments by inverting the direction of the links usually established; whereas, for example in the gender/job model, it is the family which is seen as the main influence on the capacity of women to work outside the home, Delphy argues that the patriarchal power relations which operate in the family or domestic mode of production constitute a pressure towards heterosexuality and marriage which exists for *all* women and which thus locates them in a separate mode of production from men. But there are problems here; Delphy appears to see women as a homogeneous group with more or less uniform characteristics. All women are married (or are about to marry) and care for children (or about to do so). This situation arises, she argues, because women's disadvantaged position under patriarchal relations of production, their disadvantaged situations in both paid and unpaid work, acts as an incentive for *all* women to find breadwinner-husbands. As Delphy maintains: 'The super-exploitation of all women in waged work . . . constitutes an economic pressure towards marriage' (1980a: 94). The patriarchal relations in which women's unpaid labour is then given in return for maintenance by their husbands, constitute all women as dependants whether or not they are married or have a classical relationship to production – in other words, are themselves in paid work. Delphy thus argues that women's exploitation in the capitalist mode of production articulates with their exploitation in the family, domestic or patriarchal mode of production and that this operates for all women, even for those who are not married.[6]

Delphy's work has not been without its critics however. Bradley (1989) argues that in attempting to define patriarchy as a mode of production comparable to the capitalist mode of production, two dissimilar things are being compared. Bradley argues that it is not possible to conceive of patriarchy as a structure homologous to capitalism, or indeed to the more general structure of a mode of production in the marxist sense. Barrett and McIntosh (1979) take issue with Delphy (1977) over, amongst other things, her attempts to conceptualize a family mode of production in what they see as *marxist* terms. They argue that whereas she uses marxist terms she does not define them, but merely uses them where convenient and substitutes sociological terminology where that is more convenient. Delphy has struggled to get around the difficulty of developing a systematic material analysis of the family mode of production grounded in domestic production, but, according to Barrett and McIntosh, the result appears rather unbounded, vague and descriptive rather than explanatory. The problem is that marxist theory can be grounded in a specific set of material relations – the social division of labour for the production of goods and services – whereas gender power relations cannot be confined to a single site (such as the family) or be said to originate at one level and

criticisms of Delphy

spread to others. Barrett and McIntosh are also critical of Delphy's simplistic treatment of ideology and they see Delphy's attacks on idealism as constituting an attack upon any analysis which considers ideology to be relevant to the oppression of women. Delphy claims that she accepts the materiality but rejects the autonomy of ideology and considers that there is only one direction of relationship, namely from the material to the ideological. Barrett and McIntosh see this as a failure to recognize the need to analyse patriarchal constructions in terms of language, culture, sexuality and so on. Finally, Barrett and McIntosh claim that Delphy's analysis of marriage as the universal institution of the oppression of women offers 'no distinction between the situation of wives and the situation of women in general' (1979: 102). As they point out, not all women are destined to marry.[7] Delphy is circumspect in response to this question however; she argues that since most women expect to be married, we can treat all women as if they are.

Hartmann (1979, 1981) has incorporated patriarchy into a framework which can take account of both class (and ethnic) hierarchies and gender hierarchies. In contrast to those theorists who argue that capitalist relations operate in the labour market, while patriarchal relations operate in the family, Hartmann promotes the analysis of the labour market as the main site for a feminist analysis of gender inequality in terms of patriarchal relations. She defines patriarchy as: 'A set of social relationships between men, which have a material base, and which, though hierarchical, establish or create interdependence and solidarity among men that enable them to dominate women . . . The material base upon which patriarchy rests lies most fundamentally in men's control over women's labour power'. (1979: 14–15) Hartmann's definition opens the way for a more precise account of gender power relations, firmly grounded in an attempt to trace the different forms taken by men's control over women's labour power in different historical stages. She argues that occupational segregation by gender cannot be explained by capitalism alone because it predates it. Occupational segregation by gender results, Hartmann argues, from the intersection of capitalism *and* patriarchy. Men as a social group benefit because they control access to better paid, higher status occupations and women's weaker economic position means that there is pressure on them to marry and service their husbands in return for financial support/ dependency. Capital benefits because employers can pay wives/women low wages. The system becomes self-perpetuating because women have less access to skills training and promotion because of their domestic work and family responsibilities.

Hartmann's attempts to achieve a synthesis of capitalism and patriarchy in terms of analysing women's labour market positions is a significant advancement on gender/job and classical marxist theories of gender inequalities, but there are still problems with this approach. The location of the economic base in the analysis of labour power gives privilege to the theorizing of *material production*, ignoring other aspects of the relations between men and women that are found in sexual relations, the family and elsewhere.[8] For example, the dominance and control by men of women's sexuality is given very little attention in Hartmann's analysis. As Harding (1981) and Ehrlich (1981) argue in response to Hartmann, she has improved on classical marxism by extending the analysis of economic determination from the sphere of capitalist production into the patriarchal family, but she still gives a limited economistic account of the relations between men and women.

Walby (1986a, 1986b) has claimed that Hartmann's analysis is too general to account for the variations in the extent and form of occupational segregation by gender across historically specific periods. She also argues that Hartmann overstates the harmony between capitalism and patriarchy and does not consider late twentieth century changes. Walby (1986b) demonstrates the diversity of patriarchal labour market strategies which maintain and reinforce occupational segregation in a variety of contexts, historical periods and economic conditions. She takes three areas of employment – cotton textiles, engineering and clerical work – and claims that variations in occupational segregation in the three areas are the result of the relative strength of patriarchal and capitalist social forces at particularly crucial moments in the development of these various sectors. Walby claims that there is no simple index of these forces; strategies of segregation and exclusion were deployed in all three areas of employment with radically different outcomes. She further maintains that on the surface there are few obvious explanations; cotton textiles, engineering and clerical work all contain manual work at various levels of skills but have different gender ratios. Explanations based on ideological constructions, lightness of labour or relationship to machinery do not adequately account for these differential ratios. In clerical work, for example, it is not possible to maintain that employers divided the workforce in order to control it nor that the tendency of capital to de-skill labour lead to its feminization, since the consequences were so different in the different areas of employment.

Walby (1986b) argues that gender segregation was the outcome of the compromised struggle of various groups within the articulation of patriarchal and capitalist interests. For example, she claims that changes in occupational segregation in clerical work were the outcome of a division of interests between employers, male clerks and would-be female clerks. This particular process of the gendering of clerical work proceeded unevenly; male clerks did organize against women's entry but not effectively so. In engineering on the other hand, men were organized into trade unions and succeeded in mobilizing state power. In cotton textiles, women were a large component of the spinning workforce and therefore, until they became an established part of the traditionally male-dominated weaving workforce, organized patriarchal forces within the factory system designed to oppose women's entry into textiles manufacturing were of less significance. Building upon this empirical evidence, Walby (1990) has attempted to theorize patriarchy as an interrelated system of different social structures through which men exercise power and control over women. She argues that patriarchy exists as a system of social relations which articulate with capitalism and racism, but that patriarchy is not homologous with capitalism in terms of internal structure. Walby conceptualizes patriarchy in terms of six structures; patriarchal relations in paid work, the household, the state, male violence, sexuality and in cultural institutions. She argues that: 'the specification of several rather than simply one base is necessary to avoid reductionism and essentialism' (1990: 20). Walby's model however still gives primacy of place to the articulation of capitalism and patriarchy in terms of gendering processes and practices in the labour market, such as in terms of the segregation of occupations by gender. The structures attributed most importance are the division of labour in paid work and in the household. Collinson, Knights and Collinson (1990) criticize Walby's adherence to what they see as a highly economistic and deterministic account of patriarchy. They claim it underestimates the significant and interrelated roles of biology, familial ideology and gender identity for the perpetuation of male domination. They further argue that Walby's approach fails to acknowledge the mutually reinforcing nature of patriarchal labour market processes with women's domestic subordination in the family.

There are further problems with Walby's analysis. She argues that if the segregation of women and men into different occupations and areas of work is reduced through changes in the comparative worth of men and women's work, then there is every reason to expect that other aspects of gender inequality, in terms of male violence and sexuality for example, will be reduced. This may not necessarily happen, particularly given the ways in which it can be argued that women are not simply gendered but also *sexualized* by labour market processes and practices, a point to which Hartmann, Walby and others appear to pay very little attention. For example, it is often the case for women that their reduction to 'sexualized worker' is a condition of their employment (Adkins, 1995). Coping with sexual harassment and carrying out other forms of 'sexual work' such as looking and being sexually attractive are further requirements of most women's jobs. Furthermore, sexual attractiveness is often discursively constructed in terms of 'naturalistic' qualities related to personality, appearance and so forth, rather than being seen as socially-achieved criteria for employment. Walby (1990) thus tends to deal with sexuality not as a component of the labour market but in terms of (sexualization) processes which occur outside of it; in psychic and discursive dimensions that are rooted in the private realm, for example. In short, women workers are viewed by Walby as sexualized through the social and psychic processes that occur during periods of identity-formation, which themselves are seen as occurring prior to and separate from entry into and involvement in the labour market. As the experiences of women and men workers in flatter organizations which this book sets out to analyse, will show, this is highly problematic.

While placing emphasis upon the conflict of interest and resulting struggles between capitalist and patriarchal power relations, Walby (1986b, 1990) also underemphasizes the part that women workers as subjective and active agents play in resisting and challenging dominant patriarchal structures and discourses. In the absence of an examination of consciousness and self-reflexivity, it is difficult to present an adequate account of women worker's resistance. As Collinson, Knights and Collinson (1990) argue: 'Walby's deterministic approach neglects vast areas of subtle forms of agency and resistance which are available to women in the social relations that comprise domestic work, labour markets and organizations' (1990: 49). It is to the issues of strategy, agency and resistance that Chapter 4 is directed.

Notes

1 Crompton and Sanderson (1990) draw attention to the dangers of talking of occupations in general terms because there are so many forms of division, ranging from generalized areas such as labouring or teaching, to specific, fragmented tasks. They point out that what is ostensibly the same occupation may have a very different outcome depending upon the gender of the occupant. This is true of occupations, for example, in teaching, which for many men may mean a short apprenticeship in a hands-on capacity followed by progression up the career ladder, but for many women means a lifetime of working in a low paid, low status capacity with few prospects for progression.

2 Wajcman (1983) recognizes that women's commitment to paid work, which she conceptualizes as the result of their roles in what is broadly referred to as the *domestic sphere*, differs according to each woman's stage in the family lifecycle. Nonetheless she maintains that it is women's primary roles as wives and mothers that determine their labour market participation. Wajcman's research thereby falls between two stools; it is a study of women *workers* in an all-women footwear manufacturing co-operative and a study of *women* at work and in the home. That Wajcman appears unsure which dimension to emphasize is possibly further indication of the need to formulate a more sophisticated approach which focuses upon women workers as both workers *and* women in a *gender-differentiated society*.

3 This is not just the case for married women with child-care responsibilities. The relationship between the sexual division of labour in the domestic sphere and women's experiences of paid work also needs to be examined with reference to the lives of single women, lesbians, feminists and politicized women, since they have all been neglected as subjects worthy of study in this respect and tend to be seen as atypical of women workers as a whole. It is assumed that such women reject the traditional roles of wife and mother and devote themselves to their job (Goffee and Scase, 1985). Whether or not this is the case, and what the ramifications are for theories of women's working lives, needs to be more carefully investigated.

4 Doeringer and Piore (1971) originally developed this model. They introduced a further division within the primary sector of the labour market between the upper independent and the lower subordinate primary jobs.

The upper primary sector of the labour market was made up of professional and managerial jobs, with higher pay, mobility and turnover patterns and the lower primary sector contained people in occupations with moderate levels of pay, with less variety in the content of their work and with less control and influence over the work of others.

5 Anthias (1983) argues that it is untenable to explain women's employment with reference to the benefits accruing to capitalism alone. Anthias suggests that these advantages are consequences rather than reasons; for example, women's dependence upon a male bread-winner's wage may be more of a consequence of their restricted labour market participation than a cause of it.

6 Delphy states: 'Since less than 10 per cent of all women over 25 have never been married in developed societies, chances are high that women will be married at some point in their lives. Thus effectively *all women* are destined to participate in these relations of production' (1980a: 71, emphasis added).

7 As Barrett and McIntosh ask: 'What are we to say of individual women who are destined not to marry, of the surplus women of the 19th century and of those who, like Christine Delphy herself, ourselves, and many other feminists, are not signatories to the marital labour contract?' (1979: 103).

8 Young (1981) argues that it is not logical to sustain an analytical separation between capitalism and patriarchy in this way. Either capitalism and patriarchy have the same (material/economic) base or they have separate (material/economic and cultural/ideological) bases. If they are not given the same base, if the material/economic is the bedrock for capitalism and the cultural/ideological the bedrock for patriarchy for example, they cannot explain the full range of features of both capitalism and patriarchy which fall outside of those bases.

Chapter 4

Gender, Agency and Resistance

Whereas socio-structural theories provide useful frameworks for analysing women's paid and unpaid work, it has been argued that not all women fit into easily distinguishable categories of oppressed workers. As Martin and Wallace have argued: 'Theories based on labour market segmentation or the role of women as a reserve army of labour do not, *in themselves*, explain female employment experience' (1984: 4, emphasis added). Not all women's work experiences are inevitably constrained, and there is now considerable evidence of widespread employee resistance or agency. Given that women do move in and out of the labour market and across a range of occupations once they are engaged in paid work, it has also been argued that their work identities are more unstable and fragmented than those of their male counterparts. This poses problems for socio-structural theories since they tend to have arisen from approaches which focus upon the material advantages to capitalism and patriarchy of women's work, and they therefore underestimate the role of women workers as self-reflexive, subjective agents, capable of disrupting dominant discourses and structures of capitalist and patriarchal power relations. What are here termed agency-orientated approaches take, as their starting point, groups of women and men workers who enter into, manoeuvre and negotiate their positions within structured labour markets, in ways which take on board resistance, agency and subjectivity, but in gender-specific ways.

Agency-orientated approaches reject meta-narratives or what Elshtain (1981) terms 'narratives of closure' and view features of society, such as labour markets or organizations, as fragmented by the diverse experiences of individuals and groups. Such approaches suggest that workers cannot be reduced to the commodified objects of managerial control or their experiences simply 'read off' from their structural positions within a capitalist, patriarchal society. In other words, women and men's working lives cannot be fully theorized without taking into account the ways in which they negotiate and manoeuvre within dominant social structures and discourses. This involves analysing the complex interconnections between, for example, women's commitments and motives to work, the ways in which they construct and manage their work profiles or careers, and their opportunities for progression in a range of traditionally male-dominated occupations and organizations. Clearly these issues will be differentially experienced by women and men; for example, the issue of women worker's commitment and motivation warrants further discussion in the light of assumptions that women are differently (and less) committed to work than men. This is particularly important given that Goffee and Scase (1985), Mellor, Hannah and Stirling (1988) and Wajcman (1983) have all argued that the commitment of women workers in flatter organizations should be seen as a highly *crucial* determinant of their experiences of work in such settings. Wajcman for example, notes in her ethnographic study of women workers in a footwear manufacturing co-operative that: 'working in a co-operative requires a *higher* level of commitment to work than a conventional job' (1983: x, emphasis added). Recent feminist research has linked issues of commitment and motivation (or the assumed lack of) to gender, and has argued that although women's waged work has been marginalized (sometimes even by women themselves), the loss of that work often highlights women's strong attachment to employment.[1] Consideration of the motives women identify for seeking non-traditional employment, self-employment and proprietorship are also illuminating. Whereas it may be the case that such motives are varied and complex, it has been argued that gender does play a part in determining the reasons that women give for working autonomously and for starting and running their own businesses. For example, Hertz (1986) surveyed 100 of the most successful women business owners in the USA and UK and found that the majority of them claimed that instrumental rewards were not their main motivation. They cited independence and the seizing of a challenging commercial opportunity as the main reasons why they started in business. But there were, in addition, motivations specific to their being women, including a desire to avoid domesticity and a wish to improve the social and financial position of other women. Whether such motivations are also to be found amongst women workers in flatter organizations has, until recently, been relatively neglected (Oerton, 1994).

Women's work profiles or careers have not been systematically investigated from the point of view of women as self-reflexive, subjective agents.[2] Early work gave primacy to women's domestic roles and their fortuitous approach to occupational choice, positioning women as simply drifting into jobs rather than making any explicit choices (Myrdal and Klein, 1956; Pavalko, 1971), whereas later research put more emphasis upon the changing structures of opportunity and the impact that this has had upon women's entry into the labour market (Allat et al., 1987; Astin, 1984). The emphasis upon occupational choice in the contributions to the Allat et al. (1987) volume is based upon the idea that men experience relatively simple, consistent and unitary career trajectories, whereas women's working lives are more complex, contradictory and fragmented. As a consequence, women's breaks in employment are often viewed as negative and the reasons for the gaps in their (paid) work profiles are often denied legitimacy, sometimes by women themselves. In other words, women's work profiles are viewed as somehow deviant. As Gutek and Larwood express it: 'Men had careers; women had temporary employment or jobs that took second place to family interests or obligations' (1987: 8).

A further problem is that most of the research on women's occupational choices is grounded in the sexist and class-centrist assumptions made about (men's) careers (Holland, 1980). Holland argues: 'The main conclusion we can draw from this excursion into the literature is that for women, occupational choice is a misnomer; it does not exist' (1980: 15). Similarly, Purcell (1986) has argued that women are more likely than men to be fatalistic as far as their employment opportunities are concerned and to perceive little possibility of radical alteration in their individual circumstances. In seeking to explicate in this way the different career expectations and opportunities open to women and men, there has been a tendency to position women as passive, fatalistic and prey to fortune, whereas men are viewed as decisive, rational and individualistic, and therefore capable of making informed career choices based upon their capacities, interests, values and so forth. As a result, recent feminist research on women's employment profiles has examined women's lives from the point of view of subjectivity and agency, and seeks to distinguish women's career choices or preferences from the jobs or occupations at which they finally work. For example, Yeandle (1984) has attempted to replace static pictures of women's labour market participation with dynamic ones which capture the patterns of education, employment and domestic labour undertaken by women over the course of their lifecycles. Yeandle has shown that within the sphere of suitable women's work, individual women tend to have experience of a wide variety of occupations. Three-quarters of the women she interviewed had experienced employment in three or more different types of work and over half in four or more different types. This varied experience of paid employment had been compounded by interviewees' experiences of working an assortment of different hours, under a variety of different conditions, throughout their working lives. Not surprisingly, the experience of having a part-time job was also common and over three-quarters of the women interviewed had at some time been employed on a part-time basis. Flexibility of approach in women's working lives emerged as an important theme in Yeandle's research and is, she argues, a crucial feature of women's labour market participation.

It is often assumed that most of the women and men who work in flatter organizations are graduates and/or middle class in origin, and that they will view their labour market participation in terms of career progression because of their class and educational background (Carter, 1987; Cornforth et al., 1988; Goffee and Scase, 1985). This needs problematizing since it is all too easy to dismiss them as young, middle-class idealists seeking an alternative to conventional careers, while retaining the possibility of resuming career progression at a later stage of their working lives. But the opportunities for career advancement for middle-class women in a range of white-collar and professional occupations has been shown to be highly circumscribed by gender (Acker, 1989; Greed, 1991; Spencer and Podmore, 1987) The problems experienced by middle-class women in male-dominated professions such as the higher civil service, senior management, medicine, accountancy and law often revolve around the dynamics of exclusion, marginalization and trivialization. Research suggests that middle-class, professional men have been able to exaggerate their own skills and status so as to secure labour market closure and demarcation. For example, Lawrence (1987) has shown how women general practitioners are found to be ghettoized by their men partners into gynaecology, psychiatry and paediatrics. Legge (1987) argues that women may play a central role and reach the top in occupations such as personnel management, which are seen as far removed from strategic decision-making and as peripheral to central management, organizational or societal concerns. Legge further claims that if an occupation becomes recognized as no longer peripheral and as a valid contributor to strategic decision-making, then women, if not directly removed, are politely pushed aside, often with their own unacknowledged collusion.

It is obvious that these dynamics mitigate against the full participation of women in male-dominated, middle-class occupations (Marshall, 1984). Women entering such areas have to struggle to fit into male-orientated work cultures, often finding themselves excluded from male friendship groups and social activities crucial in making contacts and fostering careers; the gatherings in clubs and pubs, the chats on the golf course or at the companies' sports matches.[3] Furthermore, it has been argued that the dominant male members of various professions engage in stereotyping activities about the nature of the professions and about the women who work in them such that a 'double-bind' for women is created (Coyle and Skinner, 1988). This operates in subtle ways; for women to be seen as competent professionals, it is necessary for them to adopt masculine attributes and values. However, to the extent that they do so, they will be perceived as having failed as women, as having become unnatural and unfeminine. In addition, because women constitute visible and deviant minorities within the professions, they have difficulty finding sponsors or role models. According to Coser (1984) professions tend to be greedy, and the idea of professional commitment often makes it difficult for women to cope with their family responsibilities by working more flexible hours or by working part-time for a period. However, the extent to which women workers in flatter organizations are similarly or differently engaged with these processes of career formation does warrant further exploration.

Cultural and Discursive Approaches

It is important to review accounts of women worker's collusion with or challenges to prevailing organizational and workplace cultures in the course of analysing their agency and resistance. This point has been relatively neglected until recently in the literature on gender, sexuality and work, despite long-standing recognition that sexist and heterosexist organizational cultures may prevent women from achieving equality with their male co-workers and colleagues in particular spheres of work and that women workers do devise strategies for dealing with these problems. In some of the career and management literature, women have been endowed with unlimited agency, as if their entry into various occupations was solely a matter of individuals' preferences. But as Nieva and Gutek argue the process of linking up with an occupation/organization is a reciprocal one, although much of the literature on occupational choice makes it appear: 'a one-way process with women doing all the deciding, whereas organizations also select' (1981: 9). Women workers' ease of entry into and successful positioning within organizations is thus not only based on individual occupational or career choices, but is also determined by the cultural features of organizations. In offering a space to women who do not wish to or cannot secure jobs in more hierarchical organizations, flatter organizations also select certain women and shape the form that their experiences take. For example, it may be the case that if certain women are highly committed to working on issues of domestic and sexual violence, they may have no choice but to work in a collectively-run organization in the voluntary sector.

Women workers, unlike their men counterparts, are typically constituted as engaging with discourses of heterosexuality and familialism within the workplace. It has been argued that women's work cultures centre on their marriages, home lives, families and domesticity. Conversations, rituals and symbols are supposedly concerned with romance, marriage, children, clothes and food; cakes and recipes are exchanged, clothing catalogues and family photographs are circulated and advice on how to handle husbands and boyfriends passed on. Workplace culture is thus a source of (femininized) identity for women, acquired largely through heterosexual and familial orientations. Much feminist research has been directed at uncovering and explaining women's workplace cultures, and it is to an outline and critique of such research that this section is directed. Westwood's (1984) ethnographic study of women workers in a knitting and hosiery company in the Midlands concentrates upon the generation and reproduction of shopfloor culture by working-class women. Westwood argues that the women workers she studied insisted on bringing home into work. She sees the attempts to separate the two systems of (patriarchal) family/home and (capitalist) workplace as mistaken since home and work are not just interrelated in the case of women workers, but are part of one world. Shopfloor culture thus reinforces women's sense of identity as women and as workers. Westwood characterizes these processes as both oppositional and collusive; the shopfloor culture of the women workers is oppositional in terms of the resistance displayed by women to the demands made upon them by employers, but collusive in its emphasis upon women's traditional roles in the home and family. Women's workplace culture was thus highly contradictory; women on the shopfloor were 'strong, active and trying to control their own lives' (1984: 101) while at the same time they were: 'enmeshed within a world of romance and sexuality which took its cues not from solidarity and strength, but from the myths and stereotypes which surround men and women and their relationships' (1984: 101).

Like Westwood, Pollert (1981) also draws attention in her study of women workers in a tobacco factory in Bristol to the importance of the family, women's role in reproduction and their relationship to social production. Pollert examines the relationships between class and gender in terms of the labour process as it is lived and experienced. Most of the factory workers in Pollert's study were young and single, and turnover in the factory was high. Waged work was overshadowed for married women by the immediate, intimate and daily concerns with the actual processes of family life. Young, single women in the factory looked not just to the escape from the daily grind of work found in the talk of emotions and romance, women's magazines, love stories, pop heroes, relationships with boyfriends and so forth, but also to a career as constituted by marriage and child-rearing as an alternative to the sense of low worth that they experienced in their jobs. Pollert argues that low status, unskilled manual work confirms the self-perceptions of these women and girls as inferior, fit only for the mundane tasks of assembly line work and housework. Unlike young men, who Willis (1977) has shown can transform manual work into a culture of machismo, these young women could only treat unskilled manual labour as an affirmation of their worthlessness. It was not surprising therefore that they elevated romance and marriage into a life solution, thereby reinforcing the identification of women with housewifery and motherhood.

There are a number of shortcomings of the shopfloor studies reviewed here, however. There is little material underpinning in these studies and they focus mainly on the discursive realm, showing how workplace cultures reflect assumptions about women and images of women as men see them. In this way, the culture of femininity thus engendered is seen as drawing upon pre-existing stereotypes about women. The women themselves are seen as negotiating their way through this workplace culture; the workplace itself is not seen as active, fluid or dynamic in terms of being a site of gendering processes, but is seen to reflect pre-existing assumptions about women that arise from outside the workplace. Notwithstanding these problems, it may be fruitful to draw upon the similarities and differences between working-class women on the shopfloor in manufacturing industries and women workers in flatter organizations, using the idea of workplace culture as a reference point. Both the women workers in Westwood's and Pollert's studies and the women workers in my research undertaking are located in settings in which face-to-face relationships with co-workers and personal emotions figure highly. The shopfloor studies also offer some interesting pointers in that they highlight how the move into waged work simultaneously opens and closes doors for women. Workplace culture offers working-class women a version of womanhood which they take on board in ways which tie them more closely to a feminine destiny. However, whether this could be said to be true of middle-class, well-educated and economically independent women of the kind assumed to predominate in flatter organizations is another matter, particularly given their (assumed) politicization and antipathy to the traditionally circumscribed roles of women as wives/mothers. Again, these are points that will be developed and explored in the course of the fieldwork presented in Part II of this book.

Other ethnographic studies have focused upon the *cult of femininity* found in non-manual workplaces in which women predominate, like offices, and these sites too have been seen as both oppositional and collusive. MacNally (1979) provides some evidence of an active manipulation of their work situations by a group of women workers not usually considered to be in a position to exercise power and control, namely temporary clerical workers. The women in her study were largely employed in jobs which comprised tasks which were highly routine, repetitive and which required little expertise. MacNally argues that by certain techniques of worker control, such as the development of self-help and supportive friendship networks, and by the more dramatic movement into and out of the labour market at their own dictate and in response to their own needs and requirements, these women were engaging in strategies of control over their working lives. Temporary clerical work was often chosen because it enabled women to work when it suited them. MacNally goes so far as to claim that: 'Temporary workers exemplify *par excellence* women's capacity to negotiate the limiting structures which confront them' (1979: 186). Other attractive features of temporary work included variety, both of job content and workplace, and the sense of freedom it generated. Temps could remain more detached from the pressures to conform to prevailing norms concerning behaviour and output.[4]

Barker and Downing have argued that an informal culture which cannot be penetrated by masculine work standards exists amongst women office workers, thus allowing women 'to get away with doing certain things that cannot be controlled' (1980: 83). For example, managers may turn a blind eye to conversations which are personalized and which centre around personal gossip and domestic concerns. Barker and Downing cite the case of the young single clerical worker who arrives late for work, mumbles something about a 'late night' and is excused amidst a host of nods and winks. Like Westwood and Pollert, Barker and Downing argue that this is indicative of a workplace culture which is contradictory, appearing oppressive but at the same time containing the seeds of a specifically feminine form of resistance. They argue that the role of women clerical workers as 'office wives', although characterized by commitment and obedience to their bosses, also allows them to create space and time for themselves, to develop their own rituals and activities such as feminizing the office with pot plants and photographs. Barker and Downing further argue that many women in offices actively refuse to comply with the expected norms of behaviour and that this was reflected in the growth of militancy and unionization amongst clerical workers in the 1970s. Nonetheless, power and control is maintained in subtle ways; the *culture of resistance* operates within capitalist and patriarchal power relations within the office, and women workers as agents are not able to negotiate and manoeuvre as freely as men workers.

It is clear that whereas clerical employment offers women workers opportunities to exercise autonomy and control, in many ways it renders them powerless. Direct experience of being at the vagaries of the market for their labour lead to strong feelings of insecurity amongst temporary clerical workers, an almost inescapable feature of permanent temporary clerical employment. In addition, it is doubtful whether temporary clerical work carries any financial advantages in the long term. Apart from the obvious material disadvantages, there is also the additional problem that temping may fail to live up to expectations. Employment agencies in their capacity as occupational gatekeepers, may be unable or unwilling to effect a match between the temp's requirements or skills and the nature of the jobs/assignments to which she is sent. Thus while a dissatisfaction with permanent clerical work may cause an employee to take up permanent temping, a dissatisfaction with the kinds of jobs she then obtains may cause her to abandon it. There are limits on the extent to which women workers can be constituted as subversive and threatening within these wider socio-structural and discursive constraints, and how this operates for women workers in flatter organizations needs addressing.

Familial Orientations and Family Symbolism

In addition to the feminized cultures operating in workplaces in which women predominate, it has also been claimed that *family* plays a complex and subtle part in most organizations, from small firms employing only direct family labour, to large corporations and even state bureaucracies not organized objectively on family relations (Scase and Goffee, 1980). *Family* in the normative sense means a set of relations based upon discourses of familialism, rather than family as a set of relations governed by ties of blood and kinship, so that organizations with no objective family basis may incorporate discursive rationalizations which are familial in form. For example, the claim advanced by many owners, managers and workers that they are 'one big, happy family' illustrates this point well. In addition, apprenticeships can be underpinned with parent/child bonds, trade unions call upon the legitimacy of brother/ sisterhood and one of the most unionized sections of industry, printing, traditionally involved not shop stewards but 'fathers' of chapels. Some of the research on family, work and organizations has explored the gendering processes involved in familial constructions of work; Eastlea (1983) for example, in his work on the international community of nuclear scientists, traces the sexual and birth metaphors associated with their work by (overwhelmingly male) nuclear scientists.

On the whole, however, the relations between the labour market and *family* in its normative sense have not been an issue of primary concern to organizational and labour market theorists. The growth of modern capitalist industry has tended to be seen as a unilinear movement towards the application of ever-increasing amounts of technology and the consequent growth in the size of units of production, such that there is an eventual transformation of the family as a productive unit to the family as a unit of consumption. However, the validity of this position has been questioned by those who argue that the historical and economic forces at work are more complex than this. The relationship between the family and the workplace is unlikely to have assumed any single, simple pattern. The material conditions of capitalism have ensured that forms of rationality other than the purely calculative remain important, especially in times of economic slump. In such periods, formal rationalities may be underscored in terms of survival and an important factor in such circumstances is often appeals based upon affective and familial loyalties. Such appeals support a system of obligations whereby pressure can be exerted by employers as and when necessary; work is then held to be an affective duty since tasks are undertaken to please another with whom workers are bonded familially, rather than as a calculative action, and as a result it is assumed that they should not worry too much about hours worked or wages received.

Familialism is also important in the day-to-day regulation of work. A quasi-familial form of integration and instruction may be bound up with informal and personalized recruitment strategies. Recruitment networks and procedures which involve families, friends and acquaintances means that employers can make indirect requests of workers by asking relatives or friends of the worker concerned to 'have a word' with them. Close familial relations between co-workers can therefore be seen to support the control dimensions within hierarchical organizations.[5] Furthermore, where there is a fusion of familial relations with more formal, calculative rationalizations, an employer may not need to reproduce the full costs of labour power. For example, in the case of organizations employing family labour proper, the hidden employment of a spouse, siblings or children may mean that specific forms of exploitation occur. This is even more disguised where such relations are discursively familial rather than being directly familial in content and/or form. Frankenberg's comments on the farming industry illustrate this well: 'Even where hired labour is employed, the idea of a family farm persists. Farmers seek out other farmer's sons as labourers and treat them as part of the family. This may raise another difficulty ... *for a family member is not expected to worry about the hours he works or the wages he receives*' (1966: 79–80, emphasis added).

Feminists have taken up the issue of familialism in terms of its significance for women workers. Familial exploitation has been held to exert such a strong grip on women workers in particular that Crompton and Sanderson have referred to it as 'moral despotism' (1990: 146). Pringle (1989) also claims that the significance of 'family' in the workplace is not simply the result of paid work being seen as an extension of women's domestic roles but arises because authority in the workplace is organized around patriarchal familial relations. She argues that the dominant influence of men in the patriarchal nuclear family is paralleled in the hierarchical relations of formal organizations. In many organizations, one person defers to another much as women and children defer to the rule of the father in the patriarchal family, and that this can be evidenced in particular in the workings of the gendered power relations that constitute (men) bosses and (women) secretaries. Despite these various attempts to analyse familialism as a component of relations in paid employment and organizational life, most sociological accounts on the whole have underestimated the importance of familialism as an element in the intersection of gender, work and organization, and have failed to analyse the ways in which familialism acts as both an integrative and divisive force in the labour market. Familialism as a major source of workplace orientations can serve to underpin, usually covertly, the strategies employed by many different types of organization to control workers. This may be as true of flatter organizations as it is of more hierarchical ones. Furthermore, implicated within discourses of familialism are (gendered) processes and practices of sexuality in general and heterosexuality in particular, which are also held to permeate work and organizational life, albeit in ways which have been until recently, under-researched. It is necessary to turn attention to these gendered processes and practices of sexuality as they inform and impact upon work and organizational life, and it is to these issues that the next chapter is directed.

Notes

1 Martin and Wallace (1984) found that women have an 'extraordinary attachment' to paid work, and although they found that there were variations in women's responses according to their employment status, age and educational qualifications, nevertheless a simple positioning of women workers as having little commitment to paid work clearly needed to be qualified.
2 Dex (1984) has substituted the term *profile* to avoid what she sees as the male-centrist connotations which attach to work when the term *career* is used. The concept of career has also come under attack for its assumption of the rational and conscious pursuit of occupational goals, or of a structuring of time in the past, present and future. Hearn (1977) has suggested a broader typology in which people can have *pure careers*, *non-careers*, *un-careers* or be *career-less* and he has since extended this to include *guerrilla careers* and *cop-out careers* (Hearn, 1981).
3 Bourne and Wickler (1978) have referred to these areas as 'discriminatory environments' where the careers of women are shaped in a less advantageous way because of their gender. They also argue that organizational belonging depends not just on involvement in officially sanctioned social activities, but upon the availability of mentors who may be largely confined to white, middle-class men, and the motivating language of the organization which may be couched in terms of male-orientated imagery.
4 Olesen and Katsuransis (1978) also found in their analysis of American temporary employees that temps experienced a heightened sense of autonomy and control because they were able to influence the assignments

offered to them. The temporary employee, they argue, is in a relatively well-placed position to negotiate for the conditions of work she most desires. Olesen and Katsuransis claim that: 'In our analysis, these women emerged not as creatures adrift in a rapacious business world but as individuals exercising critical judgments for themselves and the industry they made possible' (1978: 333).

5 Roberts and Holyroyd cite the case of a transport cafe in which the male owner employed predominantly young women staff and one older woman who, while she did not formally occupy a supervisory position, 'kept the young girls right' (1990: 14). This included making sure that they pulled their weight as well as defending them from the attentions of lorry drivers. The role of 'Mum' played by this older woman included elements of both a defensive response towards 'her girls', but she also ensured that to some extent at least, they behaved responsibly and did some work.

Chapter 5

Gender and Sexuality in Work and Organizations

Sexuality is an important dimension of workers' experiences and yet it has been relatively neglected in both organizational theory and in labour market analyses. MacNally (1979) was arguing more than 15 years ago that sexual interaction in the workplace had been seriously overlooked in sociological research on work and organizations. The situation has since changed, although some would argue that progress on this front has been slow; for example, Hearn and Parkin's (1987) review of the literature on sexuality and organizational life is, they claim, not so much a conventional literature search as a literal search for any research relevant to the issue of sex at work. One of the points highlighted by agency-orientated and resistance approaches to gender, organization and work is the relative failure of socio-structural theories to focus upon the social construction and deployment of sexuality in power relations in the labour market. This has consequences for women workers, particularly those who are feminists and/or lesbians, since although the issue of sexuality in organizations and in work remains largely underresearched, it tends to contribute to the marginalization and devaluation of women as workers, since it is hard to see the sexualized woman worker when only the asexual (but masculinized) worker is present. In denying sexuality at work in this way, it often becomes linked with the (discredited) woman; as Gutek (1985) has claimed, in organizations it often appears that sexuality is only where women are.

One clue as to why there has been this separation of sexuality and paid work in sociological research on the labour market may lie in the arguments advanced by Mitchell (1974) for whom sexuality and the workplace are dichotomous. Sexuality is the province of patriarchal power relations, whose site for Mitchell lies in the unconscious, whereas work is determined by capitalist relations. Mitchell discusses the negation of the links between sexuality and paid work/organizational life in terms of the classic separation between the two systems of patriarchy and capitalism, in which the economic level is ordered by capitalist relations, and the level of the unconscious by the forces of patriarchy. This may account in part for the separation of sexuality and paid work in much sociological research. It is also in the interests of ideal organization to control the disruption and interference posed by sexuality, emotionality and procreation as they pervade organizational processes; constituting them as private renders them invisible and illegitimate. Hearn and Parkin discuss the neglect of sexuality in terms of the ways in which 'ignoring the obvious' removes it from contention, from political argument. They see these processes as operating through, for example, 'the everyday language which says that sexual harassment is "only a bit of a laugh really" ' (1987: 5). Tancred-Sheriff suggests that sexuality has not appeared to be an explicit part of the labour market because front-line women in organizations, whose job it is to deal with customers, clients and co-workers on a routine basis, are located in areas of 'adjunct control'; namely, 'between the labour process and control systems' (1989: 520) and are therefore on the margins of more formal control and appraisal systems. Notwithstanding these differences over the reasons for neglect, there is now broad agreement that sexuality remains a strong under-current in organizational power relations, even though this may not always be made explicit.

Despite Hearn and Parkin's claim that feminists have focused too narrowly on (hetero)sexual[1] harassment of women by men in the workplace, it is fair to say that the sociological understanding of organizational life has been changed by the attention given to (hetero)sexual harassment (Hadjifotiou, 1983; MacKinnon, 1979; Wise and Stanley, 1987). MacKinnon, for example, quite correctly raises the question of why, even if capitalism 'requires some collection of individuals to occupy low status, low paying jobs . . . such persons must be biologically female. The fact that male employers often do not hire qualified women, even when they could pay them less than men, suggests that more than the profit motive is implicated' (1979: 15–16). She cites a wealth of material documenting not only women's segregation into low paying service jobs, but also argues that the sexualization of women workers is often an (unwritten) condition of employment. MacKinnon claims that central to the economic realities of women's working lives is the requirement that they will market sexual attractiveness to men; women workers have to behave in an ingratiating heterosexual manner, she argues, because this is often an implicit qualification for employment, whatever the job description. MacKinnon concludes that: 'Sexual harassment perpetuates the interlocked structure by which women workers have been kept sexually in thrall to men at the bottom of the labour market. Two forces of American society converge; men's control over women's sexuality and capital's control over employees' work lives.' (1979: 174). MacKinnon's work on sexual harassment is useful because it suggests that men managers' motives are not an integrated totality nor are they exclusively concerned with the organization and control of labour power, irrespective of the gender and sexual identities of workers. However, MacKinnon does provide a deterministic analysis which underestimates the significance of other ways in which sexualized power and control dynamics affect women workers' experiences, not least how the constitution of sexualities other than passive heterosexuality operates to position some women in complex and contradictory relations to other women and to men.

In recent years there has been greater academic recognition of the idea that organizations are themselves involved in the production and reproduction of the social construction of various sexualities (Brewis and Grey, 1994; Burrell, 1984; Filby, 1992; Pringle, 1989). Pringle (1989) for example, has located work in the context of debates concerning cultures, sexualities and subjectivities. In her study of secretaries (and bosses), she argues for the centrality of sexuality, family and personal life in the analysis of the organization of work and the production of power relations within the workplace. She claims that the boss–secretary relationship is organized around sexuality and familialism, and that such relations are often conceptualized as chaotic, archaic and marginal to the workings of 'bureaucracy proper', which is based upon conventions of legality and rationality. For Pringle, however, an analysis which draws attention to sexuality and familialism in the workplace vividly illustrates the workings of modern, bureaucratic organizations. Pringle further maintains that power relations in organizations are often based upon men's sexual interests and upon heterosexuality, although this may not be made explicit. She notes that the traditional association between masculinity and rationality allows men's sexuality to remain buried and yet dominant within the workplace. The attention given to sexual harassment at work has also highlighted how *coercive* forms of power and control operate at the expense of control through (supposedly) less coercive constructions of heterosexuality such as sexual joking and game-playing in relations between men and women at work. Finally, Pringle has argued that women's resistance within discourses of power requires strategies which recognize and embrace, rather than seek to deny, sexualities. If the normality of heterosexuality is not so much compulsory as Rich (1980) has argued, but is open to negotiation and reinscription, then patriarchal power relations cannot necessarily be seen as being enacted to censor and control *all* the various forms of expression that sexuality in the workplace might take. Sexuality thus offers a resource for resistance, even if only partial and temporary, since women's engagement with heterosexuality can for example, be directed towards embarrassing and undermining heterosexual men as figures of power and authority.[2]

These fluid, negotiable and disruptive dynamics of sexuality are highlighted by Hearn and Parkin (1987) to illustrate the powerful and paradoxical forms of interrelationship between the public realm of the organization and the private realm of the intimate/familial. In their view, organizational sexuality assumes its own erotic and developing symbolism, which is a powerful yet underemphasized current in work and organizational life. They argue that examples of organizational sexuality are everywhere – in the movement of people through organization, and in the patterns of emotions, consciousness, language and imagery in organizations.[3] They also argue that an important component of modern feminism is not just the recognition of the traditional division between paid work, organization and sexuality, but also the development of practical ways of transcending the desexualization of paid work/ organizational life. They suggest that many feminist critiques of organizational dynamics have been concerned primarily with gender segregation, the sexual division of labour, and men's power and authority, so that sexuality, where it is addressed, follows from these, rather than acts as a dynamic in itself. In short, Hearn and Parkin maintain that even in feminist research on gender and work, sexuality has been a peripheral concern.

It would appear that the interconnections between hierarchical organization and heterosexuality have not been given sufficient attention hitherto. The dominance of heterosexuality is not restricted to incidents and events within the life of an organization, but is constitutive of the hierarchical power relations upon which organizations are based. It would appear therefore that less heterosexual/patriarchal processes and practices of power and control are more likely to be constitutive of less or non-hierarchical organization, whereas hierarchical organizations are inevitably 'contaminated' by heterosexuality. The attempts by some women workers to create a space for themselves in the form of setting up and working in flatter organizations may not only represent an attempt by such women to avoid hierarchical organization, but may also involve an attempt to circumvent and escape the dynamics of *hetero*sexualized, as well as *gendered* power and control relations. In short, women workers in co-operatives and collectives may be seeking to establish organizational sites which are quite distinct from the (hetero)sexual/patriarchal form of hierarchical organization. The ways in which gender and sexuality are differently constituted within flatter organizations, and how this shapes the experiences of *women* workers in co-operatives and collectives in particular, therefore requires greater consideration.

From this brief review of recent literature, it can be seen that, for some writers, sexuality is as central to paid work, organizations and the labour market as it is to family and domestic life (Adkins, 1995). Furthermore, it can be argued that sexuality is central not only to boss–secretary relations, but to many different forms of power and control relations in the labour market. Nevertheless, those in positions of power and control may have only a tenuous grasp over the use of sexuality as a management resource; sexuality is generally constituted in terms of sexual attractiveness or personality and therefore it is neither openly articulated in managerial relations nor are audit mechanisms made available for its recognition, categorization and appraisal. More so than gender, sexuality remains uncharted territory in many hierarchical organizations and the consequences of its exposure as such in the workplace are not always predictable. This gives rise to the possibility of gendered and sexualized forms of resistance on the part of women and men workers which need addressing.

Lesbianism, Work and Organization

One aspect of sexuality which has not received much, if any, attention in the sociological literature on gender, work and organization is the differential experiences of those whose lifestyles and sexual identities do not conform to the prescribed heterosexual norm (Hall, 1989; Schneider, 1988; Squirell, 1989; Taylor, N., 1986). On a daily basis, most lesbians and gay men experience problematic social interactions within public arenas, but it is in paid work, more than other public settings perhaps, that interactional difficulties arise most persistently. The problems are not about the content of the work itself, but about all the social aspects of the job that heterosexuals often take for granted. Lesbians have commented, for example, that the only personal talk they engage in at work concerns their pets or their parents (stereotypically their cats and their mothers) which serves to reinforce discourses of lesbians as unhappy, lonely, frustrated and not 'real' women.

Most organizations tend to be dominated by heterosexuals and hetero-sexual discourses and practices, and as a consequence, they tend to be hostile places for lesbians and gay men to work in and to pursue careers. Power relations in hierarchical organizations tend to be sexualized as well as gendered; they eroticize women workers as well as feminizing them for the purposes of (men's) domination and control. However, this eroticization of women workers is not without contradictions; it can act to position women not only as passive and demure, but also as merely decorative and bordering on the useless. If women workers resist men's sexualized power and control in organizations, then they are usually positioned as undesirable/unfeminine and/ or masculinized, unattractive, honorary men. In either case, they are viewed as asexual or de-sexualized, since it is often assumed that failing to conform to the eroticized power relations of heterosexuality signifies a lack of any sexual-ity. However, if women workers are not simply undesirable/unattractive but are also or are instead positioned as lesbian, then this poses problems for the heterosexualized control of women workers in paid work/organizational life. Lesbianism can be discursively eroticized by and for heterosexual men, but such men's expressions of heterosexual interest/power are less likely to incite the appropriate sexual response from lesbians themselves; for example, they are less likely than other women to engage in sexual banter with men or to find expressions of men's heterosexuality erotically appealing.

The construction and deployment of both homosexuality and lesbianism in paid work and organizations has been one (or two) of the most neglected areas in research which attempts to address sexuality at work (Oerton, 1996). Because very little of the wide-ranging, quantitative, survey-style research on gender and work ever inquires about sexual identity, valuable opportunities for comparative analysis of the similarities and differences in the experiences of lesbians, gay men and heterosexuals at work is unattainable. The material consequences of non-compliance to sexualized controls in cases where women have resisted or complained of (hetero)sexual harassment have been identi-fied, and include removal, demotion and transfer (Thomas and Kitzinger, 1994), but whether non-compliance to such control dynamics in the form of expressions of lesbianism at work carries the same penalties for (real or assumed) lesbians as for heterosexual women has not been established. The almost complete lack of research in this area is matched only by the lack of research on the experiences of lesbians compared with gay men at work. Given Rich's claim that 'A lesbian['s] . . . job depends on her pretending to be not merely heterosexual, but a heterosexual *woman* in terms of dressing and playing the feminine, deferential role required of "real" women' (1980: 16, original emphasis), it would be surprising if the 'penalties' incurred by gay men and lesbians at work for not conforming to heterosexualized controls were the same.[4] In addition, given the importance attributed to heterosexualized power and control in hierarchical organizations discussed earlier, it would follow that the disruption to the normality of heterosexuality posed by lesbianism represents a particular threat to the maintenance of gendered hierarchy within organizations, but this too has not been systematically explored.

Most workers engage in discourses and practices in the workplace that reflect and reinforce what occurs in non-work settings, so that power relations in both work and non-work include a view of heterosexuality as the only important, real and natural sorts of relations in which to engage. Tied to this is a view that every woman needs to be connected to a man for emotional, practical and economic support. The very pervasiveness of these linked assumptions means that lesbianism is seldom raised as an issue at work, except in the form of derogatory comments and passing remarks to the 'other'. This creates problems for research which focuses upon the employment experiences of lesbians and gay men. But since lesbians are particularly vulnerable and often hide their sexual identity at work, contacts and collaborations between researcher and researchee are especially difficult. Schneider for example, discusses the problem of knowing who was and is a lesbian, in her research on lesbians' experiences in corporate organizations, and she highlights how research is affected by the fact that most lesbians hide their sexual identities in the context of work. She maintains that: 'any account of lesbians' employment experiences is at best a speculative effort to overcome a deep cultural silence and intentional invisibility' (1988: 274). Most research will rely upon volunteer or snowballing contacts through lesbian and gay networks and organizations, or will solicit respondents through the lesbian and gay press. Schneider also maintains that some researchers still hesitate however, to study lesbians and gay men for fear of being known as lesbian or gay themselves and suffering the career consequences.

Much of the recent research on lesbianism, work and organization has been conducted in the US and it is difficult to determine how much bearing these studies may have upon lesbians' experiences of work in the UK (Hall, 1989; Schneider, 1988). In her research upon American lesbians in a variety of occupations, Hall (1989) argues that lesbians are likely to experience double jeopardy in terms of their gender as women and their sexuality as lesbians. She suggests that the decision processes that lesbians undergo in relation to the disclosure or non-disclosure of their sexuality at work, is characterized by processes of doubt, confusion and ambiguity. She refers to the development of coping strategies designed: 'to maneuver in inimical environments in which any deviation from male, heterosexual norms results in less status, less opportunity, loss of co-workers' esteem, ostracism, harassment and/or firing.' (1989: 135). Hall maintains that lesbians' concealment of their sexuality sometimes occurred automatically and at other times it was deliberate and felt more stressful. The lesbians she interviewed were not only continually on guard but also had to be attuned to the hidden nuances of behaviour, values and attitudes, both of themselves and others, in order to detect where and when vigilance was necessary and where and when it was possible to 'relax and be herself' (1989: 129). This heightened awareness and sensitivity is read as positive by Hall. Nonetheless, she argues that most of the lesbians she interviewed felt hopeless about creating change in their organization and many planned to go into business for themselves or to become freelance consultants where there lesbianism would not be an obstacle.

Research in the UK is harder to come by, although Hall's arguments are borne out by Squirell's (1989) research on British lesbian and gay school teachers. Squirell argues that the lesbian teachers she interviewed tempered their feminist politics at work, either because they felt that others were likely to see their sexuality as discrediting their politics, or because they kept a low profile generally to avoid homophobic reactions from colleagues and the school community. Squirell also argues that people on the margins develop greater insights; the lesbian and gay teachers she interviewed, experiencing (real or anticipated) victimization as they did, felt that they had gained extra sensitivity to other forms of discrimination. However, Squirell deals only in very general terms with the gendering of such experiences of anti-lesbianism/ homophobia, and there are no pointers as to how the experiences of discrimination and disadvantage faced by lesbian teachers may be differently theorized from gay men teachers' experiences of discrimination. Finally, one of the few pieces of quantitative research on lesbians' un/employment experiences in the UK comes from a small-scale survey undertaken by the Lesbian Rights Support Group (Taylor, N., 1986) and illustrates how the dominance of heterosexual discourse and practice in work organizations constitutes a form of anti-lesbianism in itself – for example, in co-workers assuming that all women are heterosexual. The report concludes: 'Our research shows that heterosexism, in the form of assumed heterosexuality and anti-lesbianism, pervades almost every workplace' (1986: 30).

Based upon this research, it would appear that lesbians have a well-founded apprehension about their reception in the workplace. Many lesbians not only develop strategies for protecting themselves in inhospitable workplace cultures, but they also seek practical means of resolving the difficulties they encounter in male-dominated, hierarchical organizations. If it is the case that working in flatter organizations creates space not only for women who are seeking to circumvent the power and control relations found in male-dominated organizations, but also for women who are seeking a safer space in which to express their lesbianism outside the heterosexualized power and control relations of most organizations, then this has to be acknowledged and incorporated into research on flatter organizations. This opens up difficulties too for the arguments concerning patriarchal power relations advanced by some socio-structural theorists, who maintain that through the institution of marriage and the exploitation of wives' labour by their husbands, all women come to constitute, first and foremost, a gendered category of worker and this is held to be of greater significance presumably, than whether such women are heterosexual or not (or even whether they are actually married, or about to be married, or have never or never will be married). These arguments will be returned to later, but it is useful at this point to turn to a review of the contributions to our understanding of power, gender and sexuality in work and organizational life offered by post-structuralist analyses.

Post-Structuralism, Feminism and Sexuality

Post-structuralists' analyses of power, gender and sexuality offer no consistent or homogeneous body of theory; nonetheless they may offer valuable frameworks for the purpose of providing a context in which to theorize the experiences of women and men workers in flatter organizations. Feminist theory too has placed gender, sexuality and the embodied elements of work on the agenda as serious media for understanding how central these are to women's obedience (or resistance) to the rules and practices of heterosexuality as constituted under capitalist and patriarchal power relations, and how central work and organization is to the deployment of these power relations. In this context, the work of Foucault (1979, 1985, 1986), MacKinnon (1982, 1983, 1987) and Adkins (1995) will be discussed.

For Foucault, power is capillary, shifting and unstable; it does not emanate from above, as the possession of a particular group such as the managerial elite. The individual or subject is constructed by discourses; in short, we are positioned by how we are addressed in our situation. Foucault argues that there are a multiplicity of discourses that come into play, and when they do, power relations are created. Foucault's concern was with how the subject, or more specifically the body, was made to present itself as an object of knowledge in the exercise of power. As Crowley and Himmelweit argue: 'Power is activated when people assume identities which are included within the prevailing views of the world. By occupying certain places within a discourse, the subject, according to Foucault, is empowered to act according to the identity prescribed by that discourse' (1992: 236). Hence, there is no essential Self to be discovered; the subject is fragmented between different social positions. In other words, there is no single, unified Self which travels through history, always the same and entirely known to itself. Instead discourses recognize and position us so that how something is read is not by disclosing any essential definitive meaning, but by a plurality of alternative readings and responses. In short, the truth of a discourse lies in its non-fixity; it cannot be guaranteed by anything external to it.[5]

From about the mid-1970s Foucault argued that sex and the body are not biological facts but are an effect of discourses of sexuality and the regulation and management of sexual practices. Both the discourses and practices act as mechanisms of power/knowledge so that subjects inscribe themselves in these power relations, monitoring their own actions in an attempt to ensure that they remain within the rules set down by the power relations under whose gaze they live, even though it is not always possible for the observed subject to know how and in what ways the gaze is focused upon them. Foucault offered new ways of thinking about sex and sexuality which are embedded in power relations without being overly deterministic.[6] In theorizing sex, bodies and sexuality in terms of discursive practices, he shows how ways of producing sexual knowledge and shaping the world according to that knowledge are crucial. As a result, Foucault's analysis of discourses has enabled him to argue that everything about sex and the body is constructed by culture and history. With industrialization, Foucault argues, sex became the explosive talking point: 'over these last three centuries ... around and apropos of sex, one sees a veritable discursive explosion' (Foucault, 1979: 17). In the shift from feudalism to industrialism he argues, sex and sexuality became an arena for discourse and the target of social intervention. A regime of heterosexual conjugality emerged which was economically useful and politically conservative. The specific forms of the discourses were religious (codes of heterosexual monogamy), bureaucratic/legal (glorification of the family, toleration and persecution of normal and deviant sexual identities) and scientific/medical (scrutinization of sexual behaviours and procreation).

Although Foucault was largely uninterested in feminism and issues of gender, feminist theories have engaged in debates which draw upon Foucault's analysis of power/knowledge and discourse (Diamond and Quinby, 1988; McNay, 1992; Nicholson, 1990; Ramazanoglu, 1989; Vance, 1989). Foucault's work presents a number of problems for feminism however. First, he does not systematically consider the highly gendered ways in which individual subjects are constructed and construct themselves, hence he presents a masculinized conception of the Self (Diamond and Quinby, 1988; McNay, 1992). For Foucault, there is no significant qualitative difference between discourses about women's sexualities and bodies and discourses about men's sexualities and bodies. Hence there is no way of analysing what allows men and women to occupy certain subject positions and not others within discourses. For example, MacNay suggests: 'Foucault's preoccupation with experimental subject positions is suspicious in as much as it is the expression of a privileged, white male perspective which has already had an Enlightenment and is now willing to subject that legacy to critical scrutiny' (1992: 112). Second, power/knowledge is seen as constituted so widely that it becomes pointless to see it as restrictive and hence there is no real distinction between benign and oppressive power. It is neither positive nor negative, but is, to use Foucault's term, productive. In disregarding the context of power in this way, it is difficult to see how sexuality is or becomes a site of oppression for women, as many feminists have argued. Without an understanding of sexuality and its part in the development of forms of power/knowledge integral to women's oppression, the scope of the theoretical work that can be undertaken as part of the feminist project is limited. Third, the notion of sexuality as a social construct, while problematizing essentialist, sexological and biological theories of sexuality, leaves it free-floating and disembodied in a literal sense. As Vance argues: 'the object of study – sexuality – becomes evanescent and threatens to disappear' (1989: 137). In short, feminism needs, for its theoretical project, to retain the question of what the 'it' is that is being constructed and studied, as well as how 'it' connects with anything to do with our bodies. Finally, it is argued that Foucault cannot adequately theorize the basis of any kind of collective feminist politics through which women create space for resistance and where opposing forces to those dominant in society might assert themselves (Nicholson, 1990). The stress placed on the unstable and decentralized nature of the Self can be seen as oppressive because it denies marginalized groups the space in which to construct a coherent identity for themselves and thereby initiate a politics of resistance. As Hartsock has asked, 'Why is it just at the moment when so many of us who have been silenced begin to demand the right to name ourselves, to act as subjects rather than objects of history, that just then the concept of subjecthood becomes problematic?' (1990: 163).

Ferguson and Wicke (1984) have countered this by claiming that feminist discourses, rooted in women's experiences of caring and nurturing outside bureaucratic systems of control, provide grounds for opposition and for the development of alternative ways of organizing society. However, the problems with Ferguson and Wicke's view have their origins in Foucault's work, on which they build. Complex, bureaucratic systems are seen as disembodied sites of oppression, and gender enters only as an analogy, rather than as a component of processes of domination and control. All this leaves the feminist project in difficulty with respect to Foucauldian theories of discursive sexualities. Some feminists have argued that there are useful and problematic elements in Foucault's writings; they have adopted a prescription to treat his writings as a toolbox, suggesting that it is possible to pick and choose bits from what he has to offer. What this means can be explored through a discussion of feminist sociologists who have developed some of the threads of Foucault's writings to produce some rich and dynamic theoretical work. But before reviewing such work, it is useful to turn first to feminist sociologists who have attempted to situate the discursive relations of sex and sexuality at the centre of any analysis of the materiality of work, organizations and labour markets.

Feminists such as MacKinnon (1982, 1987) take issue with the poststructuralist view of sex and sexuality as fictions, independent of the inequalities that operate in relation to, without necessarily being rooted in, the body. MacKinnon analyses women's experiences of sexual objectification – of rape, pornography and violence – as the core process by which the inequality of power between men and women operates. She argues that sexual access to women is constitutive of the privileges which men as the dominant sex enjoy, and that violence against those without power is experienced as sexual pleasure and is therefore what defines sex. MacKinnon claims:

> Violence is sex when it is practiced as sex. If violation of the power-less is part of what is sexy about sex, as well as central in the meaning of male and female, the place of sexuality in gender and the place of gender in sexuality need to be looked at together. When this is done, sexuality appears as the interactive dynamic of gender as an inequality (1987: 115).

Furthermore, MacKinnon argues that the sexual domination of women is embedded in bureaucratic/legal organizations so that the hierarchical process of gendering that goes on in the labour market includes the 'sexualization of the woman worker as part of the job' (MacKinnon, 1979: 18). MacKinnon argues that the result of denying the sexualization of hierarchy is that behaviours such as sexual harassment are viewed as deviations of gendered actors and not as components of organizational structure. With respect to MacKinnon's claim that sexuality exists only in the context of gendered hierarchy, there have been criticisms of her work as falling into reification and essentialism, for not tolerating ambiguity and fluidity.

This is less of a problem in the research by Adkins (1995), whose work on the UK tourist industry considers the gendering of the relations of production and appropriation in terms of sexuality *and* family; the aim is to take issue with theories of the labour market which have negated or understated the role that sexuality, sexual work and familial power relations play in constituting gendered labour market production. Adkins shows how heterosexuality, sexualized and familial work relations not only inform but also construct the economic. These issues are explored using data from the hotel, leisure park, pub and catering industries; the analysis of sexuality and sex-power relations are largely located and theorized from within a consideration of two medium-sized tourist establishments (a hotel and leisure park), while the pub or hotel married management team are the focus for explicating the operation of family power relations. However, Adkins's critique of the theoretical neglect of sexuality as constitutive of gendering processes in the labour market is given greater attention than her critique of theories of family work relations, which are treated briefly in comparison.[7] There thus remains further work to be done on how the sexual and familial intersect in terms of being implicated in the processes Adkins analyses. A further problem is the neglect of issues of agency and resistance; for example, there is little or no consideration of how women workers' subjectivities, as framed within these sexual and familial power relations, might be constituted. This means that very little attention is paid to the ways in which women's resistance is possible or is practiced. Adkins argues that that form of women's work which is constituted as sexual operates in conditions which allow minimal, or virtually no, scope for women workers to resist, manoeuvre or subvert processes of familial positioning, sexualization and commodification. In the case of hotel manager's wives working under patriarchal family relations as part of a married management team, their compliance is reduced to an effect of women making the best of their limited employment opportunities, whereas the relative advantages as the women see them, of wives' labour being appropriated and controlled by husbands as opposed to male employers, are not considered. It is interesting to speculate about how these sexualizing and familial processes as they inform gendered hierarchies such as those found in tourist establishments, organize other workplaces, and whether women's resistance is as muted as appears to be the case in the organizations/industries investigated by Adkins. These arguments will be returned to later since they provide a framework from within which to approach the analysis of gender and sexuality in flatter organizations, as will be seen in Part II.

Gender, Sexuality and Organization

The ways in which power relations operate through bodies and sexualities, and the difficulties of challenging them, have meant that power, gender and sexuality are central concerns for feminist and post-structuralist theories of work and organization. For the purposes of the arguments presented here, the work of Acker (1990), Cockburn (1983, 1985) and Hacker (1988, 1989) is particularly important and will now be discussed. Acker (1990) argues that organizations are arenas in which both gender and sexuality have been obscured through gender-neutral, asexual discourses. She argues that this is partly achieved through obscuring the embodied elements of work; job positions and management hierarchies assume a universal, disembodied worker. Acker claims that men's bodies, men's sexualities and men's relationships to procreation and production are subsumed in this image of the disembodied worker, and that gender is difficult to see when only the masculine is present. She concludes that as well as comprising part of the larger strategy of control within male-dominated, hierarchically-structured organizations, these processes are part of a deeply-embedded substructure of gender inequality which marginalizes women and contributes to the maintenance of gender domination and segregation in organizations. Although Acker's work makes an important contribution in tying male-domination so closely to heterosexuality, she fails to theorize the place of (anti-)lesbianizing discourses within organizational structures, giving primacy instead to the effects of heterosexualization. In a similar vein to her criticism that gender-neutral discourses of organizations mask the power of masculinity, the focus upon heterosexuality as a component of oppressive power tends to de-sexualize and render invisible any role for the discourses and practices of anti-lesbianism and homophobia that are components of power and control in gendered hierarchies.

Nevertheless, in challenging prevailing gender power relations in this way, feminist theorists have confronted not only the ideas but also the institutions which use those ideas to justify and rationalize their exclusion of women. This is foregrounded in the work of Cockburn (1983, 1985) which, although not specifically post-structuralist in orientation, does focus upon heterosexualized masculinity and how it is implicated in the power structures involved in defining and distributing skills and in instituting technological changes in the workplace. Cockburn argues that technologies which are newly invented and neutral, become gendered by user-association, so that for example, *decor* is feminine, *pasting up* masculine. But whether the binarism of hard/soft, dirty/clean, and so forth are employed, she argues that what defines these technologies are power relations which are highly gendered. She maintains that women's exclusion is part of the process of creating certain skills, *tools* and *technologies* as masculine, and by extension, creating the *unskilled*, *non-mechanic* and *technological inept* as feminine. Cockburn is thus concerned with: 'technical competence, who has it, what authority it confers and what connection it has with rocking the cradle and ruling the world' (1985: 6). Her conclusions, based on research on fieldwork in workplaces in which craft and technical skills are gendered masculine, is that: 'women may push the buttons, but they may not meddle with the works' (1985: 12).

In effect, Cockburn argues, what is gendered feminine is more easily controlled. This arises partly because men workers' images of masculinity link their gender with their technical skills and the possibility that women might also obtain such skills represents a threat to that masculinity. It also arises because men see women as oppositional – static, domestic, private, non-workers. As a result, if women are occupiers of men's world, they are clearly out of place since it is inconceivable that women possess equal competencies. Gendering of work and workplaces is thus an active process which can intimidate women workers and let them know that they are not welcome. This intimidation can take the form of anything from trivialization to severe harassment. Production processes involve the generation of maculinized workplace cultures too; Cockburn argues that competitive swearing, obscenity, the trade in sexual stories, sexual references and innuendo forge a solidarity in the workplace that women cannot easily enter. Thus, women workers have to find ways of coping and adapting in order to survive in such workplaces. This may take the form of male sponsorship, for example, by becoming one of the lads, and by taking particular care over their appearance or avoidance, for example, by women absenting themselves from certain areas of work.

Cockburn is clear on several points. First, she points to the links between the politics of the sexed body and the politics of technology. She argues that the concerns of masculinity involve complementarity between the sexes, but a complementarity which is structured in such a way to produce inequality. Second, she is clear that work is not merely a site which simply reinforces or reflects already existing power relations, but that work is an interactive two-way process that *constructs* gender hierarchy. There are a number of problems with Cockburn's analysis, however. First, she does what she says the sex/gender system does in that she oppositionally defines women after defining men; she discusses men's gendered identities and then suggests that what is left is women's identities. Second, she seems to be fairly convinced from the beginning of women's lack of technological competence – or 'know-how' – relative to men's. Assumptions about women's lack of technological competence, however, may be an aspect of the ideological representations of technology – representations which do not permit women to be equated with technological competence – rather than a lived reality for women. If women are not technologically incompetent, then Cockburn is falling into the trap of presenting them as passively and statically so. This is evidenced in the way Cockburn sees women as 'actively excluded from technological knowledge, acted upon by the technology and not interactive with it' (1985: 9). It can be argued instead that women can be extremely resourceful in accessing technologies and exercising power through such access. Third, although Cockburn examines in detail the relations between men and women as groups of workers, she locates her analysis in the realm of theory and when she descends to the actual interplays between women and men at work, for example, when she documents and details sexual harassment, she attributes it to men 'staking a claim' over technology and showing how it is their 'private property'. This must be an incomplete analysis since sexual harassment is not solely confined to men's technological workplaces or even to paid work.[8]

Hacker's research (1988, 1989) on the other hand, is only indirectly tied to heterosexuality and takes gender instead as its central focus. Hacker is concerned with the processes of gender power relations that emerge in what she refers to as 'the pleasures of technology', both in the organization of resources to accomplish work and specifically, the passions and energies involved in making technologies work. She argues that the pleasures of technology have been harnessed to power and domination over nature, the machine and other people, particularly women. This raises questions about how the discipline and control integral to the organization of technologies shape and use the exhilarating, the sensual and the erotic, and limit them to relations of dominance and subordination. The role of masculine eroticism in hierarchically ordered power relations, Hacker maintains, is expressed through increasingly sophisticated technologies, such as evidenced in the industrial–military complex. This leads Hacker to question: 'how men are persuaded to give over autonomy and come to value a narrow, technological rationality . . . to accept as normal and right the contemporary shape of relationships, sexuality and eroticism, technology and work . . .' (1989: xii). In short, Hacker ties feminist analyses of eroticism, domination and the objectification of women, to the development of a gendered technology that is a central aspect of organizations, the economy and the military. She maintains that men lose from this reinscription of the erotic into gender domination, but that they also win in other ways. Her plea is that: 'We would more likely express playfulness and mutuality in new technologies if we lived in a society in which eroticism was part of reciprocal, egalitarian relations' (1989: 138). Finally therefore, Hacker is interested not only in the ways in which gender power inequalities are constituted through technological pleasures, but also how this is part of the *problem of achieving more co-operative and communal ways of living and working.* She argues that: 'in a fully democratic and participatory workplace, we should expect to find better relations among gender, race and technology. We shall see' (Hacker, 1989: xix).

By posing issues of gender power relations in this way, Hacker tries to envisage how technologies can be transformed along more egalitarian-feminist lines. The question is bound up with a reworking of sexuality and eroticism, technology and work, around equal and reciprocal relations between men and women. Such a project is viewed as collective and political, and the formation of democratic, participatory workplaces is seen as one of the possible paths to pursue in this quest. As Hacker states: 'Co-operative workplaces offer a contrast to military-like organization of work . . . They can jointly decide what to make or sell and how, share most of the profits, and give the rest back to the community for child-care, health and education . . . *Co-operative workplaces could also require gender equality*' (1989: 75, emphasis added). Thus in order to substantiate her arguments empirically, she presents a detailed case study of the Mondragon system of producer and manufacturing co-operatives in the Basque region of Spain. However, the conclusions drawn with respect to Hacker's case study material are not encouraging; she suggests that the experiences of women workers in co-operatives are not markedly different from those of women in capitalist or non-capitalist workplaces (1989: 238). Although she found that the co-operative structure benefited women workers in many ways, several factors continued to structure gender inequalities, namely in respect of market-wage levels, specifically in low-waged female contract labour, in women's unpaid domestic labour and in their economic dependence upon their husbands. Several women workers at Mondragon saw their co-operatives as hopelessly traditional, especially in their views of women's role in the family. An additional problem as the community modernized its technological base was the increasing reliance on professional expertise. This tended to erode the autonomy and democratic participation of workers at lower levels, where women predominated. Hacker concludes that major obstacles to democratic participation lie in the gendered structure of technology which meshes with the administrative practices of the organizations she studied.

This sounds like technological determinism; technology *is* important but so are other factors. Gender is clearly central to Hacker's analysis but her work tends to problematize the flattening of hierarchical power relations in co-operative organizations with reference entirely to gender. Sexuality is left untouched and unanalysed; she fails to relate her analysis of gendered power relations to the mixed-sex composition of the co-operatives and collectives she studied. Thus the mixed-sex composition of these organizations, the (assumed) heterosexuality of workers and the heterosexism of organizations are treated as given and unproblematic in her otherwise ground-breaking research. Bearing in mind these criticisms, it is clear that workers' experiences in flatter organizations must be studied by engaging with the fluid, interactive and dynamic character of gender, sexuality and power. Gender and sexuality are not stable or cohesive elements of work and organizational life, but provide the fluid dynamics upon which power relations are mapped out. In Hacker's analysis of the Mondragon co-operatives, sexuality is collapsed onto gender, whereas the arguments developed in this book point to the importance of recognizing not only how heterosexuality underpins discourses of power relations in hierarchical organizations, but also how discourses of lesbianism, anti-lesbianism and homophobia differentially inform and impact upon workers in less or non-hierarchical organizations.

Beyond Hierarchy?

Feminist analysis has moved on from questions of women's disadvantage and inequality to the broader problematic of the gendering and sexualization of all social structures, processes and practices. This means examining the organization of gender and sexuality in their present and emergent forms within various locations and discourses of power. From this standpoint it is clear that women's and men's experiences in flatter organizations cannot be studied using traditional organizational ideas alone, especially as systematic feminist theories of organizational dynamics are still in their infancy and also need explicating and developing (Brown, 1992; Fried, 1994; Rothschild, 1990). Socio-structural and/or agency-orientated approaches are also by themselves only of limited usefulness in theorizing the relationship between gender, sexuality, power and hierarchy. The dynamic and interactive character of gender and sexuality as they inform the power relations of flatter organizations must be explored in order to bring research to life. How this might be done can be explored by means of finding common threads in many of the writings on gender, sexuality, work and organization which have been reviewed in this and the preceding chapters. One of these common threads is that women's experiences in the labour market cannot be understood without reference to the interconnections between women's position in the family or domestic sphere, and their position in the work organizations and the labour market. In its early formulations this approach was termed the *gender/job model* of women's work, with women's (paid) work situations simply read off unproblematically as an effect of their positions as wives and mothers. Some materialist feminist theorists such as Delphy (1977, 1980a) argue that all women, whether wives or not, are materially circumscribed by the position of most women in the patriarchal, domestic or family mode of production. They are not part of the same system of theoretical reference as men, whether or not they are married and/or have children, and experience systematic disadvantage *vis-à-vis* men. For other feminist sociologists, the debate has been concerned with whether gender inequality can be understood in terms of the structural gendering processes that go on in the labour market itself

(Hartmann, 1979; Walby, 1986b, 1990) or whether gendering dynamics are located outside of the labour market, in the realm of the cultural and ideological for example (Pollert, 1981; Westwood, 1984).

Some feminists have argued that not all women workers form a homogeneous group and that different groups of women, by virtue of, for example, establishing their own democratic and participatory enterprises circumvent some (but perhaps not all) of the constraints faced by women employed in traditional, male-dominated hierarchies (Brown, 1992; Cadman et al., 1981; Fried, 1994; Gould, 1980; Mansbridge, 1980; Rothschild, 1990). Some women workers might therefore be seen as archetypes for feminist aspirations in organizations and in the labour market; they are viewed as active agents in terms of challenging and resisting male-dominated hierarchy. The matter may go deeper than this, however, since it is argued by post-structuralist feminists that gender, sexuality and family are not stable or cohesive elements of work and organizational life, but provide the fluid dynamics upon which power relations are mapped out (Pringle, 1989). This opens up the possibility of new readings of the experiences of women and men workers in one particular setting – the less or non-hierarchical, flatter organization – and it is to an empirical analysis of women and men workers in these organizations that Part II of the book is directed.

Notes

1 In nearly all cases sexual harassment is simply assumed to involve harassment of heterosexual women by heterosexual men. This disguises other forms of sexual harassment (of lesbians, for example) which goes on in the workplace and elsewhere, and which needs to be carefully distinguished from (hetero)sexual form of harassment.

2 In his case-study analysis of the off-course betting industry, Filby claims that the dominant assumptions of men's sexuality were frequently challenged by the women cashiers in the betting shops he observed, to the extent that the dominance of organizational heterosexuality was 'rumbled in ways which are far removed from the politics of lesbian and gay rights' (1992: 25).

3 Hearn and Parkin (1987) point out that in the micro-politics of organization, sexuality can be an important resource for men managers. They point to the ways in which men managers can make use of sexual game-playing and sexual jokes as a means of controlling women employees. They refer to these relations of labour in which women workers become objects of 'simpering passivity' for men as a variant of the 'reserve army' thesis, detailing what they term 'a reserve of sexual labour' which provides the foundations for the 'social and formally structured expression of the hierarchic power relations of sexuality between men and women [in organization]' (1987: 138).

4 In general, it is fair to say that there has been very little research on the

experiences of lesbians and gay men in paid work and organizational life *per se*, but what little there is confirms Hall's contention that 'Within the shadowy world of organizational sexuality . . . homosexuality must remain within the darkest penumbra, sealed away from any illuminating awareness' (1989: 125).

5 The social and the political in this sense is not determined by a particular historical process, as in for example, marxist theories of the economic mode of production as the determinant of all forms of social relations, but is instead transient and unstable.

6 This approach can be compared with that of MacKinnon who views sex as an effect of monolithic male power. For example, MacKinnon claims that: 'Sexuality is to feminism what work is to Marxism; that which is most one's own, yet most taken away' (1982: 117). Women are thus seen as carriers of their ideological sex position in the social formation, as containers for male desire.

7 Sociological theories which have tended to relegate sexuality to the non-economic by locating it in terms of the discursive and cultural are challenged by Adkins' contention that sexuality is not only deeply embedded in the gendered labour market but also organizes production. Theories which have tended to collapse family work relations onto non-waged production and assumed that all labour market work is waged are, however, problematized but not foregrounded with the same attention as given to sexuality.

8 Cockburn also obscures class by gender with the result that class relations form a backdrop upon which gender relations are mapped out; for example, she overstates the similarities between men's work, failing to take into account diversity and differences between men workers. She also plays down the processes whereby capital helps to construct and maintain differences between workers and uses gender power relations to do so; in short, she implies that capital is a homogeneous group.

Part II

Chapter 6

The Research Fieldwork

There are a number of issues that have been raised in Part I that are central to the main lines of argument which are presented in this book and which are used to theorize the experiences of women and men in flatter organizations. These arguments are discussed in the course of Part II, in which the findings from a comparative small-scale survey of women and men workers in a cross-section of different worker co-operatives and collectives in the voluntary sector are analysed. To begin with, this chapter will outline in greater detail than was attempted in Chapter 1, the two lines of argument around which the data is presented. The first line of argument maintains that workers in flatter organizations are highly circumscribed by gender and sexuality, and that working in a co-operative or collective does not offer women or men much opportunity to circumvent such intractable constraints. This in itself should not be surprising since it has already been shown that women are disadvantaged *vis-à-vis* men in the labour market. Furthermore, it has been seen that the positioning of women as subordinate arises not simply from the way that women's roles as wives and mothers are constructed within patriarchal family households, but also because of the gendering and sexualizing processes and practices that are to be found in the labour market and in organizations, whether they are sites of formal hierarchy or not.

A wealth of research on gender, sexuality and work has shown that women workers as a group are circumscribed both in the labour market itself and in public sector, private sector and social economy organizations. There is little reason to expect that the situation should be very much different in flatter organizations in the social economy, even though if gender inequalities were being overcome anywhere, these are the settings in which it would be most likely to occur. However, there are good reasons not to be over-optimistic on this score. First, because women workers are still part of an organizational culture and labour market which is dominated in numerically and status terms by men. Second, because they are working in organizations which are viewed at best as alternative and fringe, and at worst as inefficient and unworkable, by virtue of their less or non-hierarchical character. Third, (in the case of some women) because they are working in non-traditional occupations in which women have barely established themselves (such as architecture, film-making, manual trades and so on). Paid work can offer women financial independence, higher status and the possibility of self-determination or personal autonomy and several of the original stated aims of second-wave feminism were formulated with this approach to women's emancipation in mind. However, entering paid work does not necessarily remove discrimination and disadvantage from women's lives, and it can be argued that even in that supposedly most egalitarian of workplaces, the flatter organization, gender and sexuality remain potent forces for the constitution of inequalities. This means that women workers in co-operatives and collectives share some of the same material disadvantages as experienced by women workers generally; in short, that women workers in flatter organizations are subject to the same gendering and sexualizing processes and practices that constrain women in the labour market as a whole. In addition, however, there are particular forms of discrimination and disadvantage that operate specifically in the case of women workers in flatter organizations, often acting to place such women and their organizations 'beyond the pale', and limit them materially in ways that are not characteristic of the experiences of women workers in more hierarchical organizations.

These structural constraints are not only material, but are also discursive. The way work and organizations are constituted discursively along gender lines also needs to be taken into consideration. It can be argued, for example, that discourses which implicitly encourage the self- or collective-exploitation of workers in flatter organizations, in order to realize social and political goals, are informed by the (assumed) greater nurturing and caring roles of women in the family.[1] In the case of the women workers in the flatter organizations studied here, it can be argued for instance, that gender power relations are reinforced by what can be termed a sacrificial discourse based upon the idea that women workers play a support role in the workplace which involves subsuming their own attempts to exercise power, control and autonomy beneath that of being the nurturing and caring wife/mother at work. It can be argued that such a discourse is inscribed in specific ways into the flatter organization, even where women workers are themselves mostly single and have no child-care commitments.

From the viewpoint of the material and discursive constraints experienced by women workers in such organizations, working in a co-operative or collective might be seen as a personal and political cul-de-sac. The extent to which workers in flatter organizations, and women workers in particular, can overcome gendering and sexualizing processes is thus limited. Women workers' experiences in flatter organizations are less autonomous than those of their men counterparts, and they are thus not in a position to create or maintain fully egalitarian power relations at work. In short, gender inequalities are reflected by and reproduced in flatter organizations, albeit in ways which do not necessarily conform to the operation of material and discursive constraints in hierarchical organizations, but which nonetheless still place women workers in flatter organizations in a disadvantaged position *vis-à-vis* men workers. Given the explicit attempts to minimize or reduce hierarchical power relations in flatter organizations, it is important to consider the ways in which gendered and sexualized power relations are reconfigured and re-worked in such organizations. But it any case, whatever the configurations of power, women workers are nonetheless in a less advantaged position *vis-à-vis* men. It is to an empirical exploration of these arguments concerning gendered and sexualized constraints in flatter organizations that Chapter 7 is directed.

On the other hand, a second line of argument is presented as a way of problematizing some of the socio-structural assumptions concerning gender, sexuality, power, work and organization. On the face of it, the first line of argument appears radical since it draws upon theories of structured power relations. However, such an approach can provide an over-deterministic view of women workers and gloss over the possibilities for resistance. It may also fall prey to the processes and practices which are being interrogated in that it presents the capitalist and patriarchal order as the fundamental reference point for analysing *all* workers' experiences. A further criticism levelled against socio-structural theories is that they tend towards fixity, at least in the short term, and so imbue workers' experiences with an apparent inevitability. The complex and contradictory ways in which workers are positioned in relation to socio-structural forces are thus in danger of being swamped, if not lost altogether. As a result, contradictions which may be problematic for such theories can be minimized. In short, socio-structural approaches to gender, sexuality and work may not be comprehensive in terms of theorizing the full range of experiences of workers in flatter organizations.

In the case of such workers, it can be argued that they have escaped some of the traditional constraints associated with paid work, by virtue of having rejected the hierarchical (and with it the heterosexist, capitalist and patriar-chal) power relations of many private (business), public (statutory) or social economy organizations. In this view, women and men in flatter organizations can be seen as challenging and resisting gendered and sexualized power rela-tions. Consequently, it is important to consider workers' agency and resist-ance, and highlight the ways in which both women and men workers 'rattle their chains' and seek to throw off the shackles of material and discursive constraints that surround them. Workers' experiences of paid work are more than simply determined at the socio-structural level and workers are more than passive objects. For example, it is clear that many women do observe contradictions in the way they are treated differently at work from men, and they do resist and challenge those contradictions. Within the overall constitu-tion of gendered and sexualized power relations in organizations, it is there-fore important to note that workers (as agents/subjects) play a crucial part in challenging and manoeuvering within organizations. Adopting this approach allows a second line of argument to be developed – one that suggests that both women and men workers can be active agents for change. There is clearly scope here for looking at what workers *achieve strategically*, hence the adop-tion of certain stances by workers in flatter organizations towards their work-ing lives does need to be analysed. However, in terms of having any measurable impact this is difficult to specify empirically, but in terms of what women and men workers in such organizations *seek to or perceive themselves* as achieving, personally or politically, there is much scope here for exploring the ways in which they are active agents/subjects. Workers' experiences of work and of organizations is not static or fixed, and there are many opportunities afforded to workers in flatter organizations to resist, destabilize and undermine gendered and sexualized power relations. However, it must be pointed out that men workers are not seen as challenging and destabilizing gender and sexuality in the same ways as women workers, as they are not subject to the same material and discursive constraints in the labour market as women. This is not to suggest that men workers in flatter organizations cannot be seen as disruptive of traditional conventions of masculinity at work; for example, by challenging the gendered assumption that men have full-time, continuous career tracks, or that only businesses which operate with share capital and have men in positions of authority can be successful. But it is to suggest that since women workers operate within different constraints than men, subversion takes on a different meaning and emphasis for women workers than for their men counterparts. The second line of argument therefore suggests that both women and men workers in flatter organizations can strategically and symbolically subvert gendered and sexualized power relations, albeit in very different ways.

This second line of argument appears to stand in direct opposition to the first line of argument outlined earlier, since it suggests that neither women nor men workers in flatter organizations have working lives which are predictably patterned in any obvious way. By working in organizations in which there is less or no hierarchy, and by having jobs which do not involve the strict delineation of occupational roles, workers in such organizations may be doing more than simply creating an alternative space for themselves. At the heart of the second line of argument is the idea that both women and men workers can be experimental subjects, both in terms of what they do and what they represent. This approach is in contrast to the more deterministic approach outlined earlier. To put it crudely, the first line of argument is concerned with macro explanations of women's work and the socio-structural determination of gender inequalities, whereas the second line of argument is more concerned with the minutiae of women's working lives and the construction and deployment of strategic subject positions. These two sets of arguments also reflect the recent shift in sociological and organizational theory from a concern with power inequalities and how to eradicate them, to deconstructionism, differentiation and subjectivity. Both sets of arguments may therefore view the same or similar data from a different perspective.

A number of problems do need to be noted, however. The stress on heterogeneity and non-fixity in the second line of argument can provide a useful corrective to the problem of offering the over-arching generalizations that are considered characteristic of the first line of argument. Nevertheless, it carries with it the danger of falling into a kind of liberal voluntarism whereby the notion of systematically structured gender inequalities are denied. There is also the problem of reading too much from the actions of workers who fight back. Finally, if socio-structural analysis is rejected, the theoretical work that can be done, although interesting, may be limited; hidden elements of socio-structural theory inevitably end up entering by the back door. Nevertheless, women and men workers in flatter organizations offer a critical case for comparative analysis of some of the most interesting theoretical dimensions of gender, sexuality, power, work and organization. It is to an exposition and discussion of these theoretical issues as they bear upon the experiences of women and men workers in flatter organizations that Part II of the book is directed. Before that however, it is necessary to consider the background to the fieldwork research.

The Background to the Fieldwork

A study which focuses upon women workers in flatter organizations and compares them *vis-à-vis* their men counterparts, throws light upon the extent to which gender and sexuality are crucial elements of workers' experiences in such organizations. Inasmuch as the experiences of women workers may conform to the experiences of men workers, then the strong emphasis placed upon gender and sexuality in this book is weakened. Where obvious inequalities between women and men workers in flatter organizations are evidenced, the significance of gender and sexuality as crucial elements of hierarchical power relations is enhanced. When researchers adopt a critical feminist awareness, their work can provide insights into the ways in which paid and unpaid work is constructed and organized along lines of gender and sexuality. Sensitivity to issues of gender and sexuality also allows for the subtle and contradictory ways in which power relations are shaped in organizations to come to light. This is not to take the view that these two dimensions on their own provide a sufficiently comprehensive framework within which to make sense of all experiences of work in flatter organizations. The danger in homogenizing women workers or men workers as unitary categories and focusing upon a polarity which draws upon the opposition women/men is that this can disguise other lines of social division. There is a need therefore to be sensitive to issues of commonality and distinctiveness amongst and between women and men workers in flatter organizations. However, by matching workers according to their organizational location (in co-operatives and collectives) and by attempting to compare women workers with their men counterparts by, as far as possible, interviewing women and men in the same or similar occupations, it may be possible to isolate gender and sexuality more clearly as independent dimensions of power and inequality.

The methodological approach to the collection and analysis of data involved a combination of social survey traditions, which were designed to generate the data required to address the comparative focus built into the research, and ethnographic traditions, which were designed to allow for pro-gressive focusing, the evolutionary nature of the research and the develop-ment of the research focus over time. The data itself was collected by means of semi-structured, taped interviews which were designed to be relatively short – no more than 1–1.5 hours each – since they took place during working hours and were taped-recorded on workplace premises, and by means of a struc-tured, self-completion questionnaire (see Appendix 2). It was necessary to collect this quantitative data in respect of the social and demographic charac-teristics of interviewees and the organizations for which they worked in a readily accessible form. The questionnaire was a quick and easy tool for these purposes. As it was intended to supplement the taped interviews, it was administered at the end of the period spent in interview. Categories for data collection on the questionnaire included such items as length of involvement in the organization and whether employed full or part-time, etc. Data on age, social class, ethnic origin, educational levels, partnership status and household composition were also collected. The fieldwork research was clearly designed to be eclectic; qualitative data was collected by means of a more freestyle, conversational interview, although it was by no means totally unstructured. The aim was to bring to light the finer nuances of workers' experiences. It could be argued that it would have been more useful to have conducted a large-scale sample survey using structured questionnaires only, or a smaller-scale case study of women and men workers in only a single or a handful of flatter organizations. It has to be acknowledged that to some extent the fieldwork inevitably involved some trade-off between breadth and depth, but the methodological approach adopted in the end was felt to involve a useful compromise between these two extremes, and the most useful for addressing the theoretical issues raised in Part I.

Hierarchical organizations often have well-defined characteristics such as formal, stated policies, rules and regulations, whereas less or non-hierarchical organizations may not be constituted in quite the same way and the docu-mented characteristics of the organization may be less easy to specify. In the flatter organizations that are the focus of this book, there was an absence of formal hierarchy and greater scope for democratic, participatory working. Sampling procedures for the research fieldwork were two-stage; involving, first, samples of flatter organizations and second, samples of women and men workers within those organizations. In the event, these sample selection pro-cedures were less two-stage in practice than in theory as all 45 interviewees were drawn from (45) different co-operative and collective organizations. As far as possible, all the co-operatives and collectives selected were matched on three criteria. First, if the single-sex co-operatives consisted of a range of retail, manufacturing, arts/crafts, and service enterprises, then the mixed-sex co-operatives had to reflect this variation. Second, if the single-sex collectives consisted of projects directed, for example, towards providing services for women or campaigning on women's issues, then the mixed-sex collectives had to be geared towards providing services for (other) well-defined communities too. This could be for minority ethnic groups, children, young people, the disabled and so forth. Finally, all the organizations had to be matched for size and geographical spread in order to compare 'like with like'. Underlying the decision to be taken when considering the geographical spread of the research sample is the virtual impossibility of specifying the degree of heterogeneity required and the extent to which this may be affected by geographical location. It was clearly undesirable to confine the fieldwork to one (urban, cosmopolitan) area such as London, or my home city of Bristol. Eventually, it was decided to aim for a geographical spread across the urban/rural continuum and across five regions of England and Wales that could be reached in a day's travelling to and from the site of the interview.[2]

In research such as this there is no simple way to decide the size of the sample, and so theoretical sampling procedures were adopted rather than statistical ones.[3] Theoretical sampling should achieve a number of aims. First, it should generate potentially relevant categories for comparing like with like. Second, it should reflect all the important characteristics of the population under consideration. In other words, the sample should be sufficiently representative to generalize the findings to the population as a whole, in this case, all workers in flatter organizations. The criteria for the selection of interviewees was that they were either women or men workers in single-sex or mixed-sex worker co-operatives or collectively-run organizations in the voluntary sector, and that they were waged workers, not volunteers. Attempts were made to match interviewees in respect of the sectors/occupations in which they were employed. This yielded a total of 45 interviewees; 15 of whom were women in women's flatter organizations, 15 of whom were women in mixed-sex flatter organizations and 15 of whom were men in mixed-sex and men's flatter organizations.[4] This sample was arrived at by quota sampling; the first quota being drawn from women workers in women's flatter organizations. Once a fairly heterogeneous mix of 15 women workers in single-sex organizations had been interviewed, this group was then matched with the same number of women workers drawn from mixed-sex flatter organizations, and finally with 15 men workers from mixed-sex and men's flatter organizations.

Procedures for selecting samples of workers within flatter organizations also had to meet four further criteria. First, half the interviewees in each quota were drawn from worker co-operatives and the other half from collectives. Second, a concentration or cluster of interviewees from a single organization was avoided. Because interviews were taking up valuable time during busy work days, no more than one worker from any single flatter organization was asked to participate in the fieldwork. This was to avoid making too great a demand upon an organization's time and energies, and to reduce the risk of refusals and non-responses. Third, the securing of an interview was dependent to some extent upon a self-selection or volunteer process. Since workers within flatter organizations were by definition, working co-operatively or collectively, it was anticipated that if any one of them expressed an interest in being interviewed then this would have to be discussed with their co-workers beforehand. To this extent, the sample was based upon a non-random, self-selection or volunteer process. Fourth, this volunteering for interview was also likely to be based upon the sort of information that workers felt that they were willing or able to provide about their experiences, since they had to co-operate with the researcher's methods of data collection, particularly over the filling in of the questionnaire and over the timing and tape-recording of interviews. It is acknowledged that these sampling procedures may have led to some problems over the extent to which those interviewed were representative of all workers in flatter organizations. However, it is argued that the sample of 45 was a heterogeneous cross-section who, amongst other things, belied the assumption that there is a single, stereotypic co-operative or collective worker to be found.

The identification of a research field and the selection of a sample for interview are only the start of the long and complex process of data collection. The first interview took place in February 1990 and the final interview some 18 months later, in July 1991. The first stage in obtaining access for the interviews was to make direct telephone contact with the co-operative or collective to check basic details such as their organizational status and their address, to elicit interest and co-operation and to identify a named individual to whom to send an introductory letter outlining the aims of the research, requesting the assistance and co-operation of workers and promising anonymity and confidentiality (see Appendix 1). It was at the initial telephone contact stage that it had to be established that first, the organization actually fulfilled the criteria for being deemed a flatter organization – often in the case of some of the collectives, a matter of self-identifying as a collectively-run or self-managed organization; second, the organization was still in business or in operation and not, for example, in the process of imminently winding down or closing; third, that the organization did in fact have *paid workers*, as opposed to volunteer labour. The letter also reiterated the point about having a flatter, less or non-hierarchical structure and a commitment to team, joint or collective working as well as requesting that the interview be conducted with a *paid* worker/member of the organization.

There are problems in contacting any potential researchee because in all organizations there are individuals who have the power to grant or withhold access. In addition, the process of negotiating access is a continual one and does not stop once formal permission for interview has been granted. To the extent that any of the workers in the co-operatives and collectives contacted had the opportunity to decide whether or not to co-operate with the research, negotiation had to take place with each individual worker. The research had to be explained satisfactorily; this involved describing the shape rather than the specific details of the research, and a certain rapport had to be established. The question then arises of what to tell workers about the research; at the initial telephone stage, mention of their perceptions of their work, their motives and commitments, the advantages and drawbacks, seemed to suffice in terms of eliciting interest on the part of workers. However, although a researcher can set out to develop personal rapport with interviewees and thereby build trust, the starting point for such relationships must inevitably revolve around the perceptions of the research held by all concerned. This involved considerations of research reflexivity.

The Reflexive Account

Feminist research is often reflexive, by which is meant that there is a conscious attempt to render explicit the processes by which the data was produced. To a certain extent, reflexive accounts often contain the backstage material which might not otherwise see the light of day. It was necessary throughout the course of the research fieldwork to consider the data collection procedures and to record these considerations in order to provide a basis for subsequent reflection and assessment, particularly after having left the field. In the initial stages of the research, I had anticipated a certain amount of antipathy to the theoretical concerns of the research project, largely because I expected that those working at the grass-roots level would be hostile to academics.[5] In the event, a large number of the interviewees were extremely positive about the research, perhaps because in some cases, the social distance between us was minimized by the disclosure of my own involvement in co-operatives and collectives over a number of years, both on a paid but largely on an unpaid basis. My own experience has included setting up and working in a mixed-sex, radical retail bookselling co-operative for three years and participating on a regular basis in a collectively-run women's advice and information centre during the same period. Later on, I was also an unpaid worker for a further three years in a women-only collective providing a telephone help-line service. None of the interviewees was likely to have known all of this, however, and in some cases when I did mention my past involvement in co-operatives and collectives to some of them, this was not until the interview was over. Being a woman obviously made access to the women-only co-operatives and collectives easier, but it is difficult to know what effects were produced by my being white, university-educated and middle-class, particularly when interviewing black and/or working-class workers. The issue of the disclosure or hiding of lesbianism in the (feminist) research process was also fraught with problems relating to the positioning of researcher *vis-à-vis* researchee (Oerton, 1993).

I also suspect that it was easier to establish rapport with interviewees, particularly the women workers, because many of us belonged to that generation of women who, as one interviewee expressed it, 'had come up through the women's movement'. Many of us had had experience of university education, without necessarily having established high powered, linear careers for ourselves. In my case this could be gauged by my own admission of my status as a postgraduate research student, and my involvement in teaching and studying with the Open University, as several of the interviewees were familiar with that university's commitment to mature students who were enjoying a second chance at education. I was aware, however, of the dangers of over-rapport and tried to maintain something of a detached standpoint, which was possibly assisted by the adoption of a check-list of questions and the use of a tape-recorder during interview and the administration of a self-completion, structured questionnaire at the end.

What follows will to some extent attempt to make explicit the processes by which the fieldwork data was produced. The recognition and exploration of research problems within the ethnographic research tradition tends to emerge in the conduct of the fieldwork itself. Rather than provide a set of structured questions to be adhered to rigidly during the taped interviews, an abbreviated check-list of topics was devised which acted as an *aide-mémoire* during interview. This check-list was also sent out to interviewees with the introductory letter, with the intention of indicating the topics that might be covered in interview rather than acting as a list of standardized questions (see Appendix 1). Finding the best way to broach various topics during the interview itself was not always easy or straightforward. The questions asked during the course of the taped interview had to appear relevant, relating to experiences that were recognized as meaningful by interviewees. The questions put to interviewees were therefore context-dependent; this meant that they developed as each interview progressed. Some questions were asked of everybody, but generally each interview took its own course, within a broadly defined framework. With some of the later interviews, use was made of illustrative material that had arisen in earlier interviews. Furthermore, although informality was high on the agenda, it was also crucial that both the interviewer and the interviewee had some control over the interview situation. This meant that ideally the interview was conducted in comfortable surroundings, that there was a definite slice of time reserved for the interview and that the interview was not continually interrupted. Having the interviews recorded on tape was of vital importance for there is much that gets lost in a packed interview if it is not recorded on the spot. At the same time it was recognized that a tape-recorder is unlikely to fade into the background or be totally forgotten by interviewees. The design of the research also meant that interviewees could reveal significant points about their experiences in the taped interviews which were an elaboration of other responses given to more direct questions earlier on. In addition, there were attempts to adopt a non-directive interviewing strategy so that interviewees could to some extent anticipate the research focus and so pre-empt the need for a great many questions. However, it must be acknowledged that different people construed the purposes of the research in different ways.

Buchanan, Boddy and McCalman have pointed to the importance of providing researchees with feedback in the form of narrative accounts (1988: 64). Photocopies of the transcribed interviews were sent to all the interviewees in case they wished to amend or delete anything in them. If they did not wish to do so, they were told that they could keep the transcripts for posterity.

Researchees can feel that academic research has little to offer them and indeed may even do them harm in terms of making public knowledge which they would rather not have known. To counteract these worries, each interviewee was assured at the beginning of the interview that no one but me would ever listen to the tapes or read the full transcripts of the interview. Interviewees were also told that their names and the names of the organizations they worked for, plus the names of co-workers or any other identifying material, would be changed or deleted from any data used in the final analysis. In mentioning any publications that might arise out of the research, reference was made to the possibility of such publications being of benefit to co-operative and collective organizations themselves. Essex, Collender, Rees and Winckler (1986) in their case study analysis of South Glamorgan Women's Workshop provide an example of the form this type of collaborative research might take.

The review of the literature on gender, sexuality, work and organization and the collection and analysis of fieldwork data are not separate processes but are entwined, both conceptually and chronologically. The aim of the research undertaken here was to be dynamic and interactive, abandoning any attempt to fit the theoretical review undertaken in Chapters 1 to 5, the refinement of the two lines of argument outlined earlier, and the fieldwork data collection and analysis undertaken in the light of all this into any neat chronological timetable. Whereas it was necessary to be 'bounded' in conducting this research, the actual day-to-day practices of undertaking a project such as this are sometimes more messy, but nearly always more illuminating than is acknowledged in textbook accounts of the research endeavour. There is also a tendency amongst social scientific researchers to seek to present an integrated, cohesive research perspective. The intention in this case however, was to be attuned to the complexities of and variations in the experiences of women and men workers in flatter organizations, including all the contradictions that that entails. It can be argued that the perceptions of those workers themselves is highly subjective; nevertheless, such subjectivity provides insights into people's experiences both of their own working lives and the position they occupy in relation to the macro elements of work and organization. Bearing these points in mind, it is now possible to turn to the outline of the interviewees and their organizations in order to provide a background context for the analysis which follows.

Women and Men Workers in Flatter Organizations – A Profile

As already mentioned, the sample selected for this study consisted of 30 women and 15 men drawn from 45 different flatter organizations in 5 regions of England and Wales. The spread of the sample organizations in terms of location and proximity to my home city for the purposes of travelling to and from interview, meant that 18 of them were based in the South-West, 8 were in Wales, 7 each in the South-East and the Midlands and 5 were in the Greater London area. The organization were also spread fairly evenly across the urban/rural continuum, but with the majority being in large to medium-sized cities such as Birmingham, Oxford, Exeter, Bristol, Cardiff and Swansea, and several (but still a small minority) being located in London. There was very little variation across the three organizational quotas in terms of size of workforce. In most cases the organizations employed only a handful of paid workers, although in some cases they were quite sizable (60 plus) when voluntary labour was taken into account. Only one organization had more than 15 *paid* workers however, with 39 out of the 45 organizations having a paid workforce of less than 10 in total, and 23 of those (just over half) having 5 or fewer paid workers. There was a slight variation across the three quotas in terms of the length of time that the organizations had been up and running; with the average life-spans of the organizations in which men worked being shorter by an average of about two to three years than that of the organizations in which women worked. On the whole however, most of the organizations were fairly youthful, with 33 out of the 45 of them being less than 10 years old. Few however, were in their infancy, with only two being less than two years old, and five having been in existence for 16 or more years. On the whole therefore, in terms of location, size and life-span, the sample of organizations across the three quotas was fairly well matched.

It is necessary, however, to discuss the potential effects of differences between these flatter organizations in terms of the relationship between their degree of politicization and their gender composition; namely, to consider in more detail the extent to which the social and political goals of a co-operative or collective are significant in terms of differentiating between the single-sex and mixed-sex organizations studied. To begin with, this issue can be approached using the typology for classification provided by Cornforth et al. (1988), but it should be noted that workers themselves were not asked to define the organizations for which they worked in terms of this typology, so what follows is my own tentative attempt to classify the sample of organizations according to whether they were 'alternative' or not. In any case, the process of judging whether a flatter organization is alternative is based upon a belief that co-operation and collectivism is partly, but not solely, a means of pursuing radical social and political goals drawn from the ideology of the social movements of the 1960s and 1970s. Across the three quotas there appeared to be little difference in terms of the numbers of organizations that could be classified as alternative. Roughly speaking, 11 of the women's flatter organizations, 10 of the mixed-sex flatter organizations from which women interviewees were drawn and 11 of the mixed-sex flatter organizations from which men interviewees were drawn, could be categorized as having radical social and political goals. For example, this might involve the stated aim of producing socially necessary goods and services rather than production-for-(private)profit. The remaining organizations could be categorized as being primarily job-creation or job-saving enterprises, and in virtually all cases were worker co-operatives formed from existing businesses (phoenix or rescue co-operatives) or designed to create jobs (new start co-operatives). However, as Cornforth et al. point out: 'not all job creation/saving co-operatives are entirely pragmatic in their orientation; they can also be inspired by radical ideas such as worker's control' (1988: 9–10).

There are a number of problems here, however. To define a flatter organization as radical or alternative does not mean that such organizations are pure types, that they are all similar to one another, nor that they do not change over time. Flatter organizations, in seeing themselves as having radical goals, can ally with social movements as diverse as the women's, disability rights, anti-nuclear/conservationist and anti-poverty movements, to name but a few possibilities. Neither does this mean that all workers within such organizations necessarily become political activists in terms of how they organize their working lives, though some clearly do. Furthermore, politicization, collectivism and feminism are often elided in the literature; as a result, many writers judge such organizations against a pure type that is stereotypic and largely unattainable. Consequently, excessive attention gets paid to issues of bureaucracy versus participatory democracy in flatter organizations, often to the neglect of other organizational dimensions (Martin, 1990). The impact of the politics of flatter organizations on all the workers within that organization is difficult to ascertain in any case, though very broadly speaking there is likely to be some degree of congruence between the radical or alternative goals of a flatter organization and the political beliefs and actions of those working within it. For example, worker co-operatives trading in recycled and wholefood goods are unlikely to attract those who do not at some level identify with the principles behind the production and consumption of wholefoods and the recycling/renewal of waste.

Some of the mixed-sex flatter organizations have been categorized as having radical or alternative goals because of their political commitments to the ecology/conservationist, disability rights or socialist movements, whereas in the case of the women-only flatter organizations, the definition of the organization as radical or alternative often arises because it is seen as socially and politically transformative, pro-women and feminist (Freeman, 1979). In any case, there are difficulties here because *feminist* is often seen as necessarily separatist. However, not all the women workers in women's organizations identify themselves with feminism, let alone separatism, and it could be argued that at least 4 of the 15 women's co-operative and collective organizations studied were all-women as a result of the high degree of occupational segregation by gender in the sectors in which they were located (the retail grocery and cut, make and trim industries, for example). Neither can all the women or men workers in mixed-sex flatter organizations be excluded from identifying with anti-sexism or feminism, nor for that matter with anti-lesbianism and anti-homophobia, simply because they are working in mixed-sex organizations. In short, it is important to take care in making any simple or straightforward connection between the gender-composition of a flatter organization, its degree of politicization and the (assumed) politics of those working within it.[6]

In the event, the attempt to select the sample of paid women and men workers on the basis of matching 'like with like' proved complicated. Formal job titles can have little meaning in flatter organizations, where there is a tendency for workers not to see themselves as exclusive specialists in any one area, and where any of them could, and did, legitimately describe themselves as administrators, managers, members and/or workers. However, to give some substance to the sample of workers in flatter organizations, the following indicates the profile of the three groups, listed in order of the matching that was undertaken across the quotas. Self-defined job titles and the sector or industry that the co-operative or collective was in are listed for all 45 interviewees, as follows:

A. Sample of Women Workers in Women's Flatter Organizations

1. Managing director; Computing systems suppliers
2. Artist; Stained glass studio
3. Designer, pattern cutter and machinist; Fashion designers
4. Co-op member; Grocery retail
5. No response; Film/video production
6. Architect; Architectural design
7. Computer consultant; Computer training and consultancy
8. Nursery worker; Training workshop nursery
9. Co-op member; Wholefood retail
10. Joint co-ordinator; Sexual abuse advice and counselling centre
11. Employment development officer; Employment training workshop
12. Collective worker; Manual tradeswomen's advice and information centre
13. Finance worker; Domestic violence refuge
14. Information centre worker; Domestic violence advice and information centre
15. Liaison worker; Advice and information centre

B. Sample of Women Workers in Mixed-Sex Flatter Organizations

1. Co-editor; Magazine publishing'
2. Co-op member; Language school
3. Secretary/machinist; Footwear manufacturer
4. Assistant chef; Ethnic restaurant
5. Actor/deviser; Touring theatre
6. Office and development manager; Architectural design
7. Community theatre worker; Experimental theatre
8. Bookseller/cafe worker; Bookshop/cafe

9. Cafe/shop worker; Organic cafe/shop
10. Co-ordinator; Advocacy and advice centre
11. Community development office; Inflatables for the disabled
12. Joint co-ordinator; Playbus project
13. Project worker; Youth service
14. Office administrator; Environmental research and design
15. Director; Black dance project

C. Men Workers in Mixed-Sex and Men's Flatter Organizations

1. Co-ordinator; Software publishing
2. Designer; Graphic design
3. Administrator; Light engineering
4. Bookseller; Radical bookshop
5. Video producer/sales director; Film/video production
6. Architectural designer; Architects
7. Rostrum cameraman and director; Animation
8. Wholesale manager; Recycled paper
9. Wholefooder; Wholefood retail
10. Co-ordinator; HIV/AIDS advice and counselling centre
11. Transport/exhibits manager; Art exhibition services
12. Fleet organizer; Community transport
13. Organizer; Youth counselling centre
14. Funding and development officer/worker; Scrap recycling
15. Co-ordinator; City farm

As already mentioned, because workers in flatter organizations are, in theory, their own bosses/managers and often undertake a range of tasks and duties, they do not always identify with an occupationally specific job title. Occupation was not therefore a valid or reliable way of gaining a picture of the social class of women and men workers in flatter organizations. However, it was possible to use interviewees' self-definitions of their social class as being middle or working, even though 10 of them refused to respond or classified themselves in the 'Don't know/other' bracket. On the basis of the other 35 responses, it was clear that about two-thirds of the sample self-defined as middle-class (of these 6 were women in women's organizations, 11 were women in mixed-sex organizations and 7 were men in mixed-sex and men's organizations). The remaining 11 workers who self-identified as 'working-class' were fairly evenly spread across the three quotas (5 were women in women's organizations, 3 were women in mixed-sex organizations and 3 were men in mixed-sex and men's organizations). The sample was also pre-dominantly white, particularly in the case of the men workers, 14 of whom identified as white (there was one non-response from a white man worker). There was some variation amongst the women workers, however, particularly in the women's organizations, where 10 women identified as white, 2 as Afro-Caribbean, one as Black African, 1 as Asian and 1 as Jewish. Of the women workers in mixed-sex organizations, 13 women identified as white, 1 as Asian and one as Black British.

There was a wide distribution in terms of workers' ages across the whole sample, with the youngest worker being 19 and the oldest 65, but very little variation across the three quotas. Men workers were slightly older on average (39.6 years) than women in mixed-sex organizations (36.1 years) and slightly older still than the average for women in women's organizations (35.1 years). The majority of workers were in the age range 31–50 years (9 women in women's organizations, 9 women in mixed-sex organizations and 10 men in mixed-sex and men's organizations fell into this age group). In terms of marital status, a total of 17 workers were single, 13 were married, 6 separated or divorced, 2 widowed and 7 were co-habiting with their partners. There was very little variation across the three quotas, although there was a slight tendency for workers in mixed-sex organizations to be more likely to be married or living with their partners (5 women in women's organizations, 7 women in mixed-sex organizations and 8 men in mixed-sex and men's organizations were in this situation).

What is perhaps most striking about the characteristics of the sample outlined above is not the lack of variation by gender and/or gender composition of organization, but the ways in which the profile of workers outlined above belies the stereotype of the typical co-operative or collective worker as necessarily middle-class, white, young and single. Although there was a tendency for this to be true, particularly of the men workers in terms of social class and race/ethnicity, it appears that workers in flatter organizations are more likely to be people in the mid-point of their working lives, married or living with partners, than young and single idealists or self-help enthusiasts of the type identified by Carter (1987) and Paton (1991). Amongst the women workers, although those who identified as white and middle-class predominated, particularly in the mixed-sex organizations, there is nonetheless a greater range of women from different class backgrounds, different ethnicities, and at different points in their working lives, than is the case with the men workers, or than we would be led to expect from the stereotypes of such workers. This disparity between the stereotypes and the wide cross-section of people working in flatter organizations does suggest that it is mistaken to assume that there is any homogeneity amongst workers in such organizations in terms of social class, race/ethnicity, age and marital status, and this does need to be borne in mind in the course of the analysis which follows.

Perhaps the only striking difference was the finding that women workers were much more likely to have completed their full-time education at an earlier age than men workers, with 6 of the women workers in women's organizations, 5 of the women in mixed-sex organizations but only 2 of the men in mixed-sex and men's organizations having left full-time education aged 18 or under. Women workers were thus less well qualified than their men counterparts, with 8 of the women in women's organizations, 7 of the women in mixed-sex organizations but only 3 of the men in mixed-sex and men's organizations having attained 'A' level (or equivalent) or below as their highest qualification. This meant in other words, that only 7 of the women in women's organizations, 8 of the women in mixed-sex organizations but 12 of the men in mixed-sex and men's organizations were university-educated and had degrees. Again this belies the stereotype of the typical co-operative or collective worker as a university graduate, and someone, by extension, who could enter well-paid, high status employment if they so choose (MacFarlane, 1987). In particular, this sample profile highlights that whereas there was no great variation across the three quotas in terms of social class, race/ethnicity, age, and marital status, nevertheless it is women workers, and particularly those in women's organizations, who are the least homogeneous group and who are on the whole, slightly younger on average, more likely to be of working-class and/or minority ethnic origin, slightly more likely to be single/divorced/separated and much more likely to be without any higher educational qualifications when compared with their men counterparts. Clearly, all this suggests that women workers in flatter organizations are likely to experience greater difficulties in overcoming some of the constraints and disadvantages linked to the interlocking and reinforcing inequalities of gender, sexuality, social class, age, and race/ethnicity, than men workers in such organizations, who it has been established, are on the whole better placed to benefit from flatter organizations. How this manifests itself in practice is, in part, the subject of the following three chapters.

Notes

1 Self-exploitation is characteristic not just of some co-operatives and collectives nor simply of all women's work, but can also be seen as operating in many commercially marginal small businesses. However, within flatter organizations this self-exploitation can encompass everyone working there and so may be termed 'collective-exploitation' (MacFarlane, 1987).
2 The sampling frames for the flatter organizations to be contacted were drawn from a number of sources. Current directory entries for worker co-operatives and voluntary sector organizations in England and Wales were obtained. Names, addresses and contact numbers for the worker co-operatives were obtained from the *Directory of Co-ops in the UK, 1988* (Open University Co-operatives Research Unit, 1989), *The Wales Co-operative Centre Co-operatives Directory 1988* (Wales Co-operative Centre, 1988) and *Women Mean Business: The Everywoman Directory of Women's Co-operatives and Other Enterprises* (Everywoman, 1990). Names, addresses and contact numbers for collectives were obtained from letters, lists and advice supplied by the National Council for Voluntary Organizations, the National Alliance of Women's Organizations, and the Spare Rib 1990

Diary Useful Addresses section, and the *Guide to Bristol's Community Groups* (Bristol Council for Voluntary Service, 1989).

3 Statistical sampling identifies cases for experiments and social surveys, starting from a defined population. Each case sampled should then be investigated and analysed. Theoretical sampling is more flexible; the researcher selects groups and cases as she or he goes along in order to discover meaningful categories and develop theory. Some groups may be selected with maximum differences on some criteria and minimum differences on others. When new ideas and theoretical revisions are no longer emerging, the point of theoretical saturation is reached and the process is terminated.

4 The third quota consisted almost entirely of men workers in mixed-sex co-operatives and collectives. Unlike women workers who have political reasons for organizing autonomously or separately from men, the majority of men workers in flatter organizations were resistant to the idea of setting up and working in men-only organizations. In the single case where an all-men's organization was identified, this was the result of the high degree of occupational segregation in the sector concerned (light manufacturing) rather than any explicit desire to be single-sex. However, this was not true of the women's organizations, many of whom set out as or ended up as all-women or women-only.

5 There were no standard responses to my requests for interviews with workers in flatter organizations, and I met with very few refusals as such. Most of the refusals were due to the precarious state of the organization or to the heavy workload with which workers were faced at the time of my request. If an organization was in financial difficulties, was in the process of moving premises or was undergoing a restructuring, then it was often difficult if not impossible to arrange an interview. In a couple of cases, though not disinterested, workers felt that they were simply too busy to talk to me – although when reservations on this score were expressed, I did assure all potential interviewees that I would stick to a timetable of no more than 1.5 hours. A small minority of interviews had to be postponed by the interviewee due to bad weather, pressure of work or some other matter that needed attention. The vast majority of interviewees however, were very helpful and accommodating, sending me maps and instructions beforehand and offering me tea, coffee and on more than one occasion lunch, while I was there. Most interviewees made sure that we conducted the interview in comfortable surroundings and in privacy; heaters were brought out in winter and Ansaphones switched on if necessary. Only one interview took place away from workplace premises and in this case it took place in the interviewee's home in the evening, as he was too busy to see me at any other time.

6 That I myself was not immune from this tendency to make assumptions about worker's politics simply by virtue of their motives for working in an 'atmosphere with just women, an environment with women' can be illustrated in the case of a black, working-class, single parent who worked in a women-only wholefood retail co-operative. It was tempting to make sense

of her stated desire to work autonomously (from men) in terms of assuming that this connected to lesbianism. However, attempts to make this connection fit failed. It transpired many months later, and from another source, that this particular women's co-operative had explicitly set out, over the last few years, to employ working-class women, minority ethnic women and women with children. This led to an influx into the co-operative of such women, and in particular of women who had experience of domestic violence and had been living in the local refuge or involved with Women's Aid. Thus it became apparent that an exclusive focus upon the politics of sexuality can act to disguise other processes that are at work in shaping women workers' desires to work autonomously from men.

Chapter 7

The Constraints of Work in Flatter Organizations

The first line of argument suggests that the extent to which women and men workers in flatter organizations can overcome the material and discursive constraints associated with gendered and sexualized processes and practices in paid work and organizational life is highly circumscribed. It has been argued that women workers occupy a disadvantaged position in the labour market in relation to their men counterparts and the terms on which they enter into and engage in paid work reflects this. The extent to which women workers are circumscribed *as women* will clearly depend upon their social class, race/ ethnicity, age, sexuality, family commitments and so on, but in general women as women are held to be less freely contracting agents in the labour market than men, due to the operation of these material and discursive constraints. The gist of the first line of argument is that working in flatter organizations does not necessarily offer women workers the opportunity to circumvent these power relations since they are not able to disengage from being gendered and sexualized, simply by virtue of working in flatter, less or non-hierarchical organizations. In short, it is suggested that women workers in such organizations are materially and discursively positioned in ways which disadvantage them *vis-à-vis* their men counterparts. These arguments can be explored using some of the fieldwork data collected and analysed for the purpose of addressing these arguments.

Earnings, Employment Status, Turnover and Tenure

One of the stereotypes about working for a co-operative or collective organization is that such work is usually very badly paid, irrespective of whether workers are women or men. However, in the case of the 45 workers interviewed here, and despite women workers in flatter organizations evaluating their levels of earnings more favourably than men workers, it was evident that women workers were much lower paid than their men counterparts. It is interesting that women and men had different expectations concerning their earnings. Six women in women's organizations, four women in mixed-sex organizations but only three men in mixed-sex and men's organizations described their income in terms of such earnings being 'excellent' or 'good'. Nine men workers described their incomes as 'poor' or 'very poor'. This is not to suggest that women workers are entirely satisfied about their earnings, since five women in women's organizations and one woman in a mixed-sex organization also described their income as 'poor' or 'very poor', but it is to suggest that workers' evaluations of their earnings are based upon gendered expectations of what constitutes being well-paid. Furthermore, it is not the case that women workers were simply more satisfied with their earnings, but that their earnings were lower in real terms than the men workers, whose net annual income from their jobs was substantially higher. For example, seven women in women's organizations, six women in mixed-sex organizations but only three men in mixed-sex and men's organizations took home less than £6000 per annum, whereas at the upper end of the scale, only five women each in women's and mixed-sex organizations but nine men took home £9000 or more per annum (1990–91 figures). This meant that the *majority of men* workers took home *more* than £9000 per annum and the *majority of women* workers took home *less* than £9000 per annum.

Furthermore, men workers tended to feel, compared to their earning potential in more hierarchical organizations, that by working in flatter organizations they were considerably disadvantaged in income terms. As one man worker in a mixed-sex graphics design co-operative, who was earning over £12,000 per annum, expressed it:

> We don't get paid enough. We're all suffering from this at the moment. It's actually, it's almost serious, I suppose. It certainly makes you think about getting other jobs . . . I think about whether I can do without my car, which is pretty important both for my work and social life. So if I got rid of the car, I'd be able to buy some clothes. It's that kind of decision because my clothes are going to wear out soon.

Some of the constraints on earnings were internal to flatter organizations themselves, whereas other constraints arose from gendering processes which were to some extent external to the organization. Sometimes workers' earnings were reduced as a direct result of the adoption of equal opportunities and equal pay policies which sought to level (if not equalize altogether) workers' pay scales. For example, one woman worker in a women's training workshop nursery collective, who took home between £6000–9000 per annum, commented:

> We all earn the same per hour. Full-time or part-time, we all have the same benefits and everything . . . On the nursery scale, we are about halfway up the scale for trained staff. But one of our little gripes is that although we are halfway up the scale, if you were out working in a Social Services Day Nursery, you would actually be working up the increments and Jeanette and I, at our ages and stage, would probably

have taken a responsibility post by now. Once you've got a responsibility post, you're way above that, so by staying here you're keeping
your own salary not very high.

This point was reiterated by a woman worker in a mixed-sex organic cafe/shop
co-operative, who commented:

I suppose we're not all on quite the same pay but if this wasn't a co-
operative then there would be some kind of pay differential to recognize the different responsibilities that people take. Basically, there
isn't and I don't think there ever will be.

However, it is not always the case that workers' earnings in flatter organizations are reduced for reasons internal to the organization itself, such as the
adoption and implementation of equal pay policies. Gendering processes are
incorporated into and legitimated by state policies, so that flatter organizations
in which pay policies are structured in such a way as to allow workers to apply
for welfare benefits to 'top up' their wages, discover that this has consequences
for the opportunities women and men workers have to maintain parity in
incomes. For instance, men workers who were on low wages had relatively
little difficulty in supplementing those wages with welfare benefits, as the
comments from a male worker in a mixed-sex recycled paper co-operative
makes clear:

Despite us having a sensible marketing policy now and making real-
istic profit margins where we can, we can still only pay ourselves quite
low wages. But we've worked it out in a way that we pay ourselves
the maximum we can to get full [welfare] benefits, so that, you know,
you either pay yourselves £150 per week and say, 'Right, no state
benefits, no state hand-outs' or you pay yourselves £50 per week and
you can get the benefits.

But the point is that gendering processes in state welfare policies adversely affect the eligibility of women workers in flatter organizations to claim
benefits in their own right. It is more difficult for women workers, who are
constituted as dependants rather than main income earners, to claim benefits
on the same terms as men. The comments from a woman worker in a women's
stained glass studio co-operative, which had set out as mixed-sex but then
became all-women, illustrates this:

When we started we were on something called the business enterprise scheme which was a total shambles. What this was to top up
wages. There's so many ifs, ands and buts written into it. It was
based on what we would all get on the dole and that worked out to
all the women getting £40 per week and the men having £70, which

immediately blew our equal pay principles! For some reason, some-how, this bloke always managed to get paid more than the rest of us, so that went a bit hard . . . and his work wasn't all that good a stand-ard either!

This gendering of eligibility for welfare benefits also by extension adversely affects women's ability to enter flatter organizations in the first place. This point was made by a woman worker in a women's fashion designers co-operative, who commented:

We've got to expand and we've keeping our eyes open for staff at the moment . . . we have had people who have been interested. One woman in particular who was very, very talented . . . but she was caught in the poverty trap again where she was either getting housing benefit or she had to earn a lot of money to make it worth her while to be at work. And we can't offer her that sort of money straight away.

The gender specificity of the relatively low wages that workers in flatter organizations can command operates discursively as well as in material terms. The extent to which gender inequalities in earnings are reinforced by dis-courses which position women's earnings as of secondary importance to the wage earned by men, was illustrated by the same woman worker's comments about low pay in the clothing industry, where women predominate:

I think part of it is the old tradition thing of dressmakers being badly paid, and they do treat it as a dressmaker thing. *Little old ladies* sat working away by candlelight for halfpennies!

The issue of gender inequalities in earnings of workers in flatter organiza-tions is further complicated by the employment status of women and men in such organizations. Whereas men's jobs tended to conform to the traditional model of full-time employment over the course of a five-day working week, with (recognized, remunerated) overtime built in to deal with periods of high demand, women's jobs in flatter organizations were much more likely to be structured on a part-time or four-day week basis, with an unacknowledged, unpaid after-hours commitment built into them. Of the 29 workers employed in flatter organizations on a full-time basis, only 7 were women in women's organizations, 9 were women in mixed-sex organizations but 13 were men in mixed-sex or men's organizations.[1] This meant that 8 women in women's organizations, 6 women in mixed-sex but only 2 men in mixed-sex or men's organizations worked part-time or four-day weeks. Part-time working clearly carries with it lower rates of pay, as the comments from a woman worker in a women's advice and information centre, who was employed on a temporary basis for 15 hours over two days per week, make clear:

> We're not very happy with the rate of pay. It's £4.70 per hour . . . The pattern seems to be at the moment that when there's money then there's a worker funded, but there are periods when it's just volunteers and it's very, very precarious.

This higher incidence of part-time and four-day week working amongst women workers in flatter organizations might be thought to account for their overall lower earnings. But even when full-time workers only are compared, the finding that the majority of men took home £9000 or more per annum (9 men out of 13), whereas the majority of women took home £9000 or less per annum (10 women out of 16), still holds. Even taking into account the issue of whether workers were graduates or not and might thereby have been working in higher status, skilled jobs in more professional flatter organizations such as architectural design co-operatives (with higher incomes attendant upon them), there is still a significant difference in men and women's earnings. When only full-time graduates are compared in terms of earnings, the gender differential is reduced but still remains. Five of the ten men in this group earned over £12,000 per annum, whereas only three of the seven women did so. However, because the number of women workers in this category is small, it is difficult to draw any firm conclusions. It must be emphasized that the majority of women workers in flatter organizations were *not* full-time workers with degrees; 23 of the 30 women interviewed were not graduates working full-time, although 10 out of the 15 men interviewed were. The material and discursive structuring of workers' levels of satisfaction with earnings, their incomes (whether made up of wages or a combination of wages and welfare benefits) and their employment status is thus complex, but nonetheless indicates that women workers in flatter organizations are clearly disadvantaged *vis-à-vis* their men counterparts. The matter does not end there, however, as turnover and tenure in flatter organizations is also gendered in complex ways, which again tends to point to women workers' disadvantage.

In terms of turnover, the length of time that women and men workers had been employed in their present jobs, prior to interview, appeared to vary little according to the gender of workers. On average, women workers had been employed for slightly longer (4 years, 10 months) than men workers (4 years, 1 month). It can be argued that turnover amongst men workers might be slightly higher than amongst women workers because they are more mobile; their opportunities for obtaining higher status and better paid jobs elsewhere are better than women's, and so they may not stay as long in flatter orgaizations. In short, women's lower average turnover may be a reflection of their *reduced* opportunities for alternative employment *vis-à-vis* their men counterparts. The gender composition of the organization did appear to make a difference, however. Women's flatter organizations appeared to have greater difficulty in retaining workers than mixed-sex organizations, with no women workers in any of the women's organizations having been employed for more than ten years, and five women in this group having been employed for five years or less. This compared to four women and two men in mixed-sex organizations who had been employed for more than 10 years and only one woman and one man in these organizations who had been employed for less than five years. Mixed-sex organizations thus appeared to fare better than women's organizations in retaining workers.

It may be that women's flatter organizations in particular have more difficulty in retaining workers because of what is known colloquially as *burn out*. This is held to be of particular significance in women's collectives which campaign around women's issues such as domestic violence, rape and sexual abuse, or which offer support services to manual tradeswomen, or women who are undergoing employment/skills training. A black woman worker in a manual tradeswomen's advice and information collective, who maintained that most women workers did not tend to stay for longer than five years in this particular organization, put this down to the stressful content of the work: 'It can be bordering on really stressful because of the letters you get, people writing in about being harassed and so on.' Another black woman worker in a domestic violence refuge, commented:

> I do realize that working in [name of organization], there is going to come a time when you do become burnt out. Every previous worker who I have ever spoken to has got to the point where they are burnt out . . . I would say that it is a hard job to do because there is a lot of stress. So from the time you walk in here you're more likely to end up with a nervous breakdown than you are a fat bank account!

There was little evidence however to suggest that men worker's turnover rates were associated with burn out, although their turnover did appear to be affected by instrumental concerns such as whether other job opportunities were available elsewhere which offered better working conditions and better pay. However, their opportunities for mobility were seen as highly circumscribed because of the economic recession at the time (early 1990s). One man in a mixed-sex architects co-operative commented as follows on the likelihood of his leaving in the near future:

> The economy a year ago was not in recession and an architectural student could get paid more money than I can, in his first job, or as I am, in his first job at that stage. That changed absolutely and fantastically in the last 12 months. We are now struggling to keep alive at all. We're on a three-day week officially. We haven't got enough work coming in and so we're trimming ourselves. We are not making people redundant but we are talking about it and saying, 'How much money can we take off? How much money can you take off?'

Women's perceptions of their opportunities for employment elsewhere showed that women's options were also circumscribed, but in ways which were constituted differently from men's opportunities. On the whole, men's expectations of their opportunities for employment in more hierarchical organizations tended to be fairly traditional; they related more to the development of their careers and the opportunities which existed in the labour market as a whole for (men's) movement. In short, there was a general expectation amongst men workers that they would seek to build upon their previous work experience and that they would be moving to positions of greater power and responsibility when they finally left the co-operatives and collectives for which they were working now. Women workers on the other hand, were less likely to have such expectations, and were more likely to see themselves, if they changed jobs, as having to be in subordinate positions (to men) in traditional, hierarchical organizations. This was a prospect that they clearly did not relish, as the comments from a woman worker in a women's sexual abuse advice and counselling centre makes evident:

> The thing is, if I wanted to change jobs, I'd feel very strange about it because I'm not used to being told what to do. I'm not used to being told what to do by men and I'm sure I'd cope but I think I would find it quite hard to adapt to it.

This point was reiterated by another woman worker in a women's computing systems co-operative, who commented:

> I think I would find it very hard [to move]. I've been my own person for too long . . . That's why I mentioned temping before. I'm sure that if I had gone temping I would have ended up somewhere where they would have offered me a job, you know, to stay. But I would rather temp than work for someone full-time because you don't have the same degree of autonomy . . . I've run my family and I've done it single-handed [laughs] so I'm not having someone telling me what to do!

The problems associated with being in a subordinate position within a traditional, hierarchical organization seemed not to be a prospect that men workers envisaged at all, or if they did it was more in terms of dealing with a different workplace *culture*, rather than the difficulties of working in hierarchies *per se*. For example, in the case of one man working in a mixed-sex HIV/AIDS advice and counselling centre, the prospect of changing jobs was daunting because:

> I think it will be a real shock to go into another organization after being here. There are a lot of people here with whom there is a sense of a common culture and in a sense, that's a key part of the work. I think that I might find it a terrible shock to leave and might really regret it and feel that I'd made a terrible mistake! [laughs].

A further strand to the extent to which women and men workers in flatter organizations felt circumscribed in terms of their employment opportunities elsewhere relates to their tenure of employment. Many workers in such organizations, as elsewhere, are unable to specify exactly how permanent or secure their jobs are, but they are able to indicate how casual, insecure or otherwise they feel their positions are by estimating how long they think they will carry on working there. For women and men workers in collective organizations receiving short-term funding from government, local authorities or charitable bodies, tenure tends to be temporary in any case. Typically, the comments of a black woman worker in a manual tradeswomen's advice and information collective suggests that workers in such organizations feel highly *in*secure about their jobs:

> We-ll, it's secure for a year at least, if that's secure! Come the end of the financial year, well, come December time, we have to start going through the paperwork again. Nothing's very secure because you think, 'Oh my God!' and when you come up, you're holding your breath in case someone says, 'No!'

In terms of how long women and men workers in flatter organizations thought they would remain in their present jobs, about half of them had no plans to leave, although this was slightly higher in the case of the men workers, nine of whom had no definite plans to change jobs at all. However, a further half of all workers *did* feel that they were making or had to make plans to leave. This was clearly different for women than for men; in the case of six of the women workers, there was an expectation that they would leave within 12 months or less, whereas all of the men thought that they would still be there in a year's time. In short, women workers were more likely than men to indicate an intention to leave in the short-term. Those women workers who thought it was likely that they would have left or moved on in 12 months or less had a variety of reasons for thinking this. In the case of at least three women in collective organizations in the voluntary sector, this was because funding was very precarious or was definitely coming to an end. As one women worker in a mixed-sex youth service collective described it:

> We've got money, probably with a bit of creative accounting we could last through until the end of October. But it's such a short time-span to raise money. We're more than likely to have money to run a project from January through to May of next year and so really it's those months of November and December, and we need about £4000 to £5000. If we don't get the money, we're done! We can't go and do that project in January . . . I just don't know what we'll do. We'll probably have to issue redundancies because they have to be done a month in advance and then by the end of the month, hopefully we'll have had letters to say, 'Yes, here's the money' and we can carry on.

The situation of workers with regard to turnover and tenure in flatter organizations is not gendered in any simple or predictable way however. The precariousness of funding, sales and contracts, together with the opportunities for employment that exist elsewhere and the extent to which the stress-related nature of some of the work undertaken causes workers to burn out, all contribute to the likelihood (or not) of workers making long-term commitments to work in flatter organizations. However, it is not simply job or work-related issues that shape a worker's commitment since workers are not simply 'empty pegs' which slot into the various positions open to them in the labour market. It is necessary to focus upon the extent to which worker's experiences of work in flatter organizations vary according to their responsibilities in other areas of their lives, particularly their domestic and family commitments, as well as whether they have other paid employment or not. It might be thought that the difficulties workers in flatter organizations face in terms of combining their commitment to the organizations for which they work with their domestic and other responsibilities, will be highly circumscribed by gender since women have long been identified as having dual roles, primarily as wives and mothers and secondarily as paid workers. This is an issue which will be considered in the next section.

Work and Family Commitments

The extent to which the 45 women and men workers studied here were differentiated according to marriage and partnership status has already been discussed; it was suggested that gender made only a slight difference to the likelihood of whether co-operative and collective workers were married, co-residing with partners, single or separated/divorced. In terms of the households from which women and men workers came however, slightly more men than women lived in households with dependants (that is, their own or others' children aged 18 or below and/or elderly dependent relatives); nine men workers in men's and mixed-sex organizations lived in such households, compared with eight women workers in women's organizations and only six women in mixed-sex organizations living in such households. When the age of the youngest child in the household was taken into account, even more of the men workers lived in households with pre-school age children; six of them in all (including one man whose 1-year-old son lived with him for part of the week only) had young children living in their households, compared with only three women in total who had children under the age of 5 living with them. Furthermore, when it came to the difficulties of combining paid work with their other commitments, it was men rather than women who said that they found it harder to do so; 11 of the women in women's organizations, 10 of the women in mixed-sex organizations but only 8 of the men in men's or mixed-sex organizations said that they found this 'very easy' or 'quite easy'. In fact the only worker who found it 'very difficult' was a *man* in a mixed-sex software publishing co-operative, who had two children aged 9 and 6. None of the women said that they found it 'very difficult' to combine work with other commitments.

This is not to argue that men workers in flatter organizations have greater difficulty than their women counterparts in combining their commitments to working in such organizations with their domestic and family responsibilities, simply because they are more likely to live in households with young children. Two points need to be made here. First, more men than women had additional employment; just under half of the men workers (six of them) were doing other paid work, compared with three women in women's organizations and two women in mixed-sex organizations who had second jobs. In addition, none of those five women worked full-time; four of them only worked part-time for their respective organizations and the fifth woman worked a four-day week. Of the six men, five of them were already employed full-time in their respective co-operatives or collectives. It is possible to argue therefore that the difficulties men workers faced in managing their various commitments were linked to the greater likelihood that they were working full-time *and* taking on second jobs, rather than that they simply faced greater difficulties because of their involvement with child-care and other domestic responsibilities. Second, of those six men who did have second jobs, they either appeared to be doing other work that complimented their first or main jobs in flatter organizations (for example, in the case of a freelance designer and a trainer in the television industry) or they were taking on second jobs which expanded their personal interests, (for example, as in the case of the three men who did other paid work as a herbalist, naturalist and tai-chi teacher, as a ju-jitsu teacher and as a musician). Those women workers with second jobs appeared to be doing them in order to supplement the wages they earned from the part-time jobs they had in flatter organizations, since this extra work neither complimented their first or main jobs nor constituted a leisure interest; one woman from example, did some extra (paid) catering and market gardening and another woman who spoke Spanish did translations, but not on a regular basis, for academic and business people.

It could still be argued that women workers have greater difficulties than their men counterparts in combining child-care and domestic responsibilities with their commitment to work in a flatter organization, but that these difficulties manifest themselves in the *absence* from such organizations of many women workers with young children. It may be that it is the real difficulties of managing to combine domestic responsibilities with paid employment that act to deter women from working in flatter organizations, as elsewhere, in the first place. The comments of a number of the women workers interviewed here, in both women's and mixed-sex organizations, suggest the demands of working flexible and often unsociable hours, of holding meetings in the evenings, and of taking on jobs with perhaps low pay and little security of tenure, all detract from the likelihood of co-operatives and collectives employing women with young children. As one woman worker in a mixed-sex, youth service collective described it:

> The difficulty with our work, you see, is that we have to do a lot of evening work because when we do anti-sexist and anti-racist sessions, they are in youth clubs and they're held in the evening. So I think it is a fairly inaccessible job for women who are, who have dependants that they need to look after, which is a shame but I think it's the reality of the job here.

Another woman worker in a mixed-sex organic cafe/shop co-operative explained:

> People who sort of want to work a 10-to-3 day to fit in with young children are not really going to fit, because no one else is going to want to work 8.30–10 and 3–5. You don't mind if someone wants to work 8.30–1 or 1.30–6 sort of thing, because they'd rather do half days. That's okay. So we haven't really been able to employ Mums with young children, though I'd sometimes like us to be able to.

For both women and men workers who did have children and other dependants living in their households, there was a tendency to cluster in those flatter organizations where the majority of their co-workers had children (in which case the needs of workers as parents were more likely to be taken into account) or where the organization made explicit attempts to accommodate the needs of parent-workers. In some cases, women workers did feel their domestic responsibilities were recognized by the organizations for which they worked, as the comments from a woman worker in a mixed-sex Playbus collective with two children aged 17 and 14, made clear: 'I've always said I need one day off per week, and as long as I get one day off per week, I don't sort of mind doing extra hours so long as I get that one day because I feel I need that.'

However, sometimes, because of the very commitment that women workers felt towards their work and towards shared responsibility in flatter organizations, it was not always possible to manage the conflicting demands of paid work and domestic and child-care responsibilities. As one woman worker in a women's grocery retail co-operative with two children aged 13 and 10, commented:

> It does become a problem if one of the children is ill. Whereas before you'd ring in sick and say, 'I'm sorry, I can't come into work. My child's ill', now it is not so easy because you know you are letting someone else down if you don't come in. So you only do that sort of thing if you have really got to, obviously.

Some women workers in flatter organizations found the conflicting demands of their paid work and their child-care responsibilities so difficult to combine satisfactorily that they were thinking of leaving. The case of a woman worker in a mixed-sex collective supplying inflatables for the disabled, who had a 10-month-old baby, illustrates this dilemma:

> I am thinking of leaving at the moment and the two main reasons that I'm thinking of leaving aren't really anything to do with [name of organization] but the fact that I don't want to work four days a week. I'd rather work two days a week because I'd like to spend more time with my son. Because I need more money in order to be able to do that, I need to get a job that's slightly better paid. But if [name of organization] could offer that then I would stay here ... I'm certainly not desperate to leave but I'm just sort of keeping my eyes open.

It is argued that it is not simply a case of claiming that domestic and child-care responsibilities play less of a part in the lives of women workers in flatter organizations than men workers, simply because fewer of them have young children. Such responsibilities can be more hidden and disguised in the lives of women workers, and yet can have far-reaching consequences in terms of constraining their experiences of paid work. For example, one woman worker in a women's workshop nursery collective with two grown children of 21 and 19, maintained that the issue of her family responsibilities over the years had been central to her (paid) working life and had been the rationale for her involvement in a women's training workshop nursery collective:

> I do feel quite strongly that it is good to support women who are trying to do something with their own lives and are looking ahead when their own children are quite young. I think that that is the big mistake that I made, I stayed at home too long, just filling in, just fitting in work around the family and never putting myself first, which looking back now I think was my mistake that I ended up in the situation I did. I think that that's a lot to do with the way we were brought up and the way society would have reacted to me when my children were young, and that's what, 20-odd years ago now.

Hence, although it is important to note that more men workers than women workers in flatter organizations have children under the age of 5 living in their households and that they identify greater difficulties in combining paid work with their other commitments, it is also important to recognize the ways in which women are disadvantaged because of their traditionally greater family responsibilities. This might mean that fewer women with children (or other dependants) are eligible to work in flatter organizations in the first place, given that such organizations often require a casual and flexible workforce who are expected to exhibit a high degree of commitment to their jobs. When the issue of commitment generally and the extent to which workers undertake an after-hours commitment over and above the hours normally worked is taken into account, women workers fare considerably worse than men, as will be shown in the next section. This further acts to disadvantage women workers *vis-à-vis* their men counterparts.

After-Hours Commitments

In terms of the hours per week on average actually worked by full-time, part-time and four-day per week workers, there was, on the face of it, very little difference according to gender or the gender composition of the organization. The variance in hours worked per week was, not surprisingly, greater when *part-time workers only* were compared with a difference of up to 12 hours per week on average, distinguishing women and men in mixed-sex organizations from women in women's organizations. But with full-time workers only, there was less than three-quarters of an hour difference in the average number of hours worked per week by women and men. Similarly, when looking at extra hours above those normally worked, there was little to differentiate women and men, with over half the women and men in each category maintaining that they often worked extra hours, and the remainder (all but one man) maintaining that they sometimes worked extra hours. In the case of both women and men workers in both single-sex and mixed-sex flatter organizations, there was a tendency to admit to working far more hours than was desirable or contracted for, but this was attributed to the social, political and/or economic needs of the organization rather than the gender of workers or the gender composition of the organization. For example, as one woman worker in a mixed-sex bookshop/cafe co-operative commented:

> You definitely work longer hours than I think you'd be tempted to do otherwise. Certainly in the autumn and coming up to Christmas, we work very long hours, putting in one or two 12-hour days because we have to do that to keep the shop open.

The long hours associated with working in a flatter organization were perceived as equally problematic by men workers, however, as the comments from a man worker in a mixed-sex city farm collective, illustrate:

> The collective itself can get in the way of the life you want to lead outside, whether it's with family or friends, through the amount of work that you actually have to do to keep the collective together and to keep the farm running. I mean, most or all the core staff members are meant to work 37.5 hours per week but it's very rare that we don't work 50!

The need for both women and men workers in flatter organizations to put in extra hours or overtime does not therefore, on the surface, appear to be obviously gendered. When consideration is taken of whether this additional work is remunerated or not, however, a different picture emerges. Two-thirds (10 out of 15) of all women workers in women's organizations but only one-third (four women and five men respectively) of workers in mixed-sex and men's organizations did this work for no extra pay or with no time off in lieu. Furthermore, when the two-thirds of women and men workers in mixed-sex and men's organizations who did receive remuneration for these extra hours, were compared, it was clear that women workers were again disadvantaged. Mixed-sex organizations tended to make more use of remuneration in the form of time off in lieu, but this was gendered, with eight of the women workers in mixed-sex organizations taking time off in lieu as opposed to only three women being paid, whereas five of the men workers in mixed-sex organizations took time off in lieu and four men were paid for their overtime.

There is a further complication here since time off in lieu does not always materialize and so, in effect, the extra hours worked become non-remunerated. The intensity of the work load in many flatter organizations is such that workers often have no real opportunity to take their time off. Some workers described ending up with nearly a month of lieu days owed to them and being in situations where, if they did not take the lieu time off in a certain limited period, then it would be lost. Raw figures therefore do not always address the extent to which such features of work in flatter organizations are rooted in and amplified by gendering processes. The disguised or hidden workings of gendering processes and practices are further problematized by the finding that most workers in flatter organizations tend to see the need for an after-hours commitment as arising primarily from the structural or economic needs of the co-operative or collective for which they work. There was thus a tendency to see the self-exploitation (or what might more accurately be referred to as collective exploitation) of both women and men workers in flatter organizations in terms of traditional capital–labour relations, as the comments from one man working in a mixed-sex software publishing co-operative make clear:

We exploit ourselves shamelessly. If this was a company acts company, I think the shop stewards would have had us out on the pavements by now, with braziers and all that sort of thing. We are over-worked, under-paid, under-rewarded, no proper job security – abysmal! No chance, you know, of decent things like workplace crèches and so on and so forth.

There was also an expectation, particularly amongst men workers, that working in certain sectors of the social economy (as suggested by the terms the *voluntary* or *non-profit* sector) necessarily involved a dedication that was not easily quantified or well-rewarded. However, recognition of this collective exploitation is not sufficient to prevent its occurrence. The conditions which affect the ability or willingness of workers in flatter organizations to exploit themselves are complex, and need exploring in terms of the part played by gender in these processes, particularly in the case of women workers in women's flatter organizations, who have been shown to exhibit the greatest non-remunerated after-hours commitment to their work and who gave several reasons for their ability or willingness (or inability to refuse) to work these extra hours with no reward.

For some women, this self or collective-exploitation was related not just to practical expediencies but also to the political commitments they had towards the work they were doing and the organizations for which they were working. This political motivation was expressed by a woman worker in a women's film/video production co-operative, who claimed:

> We do overtime but we don't often get paid for it . . . Because the work is more rewarding and *I think you are more ideologically committed to it*, so it's not like you are paid for every last hour that you put into it exactly. It is quite difficult because we set ourselves quite a lot of things to do, and if you don't do it you feel really bad, you know.

Another woman worker in a women's grocery retail co-operative simply maintained:

> I don't think you mind *when it's your own business*. You know that it's got to be done and you just have to get on and do it. We had to have something done to the floor yesterday [Sunday] afternoon. There was no argument over who was going to have to come in, we just knew it had to be done and each of us did a turn. You just expect to do it and you get on with it because we wouldn't have come into it in the first place if we had minded doing it.

Other women drew upon ideas about exploitation being a *free choice*; as a black woman worker in a women's domestic violence refuge, explained:

> There is some self-sacrifice but at the same time I feel that you do choose. Like you're not actually *forced* to do anything here, but you choose to do it . . . it's because you want to do it and it's because you believe it, sort of thing . . .

It is worth noting that the after-hours commitment felt by women workers towards the flatter organizations for which they work extends into their free time in a number of complex ways, however, as the following account of an incident that had occurred on the evening prior to the interview, as related by an Asian woman worker in a domestic violence advice and information centre, makes clear:

> Last night I was in fact on the way out to the pub with a friend and all that had to go out . . . you know, I had to forget about it because the [office] window got smashed. So it's definitely not a 9 to 5 and I didn't expect that anyway, but there are times when your social life has to take second place to your job . . . Also I feel that some people they kind of say 'No', whereas the situation I had last night I couldn't say 'No' because basically if I had just thought, 'Oh, the window's smashed' and just carried on, somebody could have broken in and done the whole place over.

Although interconnected with these ideas of a *non-gender specific* commitment based upon practical expediency, political beliefs and free choice, the issue of after-hours working for both women and men in flatter organizations is, nevertheless, problematized by gender in subtle ways. Elements of this after-hours commitment applied to both women and men workers, but there were subtle gender differences, particularly in discursive terms, in the construction of this self- or collective-exploitation. The disadvantages of undertaking extra, non-remunerated work for their organizations did appear to be differently constituted for women, since several of the women workers felt that there was a subtle expectation that they as *women* would sacrifice their free time in order to meet organizational needs, and that they needed to be aware of this in order to build in formal forms of protection against self-sacrifice. As a woman worker in a women's employment training workshop expressed it:

> Here I can easily do over my 24 hours. I don't mind doing that but it's very easy in a lot of women's organizations. You tend to get burnt out very easily if you do that. Because I enjoy coming here so much and because I enjoy the work that I do, I tend to do more than I'm actually paid for and so we've set up a new supervision and support system for us to try and avoid doing that because it's not being fair to us. You know, we're telling other women that you must go out and fight for better wages, better working conditions and yet if we continue to exploit ourselves, then it's not really a very good example, so we recognize that.

Having a supervision and support system in place with the aim of protecting women workers against doing too many non-remunerated, extra hours can reinforce the gendering of overtime, however. Several women workers made reference to feeling guilty about making claims upon their organizations for additional payments for the extra work they undertook. As a black woman worker in a mixed-sex dance project described it:

> I mean, it's weird but sometimes I feel guilty about it. Writing down all your time and so on. It sounds strange but it does sort of make you feel a bit guilty and people keep telling me, 'No, don't! Write down all your time! Write down all your hours!' Then sometimes you say 'Yes' to things because you feel that it is right and maybe you shouldn't be doing it. I don't know whether that is to do with all our conditioning over the years, that we're the carers, that we should care and that we should jump in at that specific point in time when asked to, rather than saying or thinking, 'Well, why should I? That wasn't on the records when we planned this, you know, x amount of weeks ago' . . . I don't know whether other women have felt like that but sometimes I do and feel like I should, you know, go ahead and do it even though I might be missing out on something else I would have liked to be doing.

It is difficult to separate out whether the tendency towards an inability to refuse additional work manifests itself in terms of being *women workers*, or whether it is as *workers in flatter organizations*, undertaking *work with a specific content*, that the problems arise. The same point regarding an inability to refuse to do extra work, and the guilt associated with making claims for payment for this, was made by a man worker in a mixed-sex HIV/AIDS advice and counselling centre, who commented:

> It can sometimes be very uncomfortable to say 'No' and actually not be able to provide something, because one of the reasons that I'm here is actually because of the subject matter and that's very important, feeling passionate about it. Actually saying, 'No' and if necessary, feeling bad about it but still hold the boundary, is something that I have had to learn. I know that I have exploited myself in work and still do exploit myself. I have a tendency to assume that I can do more than I can actually do at any time and at some level hold myself responsible for not being able to do it all. I set myself less of that now, that's one thing that's really handy.

Nevertheless, notwithstanding the possibility that men workers were also subject to self or collective exploitation, there were still ways in which this self-sacrifice was gender-specific, as the next section will demonstrate.

Women Workers' Familial Orientations

Despite the difficulty of specifying the gendering processes at work here, there was evidence of a link between the greater tendency for women workers in flatter organizations to adopt this sacrificial approach to undertaking extra work *and* the discursive positioning of women in the family in terms of their assumed nurturing and caring roles. Discourses of familial support and self-sacrifice in flatter organizations are subtle, as the comments by a woman worker in a mixed-sex language school co-operative illustrate:

> I think that women take on those [maternal] roles anyway and I think that in the past if a man has not been pulling his weight, we will pull it for him. That's part of not being maternal now ... but the caring approach is much more a women's role traditionally, and I think we've all inherited it, for good or bad.

The form that this familial support and self-sacrifice takes for women workers in flatter organizations may include playing not only a caring but also a housewife role at work, as the comments from a woman worker in a mixed-sex organic cafe/shop co-operative demonstrate:

> Occasionally you think, 'Why the hell do I have to do that? You know, again!' It's even down to ever such silly little things and it so happened that I started doing it because it wasn't getting done, that I now take all the dirty washing [points to tablecloths and tea towels] home from here and I wash it, and I think to myself, 'Why? Why do *I* always take it home?' [laughs].

Another woman worker in a mixed-sex ethnic restaurant co-operative made a similar point about playing a housewife role in relation to her co-workers, all of whom were men:

> You know, the worst thing is the cleaning ... It's not so much that they are untidy or messy or that everything's dirty. It's a case of things lying around, papers and things ... I say, 'Look, you've got to keep things tidy!' Customers are going to walk into the toilet and think, you know, 'It's like a bomb's hit it!' and I say to them, 'Look, you want to sort everything out', and they say, 'I do' but they don't ... [laughs].

Clearly, this suggests that the greater tendency for women workers to undertake additional, unpaid work for their organizations is underpinned by orientations to work which are specific to women and which reflect their caring/nurturing roles in the family. As was argued in the previous section, there was little evidence to suggest that women's domestic and child-care commitments in any material sense were specifically linked to their levels of support for their respective organizations and, in fact, there was some evidence that those women workers with young children were less likely to take on additional, unpaid work *because* of their family responsibilities. However, if this lack of any links is valid at the material level, the same is not true for the discursive level. It is clear that women's greater involvement in undertaking non-remunerated, extra work is illustrated by women's subject positioning in relation to familial discourses which draw upon ideas of women's (assumed) emotional, relational and reproductive capacities. This meant that women workers were more likely for example, to refer to the atmosphere in their organization as caring and nurturing; in short, as being family-like in its support of workers. It was striking how often women workers adopted explicit familial orientations towards both their work and their organizations, often during the course of answering questions on unrelated topics. In every case, these arose unprompted, as in the case, for example, of the woman worker with a mixed-sex magazine publishing co-operative who commented:

> I think there is a feeling that *it is a sort of family in a way*, that you have a relationship here with people that is quite special. It can be strictly professional but you know, it's a little bit more supportive than perhaps in another organization.

Another woman worker in a mixed-sex footwear manufacturing co-operative, who was widowed as well as being over the age of retirement, saw the organization as her substitute family:

> I shall be 66 this year and they don't want me to go. Mind you, *they have been a real family to me*, each and every one of them. Because I lost my husband and they just look after me ... I've got nothing to stay at home for. I can't imagine what I would do all day long at home!

It should be noted that not one of the 15 men workers interviewed expressed their commitment to their flatter organization in this way. Furthermore, to support the argument that there may be a link between women's discursive positioning and material rewards, between their familial orientations to work and their greater tendency to undertake less well-remunerated, additional work, it should be noted that, in the case of the woman worker above, she often took work home with her to do in her free time: 'I mean, we've taken work home at night, to do at night to keep going. If it's been work that you could take home to do in the evenings, then you take it home and you do it.'

But the matter of women workers' familial orientations towards work in flatter organizations goes deeper than this. Several other women workers expressed their commitment to their work and organizations in ways which reflected not just a housewife, but a *mothering* role, referring to their organizations as their babies. As a woman worker in a women's grocery retail co-operative expressed it: 'It's our baby, if you like, yes, it is ... [and later] This is, as I said, our baby and we're going to make sure that we look after it as best we can!' This particular woman worker often worked extra hours and had been involved during the formation of the co-operative in the repair of the shop premises. The adoption of familial orientations which situate flatter organizations as women workers' babies can be seen to underpin the material/ maternal responsibility taken by this woman in relation to her work. As she went on to explain:

> When the floor started to give way, it was us, our responsibility to do it. We didn't have the choice because it was becoming dangerous, we wouldn't have let the customers in as it was. I mean, we worked so many hours on that. It's the kind of thing that makes you realize how committed you are to your business, when you are here at two o'clock in the morning, clearing rubble out from underneath the floor for three nights running. You know, you think, 'Well, I really must think a lot of this place!'

Another woman worker in a mixed-sex experimental theatre co-operative similarly commented, again unprompted:

> I often say to people when they first come and think about joining the co-operative, you know, that the business itself is *like a baby that never grows up*. You're continually having to service it, you're continually having to change its nappy, you're continually having to feed it and you have to care for it. If it needs servicing at two o'clock in the morning, then that's what you do. With our particular kind of work that can be so. So we are in a situation where the commitment to the work and working co-operatively is absolutely essential . . .

The last two women workers from whom quotations were taken were themselves the mothers of school-age children, but not all the women who referred to flatter organizations as their babies had their own children, as the comments of a lesbian worker in a women's advice and counselling centre for survivors of sexual abuse illustrates:

> It's very difficult to separate out your personal needs and the needs of the organization. It is for me and the others that have been very close to it. This is like our baby really.

> *SO*: You're about the second or third woman who has said that about their organization! [laughs]

> I haven't even got children and yet *this feels like my baby*!

All but one of the women workers who referred to their organizations in this way had been involved in the setting up of the co-operatives or collectives for which they worked. For other women workers who drew upon familial orientations towards their work, however, the sense in which they did so was more complex and reflected certain ambiguities concerning gendered power relations. As one woman worker in a mixed-sex language school co-operative expressed it, in describing the relationships between the five women and one man in the co-operative:

> Tom is a very privileged male to be surrounded by such strong women! [laughs] He doesn't always see it that way, I'm sure, but I think we have a tendency to be quite maternal and we're trying to get away from that in terms of being, uh, directive people and we're very much trying to encourage the self-empowerment of workers these days, including ourselves . . . That is going against being maternal, so that we get a view from everybody and so then they can voice their own mind and help make a decision on it, rather than us saying, 'Right, we think this is good for you.'

There is some support here then for the argument that women workers are more likely than men workers to position themselves in relation to familial discourses, as specific family members (housewives, mothers), and in particular as mothers to babies, when referring to their commitments to their work and organizations. However to argue that these familial orientations entail a form of self-sacrifice which explains women's greater tendency to undertake non-remunerated, extra work for their flatter organizations is tenuous and might be stretching the point. Nevertheless, women workers have been shown to adopt emotional, relational and familial orientations towards their organizations and to engage in more unpaid extra work than their men counterparts. It would seem strange if this had no relationship whatsoever with gendering processes at work. However, the gendered constraints under which women and men in flatter organizations operate can be shown to extend beyond the issues of familial orientations, self-sacrifice and collective exploitation, and it is possible to argue that women workers in flatter organizations generally, but in women's organizations in particular, are systematically marginalized in ways not experienced by their men counterparts, and which constitute them as 'beyond (hetero)sexualized hierarchy'. These processes do not simply have discursive effects, but have real material consequences for the survival and success of women's co-operatives and collectives, as Chapter 8 will demonstrate.

Note

1 Gender disparities in earnings are further complicated because some women workers in flatter organizations may work a full five-day week, but not in a job that is designated as full-time; for example, one black woman worker in a domestic violence refuge worked on a full-time basis but in two different, part-time jobs, namely as a refuge worker *and* as a child-care worker.

Chapter 8

The Marginalization of Flatter Organizations

This chapter seeks to explore the ways in which the discourses that surround flatter organizations and the people in them operate to position such organizations as 'marginal' and 'beyond the pale'. It needs to be noted that discursive constructions that operate at the level of both the organizations themselves and the individuals within them are often indistinguishable, with both being coded in similar, but nevertheless gender-specific, ways. In short, the collective group of workers that make up the flatter organization, tends to *be* the organization, just as all members of the family are the family. Some attempts to separate out stereotypic views of flatter organizations themselves, as distinct from the stereotypic views of the workers who found and run such organizations will be made, but it is an important part of the argument being presented here that discursive representations attach at both the organizational *and* individual levels, with both often being collapsed together, so that both workers and their organizations can be marginalized, albeit in gender-specific ways. This has serious material consequences for the survival and success of flatter organizations, as this chapter will demonstrate. To begin with however, the organizational stereotypes will be discussed.

Organizational Stereotypes

On the face of it, the less or non-hierarchical structure of the organizations being studied here appeared to be a matter of public confusion or indifference. In general, it was felt by both women and men workers that their customers and clients were either not very well informed or were simply not very interested when it came to an understanding of co-operative and collective forms of organizations. In the case of some of the worker co-operatives, both women and men workers made mention of the popular associations that were made with the Co-op retail and wholesale societies. This was compounded by the reluctance on the part of some workers in flatter organizations to draw attention to the less or non-hierarchical structure of their businesses and enterprises, so that they sometimes for example passed as a more conventional organization by describing themselves as partnerships, or by avoiding the use of the word *co-operative* or *collective* in any of their publicity. In short, several workers downplayed the ways in which their organizations had been set up and were operated, although this tendency was more common amongst men workers than women workers. Underlying the reluctance to name their organizations as co-operatives and collectives were a number of important considerations concerning the extent to which the organization might be negatively stereotyped as a result. For example, one man worker in a mixed-sex art exhibition services co-operative commented:

> I think we made a conscious decision in the beginning that being a co-op, although we thought that it was important and that we wanted it to be that way for practical and ideological reasons, when it comes down to the day-to-day commercial world, we didn't want to be seen as something that was strange or different or alternative.

Another man worker in a mixed-sex animation co-operative expressed similar views:

> Because we are involved in something which is essentially within the television industry, people just wouldn't expect us to be a co-op. They expect television to be very well paid, carpets on the ceiling and all that kind of stuff. I have to say though at this point – I'll commit myself on tape! – a lot of the co-ops, well, not a lot but some of the co-ops, existing co-ops, the older established co-ops, feel a bit resentful of people, like I was saying, who don't put co-op on their letterhead. They want to be seen as co-ops and they feel that we're sort of selling out. I think that that's a daft point of view; it perpetuates the myths about left-wing co-ops and it doesn't do anybody any good. Co-ops work quite well in the way that they work and the people who work in them benefit from the structure, and that should be encouraged, but we do everything possible to get away from that image of sort of 'wholefood' – I'm going to start ranting in a minute! – [laughs] 'woolly jumpers' and so on.

Interestingly, for many of the men workers who expressed views about the kinds of discourses that were popularly used to mark off flatter organizations from other kinds of (more hierarchical, traditional) organizations, such discourses were see as gender-neutral. This lack of any role for gender in the discursive construction of flatter organizations as marginal, is clear in the comments of a man worker in a mixed-sex software publishing co-operative, who argued that being a worker co-operative:

> occasionally gives us a few Brownie points. I wouldn't put it any stronger than that. I think for the vast majority of people it's an irrelevance. For a small minority of people it's a positive discouragement . . . Why do I think it is a disadvantage? Well, there are a whole

set of reasons why I would be quite hesitant about telling a prospective customer anything about us. The first fact is that we are in a foreign country. You know, serious business isn't done in Wales and we know from first and second-hand reports of the large number of occasions on which people have disregarded us simply because of where we are ... The second thing is that we're small and that again is a major negative thing in many people's minds. The IBM factor, you know ... they're large so you won't get into trouble buying IBM. You might get into trouble for dealing with people as dangerous as [name of co-operative] and as small as [name of co-operative] ... The next thing is our youth. Happily we're doing something about that, we're surviving ... So right, having set up those lists of prejudices, the final one is, 'And we're a co-operative!' Madness finally strikes! ... 'You mean, you're going to do business with this bunch of Druids, on the wrong side of the Severn Bridge, who've only been in business a couple of weeks and who probably be down the liquidators right now, yeah, and there's only half a dozen of them and they're a co-operative! You're off your heads!'

As far as the discursive construction of flatter organizations as marginal and peripheral is concerned then, there appears to be little to suggest that men workers saw gender as a major player in the discourses that constituted their organizations. Nevertheless, it could be argued that gender was deeply embedded in these accounts, since the gender of (men) workers and the gender composition of (mixed-sex) organizations is not so far from the norm of organizations *per se*, which are predominantly set up and run by men, both in numerical and status terms. On the whole however this remained unacknowledged in the accounts given by men workers and it was assumed that discursive representations of flatter organizations as marginal, inefficient, hopelessly utopian and so forth tended to operate for *all* co-operatives and collectives, irrespective of their gender composition. This assumption however was complicated by other discursive constructions, very often noted by women workers alone but sometimes mentioned by men, which positioned women workers as subordinate to their men co-workers, so that when women and men worked alongside each other, even in that supposedly less or non-hierarchical environment of the co-operative or collective organization, women were typically positioned as *secretaries* and men as *managers*. This point is illustrated by the comments from a woman worker in a women's stained glass studio co-operative which had originally been mixed-sex and whose workshop space and equipment could be accessed by other artists of both sexes:

What we got is that anyone coming in to speak to someone, of course they'd go straight for Mick. They'd be talking about some legal matter on the premises or something and Mick would be going 'Yeah ... yeah' and understood nothing! We'd have to go over and rescue him . . . It's just the nature of things that there usually is a man in charge so there's usually an assumption that we're just secretaries or helpers, but I myself have learnt very quickly to put them straight on the matter and say if someone phones up for a colleague, one of our male colleagues, and says, 'Well, when will he be in?' and would I do this, or would I do that, would I look up something, quite frankly I say, 'I'm not a secretary, I'm a colleague. I can take a message for him to ring you back and that's it.'

This is not to argue that men workers were immune from these gendering processes but it is to suggest that gender power relations clearly position women and men co-workers as *unequal* in terms of their managerial/support functions, as the account of a man worker in a mixed-sex scrap recycling collective, illustrates:

We get a awful lot of, 'Can I speak to the manager?' or '. . . the co-ordinator?' and although I'm not the only man at the moment, when Martin leaves I'll be the only man here and I do tend to talk about funding and development, so I'll be meeting people in the local authorities who come in to talk about it, so I'll come in and shake their hand and sit down, try to meet them on their terms. They'll say, 'This is John, the manager' and I have to say, 'I'm not actually the manager, we don't have a manager' and they'll say, 'Oh, fine!' and think, 'Oh, fine, okay, he's just saying it . . .' The awful thing is that they assume I'm the manager because I'm the man, so there's an awful lot of that goes on as well.

Clearly then, women workers in mixed-sex flatter organizations have to contend with assumptions that their men co-workers are their bosses; even in women's organizations, there are expectations that a (man) manager exists somewhere in the background, as the comments from a black African woman worker in a women's wholefood retail co-operative suggest:

We have the problem here where you have a letter written to 'Dear Sir . . .' You know, we ignore it now but there was a time when the group of women here were infuriated. They'd just get right down and write a letter saying, 'How dare you say we are managers? We are a co-operative, we're a collective!' Because some people just don't understand. They ring you and say, 'Can we speak to the proprietor?' and we say, 'No, sorry, we're a co-operative' and they say, 'Who's the boss? Who owns the business?' and you say, 'Nobody!' – 'Nobody?' [laughs]. They find it very strange. People still don't understand what co-ops are all about . . .

Discourses surrounding the mixed-sex flatter organizations which were the subject of this study do confirm existing research on co-operatives and collectives in that both women and men workers in such organizations were conscious of their oddity, and this was largely seen to arise because of the less or non-hierarchical structure of co-operative and collective organizations. Since it is already well-established in the existing literature that such organizations are stigmatized because of their less or non-hierarchical structure, this is no surprise; flatter organizations tend to be seen as somewhat strange and unusual largely because the absence of traditional employer–employee and boss–worker relations appears to many to be unworkable. In the case of many of the mixed-sex flatter organizations their discursive positioning was not problematized by reference to gender at all, except in the case of the recognition that gender power relations tended to elevate men *managers* over women *subordinates*. As will be argued shortly, this was a very different matter for women workers in women's (and in particular women-only) flatter organizations, where complex imputations regarding their (*deviant*) gendered and sexualized identities were routinely made.

Before exploring the case of women's and in particular women-only organizations, it needs to be noted that other negative discursive imputations were identified by both women and men in mixed-sex co-operatives and collectives and concerned a number of fairly common stereotypes about less or non-hierarchical organization(s) generally. First, the down-market, under-capitalized and inefficient image that attaches to flatter organizations was frequently mentioned and second, the idea that they were all typified by being hippies was acknowledged. As a woman worker in a mixed-sex language school co-operative put it: 'It's the green-sandalled person, isn't it? You know, spinning wool and throwing a pot here and there . . .' On the face of it, these negative imputations appeared to be non- gender-specific and were used as a rationalization for why a co-operative or collective was considered to be inefficient and unworkable. As a man worker in a mixed-sex city farm collective explained:

> It's this sort of beardie-weirdie image, almost universally. I think it's to do with being a collective because . . . as soon as you tell people that it's a collective they seem to immediately think of that as a excuse why various things have happened in the past . . . and because of what has happened in the past, for historical reasons, people think that co-ops are all about people sitting about, wearing beads, and talking more than actually doing anything . . .

The popular image of flatter organizations that women and men workers in mixed-sex organizations mentioned most often however, was that of being radical and left-wing. To some extent, this was rooted in the actual political orientation of some of the organizations themselves; in terms of the goals of the co-operatives and collectives studied, only a small minority could be categorized as predominantly job-creation or job-saving enterprises, although the majority could be categorized as politicized, namely as having radical or left-wing political orientations. As a man worker in a mixed-sex radical bookshop co-operative commented:

> There is a sort of interlinking that goes on between us and various feminist groups in town and um, elements of the black community and various political groups. I mean, in no way do we represent those as they represent themselves, but we do act as post office box number for some of them. We're always willing to lend people books to sell on stalls and so on . . . The press in particular see us as representatives of radical groups so we do tend to get phoned up for numbers . . .

Other workers in mixed-sex organizations however, suggested that this negative imputation of *all* flatter organizations as radical, left-wing and hippie was undeserved, or at least, misleading. For example, one woman worker in a mixed-sex experimental theatre co-operative commented:

> We're a theatre company and people immediately have an image of you if you're a theatre company and working in a place like [name of town] which is a very conservative, very nice, well-monied area. We're not well-monied so it's taken us a long time to establish ourselves. One of the good things about establishing ourselves with people in the community is that we do have ordinary people coming in who do jobs and who go back and say, 'Well, no they're not a hippie commune! They actually work very hard!' [laughs] Well, we all know that actors spend all their time taking an amazing amount of drugs and indulging in orgies! They go back and say, 'They don't have time to do any of that because they're too tired in the evenings. They go back and watch programmes like *Neighbours* and *Eastenders* like everyone else!' [laughs].

Furthermore, many of the workers in mixed-sex organizations attempted to play down their radical, left-wing, alternative or fringe associations; in any case, there was certainly an uneasiness about the extent to which the organization might suffer commercially if it were assumed to be a very radical co-operative or collective. This image of *any* flatter organization as radical, left-wing, fringe and so on can have material consequences which work to the economic detriment of the organization. As a woman worker in a mixed-sex advocacy collective expressed it:

> [There are stereotypes] about tatty furniture and all that stuff . . . You go in and it'll be tatty old sofas, damp smell and really

down-market . . . ideally we wouldn't be in a basement, a basement is a terrible place to be. We wouldn't be in a damp basement and we would have it cleaner than this . . . you would pay attention to that kind of stuff because it's passing on the image, you know, of who you are working for . . .

Some workers in mixed-sex flatter organizations were concerned about challenging, or as one of the men workers put it 'cleaning up', the image of their organizations. To some extent, considered and careful self-presentation was an integral part of the work of all of these organizations, as in the case most obviously of the publishing, actors' and video/film makers' co-operatives and collectives who were dealing every day in the business of image-production. There was little reticence amongst the great majority of them concerning the need for flatter organizations to present a serious and professional image. There was, however, an interesting gender dimension here, for when men workers sought to break away from being seen as unprofessional, it was in the sense of seeking to offer quality *goods and services*, whereas for women workers it involved both this and presenting *themselves* as serious, skilled and efficient. As one man worker in a mixed-sex film/video production co-operative argued:

I know as we've progressed through different sort of areas we're seen as more professional. Until we get to the marketing people, let's say fully aware marketing people in companies. The comments we've had range from *worthy* to *competitive* which are sort of code-words for *ordinary* and *low budget*, which we have to accept is where we are coming from. We don't have enough money to spend on our marketing but people like the logo and the identity, that's all. That's coherent and people understand where we are coming from.

For women workers, the down-market, low-budget image manifested itself additionally in ideas about their *own self-presentation*. It was women workers therefore who were more likely to refer to the appropriateness of the clothing that they wore in the workplace, and how they had to dress the part in order to be taken as professional and serious. This point was illustrated by a woman worker in a women's employment training workshop collective, who commented:

Um, local employers up until about a year ago, I guess, nine months, a year ago . . . [saw us] as a loony left bunch of feminists who taught typing or something. It's really bizarre . . . [We have to] give a image that they are not expecting, I think, when you go to visit them. When we went to visit [name of Head of Regional Technology Centre] I mean, I put on a smart pair of trousers and shoes, a shirt, rather than whatever I wear here which is usually whatever I see first thing in the morning. The woman I went with is a ex-city chambers councillor and she wore her city council chambers suit and it just gave an image that they were not expecting. I think that they were expecting two women with earrings coming out of their noses, with long skirts or something and clutching three kids, to turn up. I don't know, they had a really weird image of who we were and we weren't who they had perceived.

None of the men workers referred to their presentations of self in this way. This may be related in part to their gender *and* to the gender composition of the flatter organizations for which they worked. Mixed-sex organizations are less likely to be so openly associated with feminism and lesbianism, which are discursive imputations reserved specifically for women's, and particularly women-only, co-operatives and collectives. This chapter will go on to argue that even and perhaps particularly in that supposedly safer, politicized organization – the women-only co-operative or collective – assumptions concerning women workers' legitimacy act to routinely trivialize and marginalize women workers and their organizations in ways which are highly gendered and sexualized. This argument will be explored in the next section.

The Marginalization of Women Workers and of Women's Flatter Organizations

The specific trivialization and marginalization of women workers in flatter organizations and women's (and women-only) organizations in particular, operated in four gender-specific ways. First, women workers were more likely than men to perceive themselves and to be perceived as occupying a peripheral position in relation to the real world, even when that real world had no singular or unified definition. Second, women workers were less likely than men to be seen as fully competent adults, and more likely to be constituted by a lack of maturity and a related tendency to be playing at business. Third, women workers were less likely to be listened to or taken seriously because women are typically constituted as secondary workers, occupying positions which are necessarily seen as subordinate to men. Fourth, women workers' sexualities were assumed to be deviant, particularly when they worked in women's (and more specifically, women-only) organizations. As a result of these gendered and sexualized discourses which operate to demean and pathologize women workers and their flatter organizations, their ability to secure contracts, sales, grants and loans, is severely curtailed. Each of these constraints will be discussed in turn, bearing in mind that such data arose unprompted and unsolicited in the course of the interviews.

Some women workers in both mixed-sex and women's flatter organizations clearly experienced a sense of estrangement from what they termed the real world. In several cases they saw themselves as occupying a separate space which set them apart from the mainstream. Men workers in flatter

organizations, on the other hand, did not appear to exp
pronounced sense of being on the margins of reality. As one wo
a women's film/video production co-operative described it, 'I've
in any other set-up so I don't know what the *real world* is like.'

In some cases, this real world was seen by women workers ѕ   ...er-
ized by hierarchical power relations, particularly as associated with gender.
This point was illustrated by a woman worker in a mixed-sex experimental
theatre co-operative. 'Sometimes it can be a real shock for us because in our
working life, [sexism] is not there and when you hit it, it's like hitting the *real
world* outside. Oh my God, someone has passed you over because you are a
woman!'

Another woman worker in a mixed-sex magazine publishing co-operative
reiterated a similar point about coming across sexist attitudes and practices in
the real world outside:

> I find it quite shocking when I go out into the *real world* and see the
> sexism and discrimination that is around and I just think, 'Christ, we
> are so lucky here!', because the men are, if you like, well-trained.
> They actively make sure, you know, that the women are listened
> to . . . recently I travelled somewhere and I met a different set of
> people, academics, I mean they were very nice, *nice* people, but I was
> amazed at the men and people that I wouldn't have expected, quite
> unreconstructed in a lot of ways which I found quite suprising. I know
> I am a million miles away from how the *real world* is in terms of both
> where I am at home and also in terms of where I am in the office, but,
> of course, you come across it in other places so I am aware of it, that's
> what I'm saying.

Not surprisingly, none of the men workers referred to this ghettoizing of
their working lives in this way, nor did they suggest that by working in a flatter
organization, they felt they were somehow set apart from the real world. When
they did refer to the real world, as some of them did, it was to characterize the
need as they saw it, for flatter organizations to engage fully with the realities of
hard-nosed business and commercial dealings. As one man worker in a mixed-
sex recycled paper co-operative expressed it, 'It's very hard but then we're
living in a market economy. We're not living on a desert island dealing in
coconuts. *We're living in the real world* and I think that that's a problem a lot
of co-operatives have, *not* living in the real world.'

A similar point was made by another man worker in a mixed-sex
wholefood retail co-operative: 'What we're here to do is to survive as a food
shop in a very competitive medium. But to do that we can't hold on to our co-
operative principles all the time. We've got to realize that *we're in a world,
whether we like it or not, that's dictated to by business and commerce.*'

Thus men workers in flatter organizations saw the real world as a place in
which they should be sited, or perhaps more crucially, were sited. As a result,

not only were those flatter organizations who failed to situate themselves in and face up to the real world seen in a critical light (by some men workers and by significant others like customers, clients and funders), but also there were suggestions that in founding and running less or non-hierarchical organizations in the first place, some people might only be going through a fad or a phase; in short, this was something they would or needed to grow out of. However, it was women workers, and women workers in women's flatter organizations in particular, who were routinely constituted in this way, namely as lacking in maturity and as playing at business. This clearly is not something that women workers and their organizations can easily grow out of because such discursive constructions are deeply embedded in gendering processes and practices which position women as less serious and less effective in founding and running successful businesses and/or project enterprises than men. It is not something that women can simply grow out of with age. This point was illustrated by a woman worker in a women's film/video production co-operative, who described how 'We're trying to establish ourselves as a resource that's based here . . . and when we go up to have meetings with [name of local council] it's like, "Oh, come in, girls!" and "Come and sit down, love!"'

A similar point was made by a woman worker who had founded and worked in a women's computing systems co-operative:

> A lot of people didn't think that we would last, partly because of the nature of the business, partly because of the structure – because of it being a co-op. From businessmen who didn't know anything about the co-operative movement, they thought it was just a load of Greenham Common women [laughs] which was said to us in a joking kind of way. They didn't think that we would last and [thought] that we were *playing at business*. They didn't take it seriously, not traditional businessmen.

But there is more going on here than is suggested merely by women's lack of maturity, their girlishness and their inability to grow out of a pastime attitude to business. On the face of it, what appears to connect a women's computing co-operative with a women-only peace camp is both the commitment to less or non-hierarchical organization and the gender of those involved. However, there are underlying issues related to women's sexualities that need addressing since Greenham Common has been shown to be encoded in dominant discourses in ways which specifically lesbianize women, and situate them as 'militant, butch and burly' (Roseneil, 1995). This point will be returned to shortly.

In mixed-sex flatter organizations there is a tendency for women workers to find that if they are not being taken seriously, rather than imputations of being *girls* or *peace-campers* (both associated with single-sex groups/activities) being made, they are instead seen as *students*. As one woman worker in a mixed-sex touring theatre co-operative explained:

We get people coming up to you after a show and saying things like, 'What's your day job?' and you've just spent four hours putting a set up and two hours doing a show and two hours taking it down again! You think, 'Aggh! You've got no idea!' People come up and ask you, as I say, what your day job is and, '*Are you students?*' because we look quite young, I suppose.

Lack of maturity (and the implied lack of credibility) appears to be contingent here upon the gender composition of flatter organizations since where there are men workers present it seems there is a greater likelihood that a higher age-graded status (students) will be imputed than when the organization is all-women or women-only, in which case women workers are simply taken for a bunch of (game-playing) girls. One important point needs to be noted however; the consequences of this assumed lack of maturity on the part of women workers and women's and/or women-only organizations can have very real, material effects. This is illustrated by the comments from a woman worker in a mixed-sex advocacy collective, who, having discovered that she was being paid less for the same job than an older (woman) co-worker who had been there for longer, had fought for and was undergoing a salary review, about which one of the members of her support group had:

... expressed quite dreadful attitudes. You know, he would like to get away with paying *little* and *younger* women, which I was at that stage, less than anybody else ... [It was] my stuff about, bloody hell! One of the important things when I came to work here was that it was about co-operative working, and it would no longer have felt the same you know, because bugger it, we do exactly the same things. I was just as good if not better than her in terms of my achievements ... I thought, 'No, I've got to sort it out', because it would have been too painful and too undermining otherwise and I wouldn't have been able to carry on ...

Clearly then there is evidence of a credibility gap related to maturity, which has material effects, as far as women workers in flatter organizations are concerned. Women workers in flatter organizations are therefore more likely than their men counterparts to feel they are being patronized, trivialized and not taken seriously because of their gender. As a result, both they and sometimes the organizations for which they worked are more likely to experience ridicule and derision. The ridiculing of women's work was illustrated by a woman worker in a women's fashion designers co-operative, who had done some outreach work for her local Co-operatives Development Agency, with fifth and sixth formers in a local school. This took the form of an Open Day at which:

... there was a board of five or six or seven of us and there were two co-operators, me and a guy called Ian who works in a computer co-op, and all the other companies were terribly hierarchical . . . the woman who was organizing it, the careers officer, her attitudes were very typical. You know, we weren't from a hierarchical business, she didn't understand co-ops at all and she referred to [name of the co-operative] as a little business . . . and all the kids went, 'Ooooh!' I think it was partly her attitude to me being a woman because she didn't say to Ian, 'You run your little business', and also it's a high-tech co-op that he's in . . .

The point about women workers in flatter organizations being ignored or ridiculed was supported by the comments of a man working in a mixed-sex architects co-operative, who maintained:

We had a very nice example the other day . . . I don't know if other people picked it up. We had a man in from our insurers to talk about some of the great dangers that architects were being put in . . . we had a long talk and he told us about this and we asked lots of questions and we all joined in. There were five of us around the table and at the end, he shook hands with John and with me [laughs] and in the end, we more or less pushed him to shake hands with at least one of the other women. But he didn't see them as being part of the deal at all. *The whole idea of co-ops not being regarded as serious because they're full of women is something I have heard.*

It is apparent that as a consequence of this gendered lack of credibility, women workers in flatter organizations feel that the work they do is less highly valued than it would be if done by men. The difficulties encountered in this respect were illustrated by a woman worker in a women's architectural design co-operative:

We are really marginal in some ways I think, or we're perceived as marginal, partly because we call ourselves feminist, partly because we're all women and a co-op . . . We don't want to be necessarily type-cast into small, low profit, badly paid, overworked, you know, bitty little jobs for worthy causes . . . We just don't want to get type-cast partly because we are women and we are a co-op as well. *They just don't think we can do things.* They're prepared to go along to you, like local authorities for small community centres but not for large-scale re-habs of existing council estates. *They go to big private practices for that because they are proper men with suits on and suddenly it's too much money for us to handle or whatever.*

The complex workings of this credibility gap also found expression in the extent to which motherhood was deemed to be an unprofessional attribute for women to bring into the workplace, and specifically to bring to the notice of potential customers, clients and other supporters. The comments of a woman worker in a mixed-sex advocacy collective illustrate this point:

> The thing that really upset me last week was that we had a management committee meeting and we had a guy who is a lawyer come along in his suit and everything and we all dressed as we are, sort of thing. One woman was breast-feeding her baby and it was fairly relaxed and so on. He is going to think about whether he wants to join and we were saying, 'Oh God, I bet he thinks we're terrible!', and someone just jokingly said – in fact it was the woman who has got the baby – said, 'Oh God, he must think we are so unprofessional!', and it really struck me, just that phase. It clued into me and I felt terrible about it. She was only joking, you know, it's not a real issue and I think that we should be exactly the way we are in terms of finding a place in the world . . . but I think that that's quite a common view that people don't take you seriously and in the end, you don't take yourself seriously.

The extent to which this credibility gap operated in relation to gendering processes *per se*, as opposed to relating to views of co-operative and collective organizations as inefficient, unprofessional, unworkable and so on, is hard to specify, since both can be seen as deeply implicated in the ways that women workers experience their marginalization. As a woman worker in a mixed-sex language school co-operative expressed it:

> It's very hard to tell how far people are gauging us, when we go out to fairs to sell our wares sort of thing, how much they are taking us seriously. You wonder when you are there next to the man with the shiny striped suit how far you are actually losing out.
>
> *SO*: Do you think that that's because you are a woman or a co-op?
>
> It's hard to tell . . . a woman, yes. I would think more woman than co-op, but I don't know. That's pure speculation. I mean, any business, if you are a woman next to a man with his company, how far do you lose out and how far do they benefit?

There are difficulties in separating out the processes which are implicated in the marginalization of women workers and their flatter organizations. However, there were further dimensions to this which suggest that not only gender but also sexuality plays a significant part in positioning women workers as somehow 'beyond the pale'. These processes need exploring carefully. To begin with, it needs to be noted that there were several references by both women and men workers in mixed-sex flatter organizations to the extent to which their organizations appeared eccentric and odd which on the face of it did not appear to be gendered in any obvious way. To organize co-operatively or collectively is often thought to be odd or weird, irrespective of whether an organization is single-sex or mixed-sex. This point about the strangeness of organizing co-operatively or collectively was supported by a man worker in a mixed-sex architects co-operative, who explained:

> We are a *funny outfit* and if you talk to other people and explain how you work as I did to one of the partners of a pretty large firm that works in our sort of field – I was at some little seminar on some technical matter – and I was chatting to him afterwards and he said, 'Oh yes! I've heard of you! How do you actually work?' and I said how we worked. I said, 'We try and do what you do but we just try and do it together', and he said, 'You call yourselves a co-op, you're not really are you?' I said, 'Well, no, I don't suppose we are really! [laughs] But we have a go. What do you mean, how would you define it?' He said, 'You don't all get paid the same amount of money do you?' I said, 'Yes, we do' and he said, 'What? Whatever your experience?' and I said, 'Yes, and our typist gets paid the same amount of money too', and he just threw up his hands and he laughed and said, 'You're bloody mad! Loony stuff! You can't work that way . . .'

This madness or strangeness was further compounded by discursive constructions of flatter organizations which positioned *all* co-operative and collective workers as funny and peculiar, irrespective of gender. Being the butt of ridicule and jokes was one of the clearest ways in which workers in flatter organizations reported being trivialized. Being ridiculed or laughed at however, operated in a gender-specific way, particularly when women workers worked in women-only organizations, and this does need to be addressed. A woman worker in a women's computer training and consultancy collective illustrated this point about how gender was implicated in the derision she experienced, as follows:

> [*People*] *just laugh*, I think, that's all that happens. They laugh and say, 'What *is* she doing?' . . . *They also think it's really weird*. They can't quite understand what it means. I get that all the time. '*Why are you doing it for women?*' You know, '*Why women only? Isn't that sexist?*' That comes up so many times . . . I think most people just think it's really odd!

Women workers in women-only flatter organizations who report these forms of derision and ridicule are in a double bind situation with regard to their assumed oddity; if they want to be taken seriously they have to present an efficient and professional image and yet when they attempt to be taken seriously as mature workers, they are castigated for their childishness, game-playing and lack of humour. The assumed eccentricity of women workers in women-only flatter organizations, together with an assumed refusal or inability on their part to enter into good humoured banter with men, thus places such women workers not only in a position of being open to ridicule, but also harassed in terms of being sexually joked with, by men. The comments of an Asian woman worker in a domestic violence advice and support centre highlights this point:

> That's another thing about being in a women's organization, you tend to get patronized a lot because, you know, they feel like, these women are all weird and they can't possibly know what they are talking about . . . I think *it's because we don't play the game . . . I don't know, I meet some women and they have a little flirt and you know, they say all the right things and we don't.* I think that's difficult for some men to handle as well. Like we don't find their jokes funny! [laughs] and it's just too difficult for them to handle.

Sexual joking thus acts as a form of harassment and is another way in which women workers in women's (and specifically in women-only) flatter organizations are marginalized *as women*. This issue arose in several of the interviews with women workers but in none of the interviews with men. It can also operate in the case of women workers in mixed-sex flatter organizations though, where they can become the subjects of their men co-worker's jokes. For example, one woman in a mixed-sex ethnic restaurant co-operative described how one of her men co-workers

> took advantage of me working here. I can't explain . . . he'd joke with you but it wasn't very funny and he doesn't realize he's doing it. But he'd talk to me really funny, because I was a woman. He'd say, 'Oh, you can't do that' and 'You don't know what you're doing!' I mean, he used to think that because I'm a woman, I can't do this and I can't do that. But in the end, I can! [laughs] But he didn't want to believe that I could . . .

Clearly then, women workers in mixed-sex but particularly in women-only flatter organizations are viewed and treated as intensely problematic, not only because of the threat they are seen to pose to men's power and identity, but also because they are seen as *beyond the control of heterosexualized hierarchy*. It is important to recognize the extent to and ways in which gender power relations in most, if not all, mixed-sex and all-men's organizations are constituted through and by heterosexuality. Some mixed-sex flatter organizations are clearly not immune from the discursive practices which reflect the dominance of heterosexualized power and control relations in organizations. The comments from a man worker in a mixed-sex software publishing co-operative illustrate this:

> I mean, the way this co-operative runs is on sublimated sex! I suspect that the way the place is run, the way co-operation operates most

> effectively here, is on the basis of a network of personal relationships ... at the core of which is a very important balancing relationship between men workers and women workers. Those are some of the most effective balances. I can give you a couple of examples to put flesh on to that. The simple example of chasing bad debts with a customer that you do not want to alienate ... it helps greatly to be able to play good policeman/bad policeman and typically you need a man and a woman to do that. I'm not saying who the good policeman is and who the bad policeman is! But actually you can play things off very, very effectively if you do that. You don't even have to do it consciously, it just comes from different styles, different feelings about the way in which one should handle a relationship with a customer or a supplier. It simply arises, if you like, through gender differences in attitudes towards relationships with the outside world.

The dominance of heterosexualized power relations in organizational life can also be seen to operate in relation to women workers and their organizations, about whom and which assumptions concerning their deviant sexualities attach in various ways. The processes here are complex, as the following comments from a woman worker in a mixed-sex youth service collective illustrate:

> Actually, that's made me think about another thing [laughs] about our reputation because I think we're seen as radical feminists. Well, we're sometimes given that label and we were, I mean, there was myself and another woman worker even more so. *People thought that we were having a relationship together and so what if we were?* But anyway, we've been very aware of that because we don't label ourselves as radical feminists and we both have differing viewpoints as well. Basically, I think that labelling comes from being or appearing to be two strong women who are running an organization and who know what they are doing and are fairly confident ... We've been doing work on issues of sexism for years and so it's been these two strong women workers going out ... But then one of the male workers did this whole project doing anti-sexist work with young men in youth clubs. *I think he was thought to be gay!* [laughs].

What this suggests is that women workers in both mixed-sex and women's flatter organizations can be assumed to be lesbian simply by virtue of being beyond the control of heterosexualized hierarchy, irrespective of whether or not they are lesbian. Such lesbianization is discursively imputed to those flatter organizations which are women-only, and as a result they are routinely constituted as suspect and stigmatized. Men workers, on the other hand, appear not to be homosexualized unless the *content of the work that they do or the organization itself* is explicitly concerned with anti-sexist or gay issues, as in the case of the man co-worker referred to above. For most men workers in mixed-sex or men's flatter organizations, the attachment of a 'deviant' sexuality did not occur at all, unless the workers in such organizations were constituted as gay on particular and specific grounds. This imputation of gayness tended not to arise in the case of men workers, as lesbianization routinely did in the case of women workers and their flatter organizations. This suggests such processes are informed by a complex combination of the gender of workers, the gender composition of the organization, and the less or non-hierarchical structure of the organization, since the experience of women and men workers clearly differed. For men workers, gayness is predicated only upon *the issues with which an organization is concerned*, and not by its gender or organizational structure. The comments of a man worker in a mixed-sex HIV/AIDS advice and counselling centre suggest that it is the *content or area of work* with which the organization is explicitly involved that is central to the attachment of stereotypes concerning workers'/organizations' sexualities, at least as far as men workers and mixed-sex organizations are concerned. 'There are certainly ways in which we as an organization get perceived as a gay organization, which isn't true, but it's seen as a demerit very definitely. Our problem is that . . . heterosexual people might not feel very comfortable coming in here because there are some confident gay people around.'

These imputations of gayness appear to relate not to the less or non-hierarchical structure of the organization, nor to its gender composition, and not even to the sexuality of workers (since the workers were not *all* gay men, though clearly many were) but to the issues with which the organization is explicitly concerned, and HIV/AIDS is seen as a gay issue. Nevertheless, the content or area of its work and the sexualities of both workers and their organization are difficult to separate out, as the same man worker went on to illustrate in relation to a particular incident:

> Very early on we made one error which has dogged us ever since . . . in this specific instance we did a piece of work in a school. It was a sixth form college. We happened to have included on our information stall some safer sex information for gay men which was fairly explicit, without even thinking twice about it . . . It happened to get back into a parent's hands . . . who was incensed and outraged and subsequently questions were raised in the House of Commons. That has been attached to us quite a lot, *that somehow we'll do something outrageously inappropriate* . . . So that kind of thing can get used and does get used.

The point here is that men's gayness is discursively constructed as necessarily outrageous and inappropriate and as a result, assumed gay men workers and their gay organizations are seen as suspect and stigmatized. However, I would argue that the homosexualization of this particular collective organization, unlike the routine lesbianization of women's flatter organizations, cannot be understood without reference to the work under-taken, and that without this dimension neither men's nor mixed-sex flatter organizations are liable to be discursively homosexualized. How this operates in a very different way, however, for women workers in women-only flatter organizations needs to be carefully specified.

The discourses attached to women's 'deviancy' mean that those women workers whose sexuality may conform to the heterosexual norm are neverthe-less routinely considered to be suspect and threatening, *when and if they live and work outside the gender relations of hierarchical power and control*, for example, when they are in a women-only living and/or working environment. This gendering of hierarchical power and control necessarily positions women and men differently, with women workers' 'deviant' sexualities being used as a means to trivialize and marginalize them as separatist, man-hating and so on, in a way that imputations of gayness cannot be seen to operate. In short, the issues involved in the discursive imputation of men workers' gayness is not that they are beyond the control of hierarchical power and control relations, since organizations are sites of *men's* power and control, and as such are not being threatened. But clearly this is not the case for women workers in wo-men's flatter organizations who are perceived to be threatening, and where, according to a black woman worker in a women's domestic violence refuge, 'a lot of the time people are just humouring you . . . a lot of the time you come across people who think, "She's a man-hater" and stuff like that.'

Such discursive practices mean that it is not simply individual women workers, whether lesbians and/or separatists or not, who then tend to be constituted in ways which mean that they experience derision, ridicule and even intimidation. It also means that in the case of women-only flatter or-ganizations, *the organization itself* can be subject to trivialization and marginalization on specifically sexualized grounds, *irrespective of whether the women workers in that organization are lesbian or not*. This point can be illustrated by the comments of an Asian woman worker in an domestic violence advice and information centre, who maintained:

> Oh, they're – especially men – very threatened by it because accord-ing to a lot of men we must be a bunch of lesbians because there's not a man around . . . I think that's why we don't actually appeal to the whole of the female population that needs us because I think that quite a few women are taken in by that image as well. You know, that we're a load of lesbian lefties . . . But if you were upset at being accused of being a lesbian or whatever, you wouldn't really survive here.

Another woman worker in a women's drop-in advice and information centre reiterated this point:

I mean, we just can't win; it's a no-win situation . . . When we opened here the comments from one of the local papers was that it would be a mecca – what was it? – 'a mecca for all man-hating feminists this side of London!' . . . That's particularly distressing because if women in the community are picking up on those messages, a lot of women come to the door really anxious about how we will be.

For both these women workers their own sexuality remained undisclosed during the course of the interviews but they both made references which suggested that they were not lesbians. However, they were clearly conscious of the ways in which discourses of feminism, lesbianism and separatism were being used to demean themselves, the worth of their work and their organization's survival and success. Underlying women workers' concerns about presenting an efficient and professional image in order to be taken seriously therefore, lie complex discursive power relations based upon gender and sexuality. Unlike other (mixed-sex and men's) flatter organizations, women-only co-operatives and collectives are constituted by discourses of feminism, lesbianism and separatism, with these three often being elided in ways which cannot operate for other hierarchical and less or non-hierarchical organizations. Whether women workers in women's co-operatives and collectives are lesbian or not (or for that matter whether all women and men workers in mixed-sex and men's flatter organizations are heterosexual) is often immaterial to this sexualization of women's flatter organizations because lesbianizing discourses can attach at the organizational level as well as at the level of the individual or body. This point was borne out by a woman worker in a women's sexual abuse advice and counselling collective, who claimed:

I think that that's why we're pushed to the sidelines. Because I do honestly believe that a lot of the negativity that comes out in the press is because if you are doing it on your own as women, you automatically hate men or you're all lesbians, which obviously isn't true in any of the cases unless you are an all-lesbian co-op . . . That is in a way why we are marginalized. You know, *because it's a part of a rationalization for the fear of women doing things on their own and actually enjoying doing things with women and not necessarily putting men first.*

Even in the case of those women's flatter organizations which on the surface bear no obvious relationship to feminist issues like domestic violence or sexual abuse, as in the case of the collectives discussed above, it is clear that some of the lack of credibility that attaches to them is associated with challenges by women to (gendered and sexualized) hierarchical power and control. Most women's and certainly all women-only flatter organizations are thus subject to specific forms of lesbianization which can apply even when the sector in which they are located and the content of their work is unrelated to explicitly feminist issues. This was the case in relation to the analogy of the Greenham Common women drawn by the traditional businessmen referred to earlier by a woman worker in a women's co-operative which supplied software to engineering companies. There are clearly imputations here then, that women who organize co-operatively or collectively, and on their own without men, for whatever purposes (even computer systems suppliers), must be separatists and therefore it supposedly follows, lesbians.

As a result, the criteria for determining the professionalism, merit and worth of women's flatter organizations is deeply implicated with the lesbianism, real or assumed, of women workers and the organizations for which they work. Such 'deviancy' is unlikely to be well received or well rewarded according to traditional discourses of professionalism. This point about the imputed weirdness of lesbians and lesbianism, and the consequences for women's flatter organizations, can be illustrated by comments from a woman worker in a women's architectural design co-operative, who argued:

> The sort of thing that concerns us and we've talked about, never even generally reaches the light of day in most [architectural] practices. For example, the development of an equal opportunities policy . . . probably the vast majority never think about it. And also wanting to work for a specific section of the populace that is least able to get access to architecture, i.e. women and within that, black women, ethnic minority women, lesbians and all that . . . targeting those people, well, *that's weird, particularly lesbians, that's really weird, or perceived as being really weird, really extreme, by the mainstream of the profession.* And they pick on, when they see that list of prioritized people, they always pick on lesbians, because that's weird!

One important consequence of this discursive sexualization and marginalization of women's flatter organizations is that they tend to be routinely excluded from access to grants, loans, sales and contracts, not only, like other (mixed-sex and men's) flatter organizations, because of their supposedly radical, inefficient and unworkable structures, nor, like other (mixed-sex and men's) flatter organizations, because of their supposed lack of credibility, but *because they are sexualized in specific ways which are particular to women.* Lesbianizing discourses are deeply implicated, but also remain buried, within the construction of women's flatter organizations, partly because sexuality can be coded as political, so that lesbianism, for example, is simply collapsed into feminism. The difficulties of organizational survival and prosperity in the case of women workers, are elided with imputations of radical feminism, which can be negative, but not as negative as imputations of lesbianism, for flatter organizations. The comments from a woman worker in a women's drop-in advice and counselling centre illustrate the difficulties here:

We've had some very good references just on a personal level. You know, letters saying 'thanks for this' and 'thanks for that', and also recognition that we've done a really good job. So at the moment we're planning to go to all these bodies, these statutory bodies, and say, 'Fine, you've said this of us, please will you give us written references we can take to the borough council and get funding for workers?' But those are individuals, not the organizations, and I *still sense some anxiety about dealing with us because we're perceived as a radical feminist organization with radical feminist politics*

The material consequences of such processes are related to the sexualization of women's organizations, since radical feminism is often discursively coded as lesbian. Hence the lesbianization of women's collectives can have the effect of denying or withholding local authority funding to women's projects, as a woman worker in a sexual abuse advice and counselling collective explained:

I think that it is quite significant that the media choose to focus on lesbians. 'Your poll tax is nearly £500 because lesbians have been given money!' You know, 'Lesbians are now the only employers!' We're definitely seen as non-deserving. They don't want money spent on women, ethnic minority groups and lesbian and gay groups. I think that what happens is that in the end if you are used as a reason for bankruptcy or bad policy, then the people who support you are going to get scared and they are going to cut back even more . . . This is a point that we've actually had from sort of liberally-minded people, which actually puts us in quite a vulnerable position . . . We're much less likely to get support for whatever we're doing which is obviously contributing to the community.

In the case of women's flatter organizations where there is some degree of congruence between the political/feminist orientations of the women workers themselves and the sexualizing discourses to which they and their organization are subject, the effects upon the continued success and survival of the organization can be dramatic. The comments of a black woman worker in a women's wholefood co-operative illustrate this point:

Customers didn't want to come in. In 1982–83, when I came in, the women were radical separatist feminists and well, you couldn't be a separatist feminist and tolerate men walking in and serving men and smiling at them! It got to the point where only the brave, the really brave, came in here! [laughs].

The specific marginalization of women workers and women's (and particularly women-only) flatter organizations, their vulnerability on the grounds of imputations that they are feminist, separatist and lesbian acts to place such organizations on the economic periphery. These problems can partly be overcome by organizational longevity; in other words, they are less likely to have damaging effects once a women's organization has been successful in surviving for a number of years, often against the odds. However, this in itself is problematic since funding for collectively-run women's projects in the voluntary sector is highly constrained and often short-term, and worker co-operatives are often subject to start-up financial difficulties, particularly when they are being set up by women alone. The lesbianization of women workers and women's flatter organizations has very real, material consequences. Women and men workers in mixed-sex and men's flatter organizations are closer to the norm of male-dominated, hierarchical/heterosexualized organization, both in numerical and status terms, and therefore do not experience comparable stigmatization and suspicion. Even if mixed-sex and men's flatter organizations are constituted by homosexualizing discourses on the basis of the issues with which they are concerned (for example, anti-sexist youth work or HIV/AIDS), they are nevertheless likely to be less acute. It can be argued that this is because when men organize (even and perhaps especially when on their own) they pose no real threat to, and in fact validate, men's identity and power. This is a point to which we will return in Chapter 10, but first it is necessary to turn to the second line of argument concerning the experiences of women and men workers in flatter organizations, one that presents a very different picture of the benefits and opportunities flatter organizations offer for both women and men workers to overcome the gendered and sexualized constraints under which they labour, and which have been outlined and analysed in this and the previous chapter.

Chapter 9

The Benefits of Flatter Organizations

The first line of argument, presented earlier and used to analyse the data in the preceding two chapters, tends, it has been argued, to gloss over the possibilities for resistance and manoeuvre in people's working lives. In contrast, the second line of argument developed in this book suggests that structural and discursive constraints *are* countered and resisted; people reflect upon their working lives, they observe contradictions and constraints in their experiences and they challenge them. In short, the second line of argument highlights the ways in which workers 'rattle their chains' as it were, and seek to throw off the shackles of assumptions surrounding their experiences of paid work in flatter organizations. However, this is not to suggest that the gender dynamics of workers' attempts to challenge structural and discursive constraints is unimportant. Men working in flatter organizations do not resist such constraints in the same way as women workers because they are not subject to the same cultural, social or discursive forces, the same discrimination in the labour market or the same position in the family as women. Resistance therefore takes on a different meaning and emphasis for women than for men. In order to explore how this resistance may operate differently for women and men, it is necessary first of all to look at what benefits workers perceive as accruing to them as the result of working in flatter organizations and what they feel they have achieved in spite of the particular difficulties they identify, as outlined in the previous two chapters. In the case of each of the various benefits and achievements, it is possible to highlight the degree of gender-specificity involved and the extent to which this allows differential room for manoeuvre and experimentation on the part of women and men workers.

Responsibility, Control, Decision-making and Flexibility

The taking and sharing of responsibility, the process of having control over working situations and a voice in decision-making are all benefits which have been perceived to be associated with work in flatter organizations. However, on the face of things, there was very little in the empirical data that indicated that these benefits were gendered in any obvious or predictable way. Fairly typical comments, which tended to replicate those of a range of women and

men workers, can be gauged from the accounts of a woman and a man worker
as follows. First, a woman worker in a mixed-sex magazine publishing co-
operative, who argued that some of the benefits of her job included:

> [Feeling] that what you say actually counts and that your views are
> worth hearing and it isn't just left to people who think that they have
> a better view on the way the company should be going or what it's
> doing. I think that in terms of maturing and taking responsibility, it's
> good because you can't just say, 'Oh, I didn't know about that' or 'I'm
> not an accountant, I didn't know about that.' Everyone is expected to
> take responsibility for financial management . . . all of us are ex-
> pected to take an interest in and understanding of the accounts when
> they are presented and I expect that's also another big advantage,
> that you are very much feeling supported by people in the work that
> you do and if you have got a problem with something, and you're
> finding something difficult, then you can share that with other people
> and they will help. I think that is a very great advantage to it. You
> don't actually feel as isolated as you might do in a more hierarchical
> organization. We have to account very strictly for what we do. We
> have to report quite rigorously, particularly on the financial aspect of
> things, any projects and so on, but because you do that really as a
> process of dialogue all the way through, it's unlikely that people will
> turn around and say, 'This is awful. Why didn't you say something
> about it?' because you've had that sharing connection all the way
> through, which is good . . .

The second quote is from a man working in a mixed-sex scrap recycling
collective, and illustrates the point that in terms of taking responsibility, having control and contributing to decision-making, there was very little difference on the face of it, between women and men's experiences. As he argued:

> You don't carry any weight of decision on your own shoulders.
> You've obviously got a good support network and you can share your
> problems with – and share your achievements with – everyone around
> you. People say, 'That's well done!' and so you get positive feedback
> as well as negative . . . so that's a good thing. You get critical feed-
> back as well. What I liked in the first month that I was here was that
> people were saying to me, 'Actually, I don't like you doing that. I
> don't agree with that', which is fine, it clears things. Just recently
> we've had a big review. We've had a group consultant in, a facilitator,
> and it's brought home ways of giving feedback and receiving feed-
> back, ways of, you know, if you're unhappy with something, then talk
> about it. It's been very healthy . . . We see the whole spectrum of it
> here in the collective. Like we'll say, 'Okay, we need a new computer
> programme', 'We haven't got the money', 'Why haven't we got the

money?' 'Well, because of the budget this year' . . . We'll go into the whole of what our budget is and our financial cash flow. You won't get that in a hierarchy: 'Can I see the books please?' . . . But the information here is wide open and if you want anything explained then it gets explained.

Closer analysis however of how these benefits were perceived as operating by women and men workers suggests that there were ways in which they were experienced differently according to gender. For example, women workers made more comparisons with what was typically denied them or was lacking in hierarchical organizations, something that men workers did not tend to do. The comments from a black African woman worker in a women's wholefood retail co-operative illustrate the types of comparisons women workers were likely to make:

I hope it is easier to communicate here than if you worked somewhere else. If you went to Marks and Spencers you would just be told, 'Oh, do that!' That would be it, that's your job and you're not involved in any way with what's going on higher up, whereas here . . . you are responsible to the co-op and to each other, you know, accountable.

Without making specific reference to gender, the point that many women workers in flatter organizations seem to be making is that more hierarchical organizations are relatively unlikely to give their women workers responsibility, control or a voice in decision-making, since most women in the labour market are crowded in the lower positions. This is not seen as necessarily connected with the position of women as workers *per se*, but with the way hierarchies are gendered and sexualized, and the way flatter organizations are attempting to overcome this. As a woman worker in a women's film/video production co-operative explained:

We don't want to reproduce the hierarchies of mainstream television. We do think that you can work differently . . . we try to integrate the various different areas of work . . . we have a lot of freedom, we have complete copyright over all our work. We shoot, we research, we write it, we edit and we distribute it ourselves, so that's good.

A woman worker in a mixed-sex youth service collective also explained:

I feel much better about sitting down and talking about things on an equal basis. I mean, I've always hated hierarchy, so I think that's probably one of the things about being here. I think I probably feel more valued and respected than maybe I would do in other situations and I think that maybe because of that, I care more. I know that if I

went into another job where there was a hierarchy, I wouldn't care so
much about what I was doing.

In fact, it could be argued that it is because women have traditionally been
denied responsibility, control and decision-making powers in more hierarchical organizations, that these benefits were seen as particularly important
advantages to women workers in flatter organizations. Some women workers
did see these aspects of work and organizational life as specifically gendered,
as the comments from a woman worker in a women's computing systems co-
operative suggest:

> I think that if we were an organization that was more hierarchical,
> it wouldn't be quite so easy because for one thing they would
> be allocating the jobs, plus if there's a man and a woman in there
> and an interesting job came up, it would be the man who was sent and
> the woman would be behind bringing the invoices and doing the
> paperwork!

It could be argued that since women do not tend to occupy the most
powerful positions in hierarchical organizations, the opportunities that flatter
organizations offer women to take and share responsibility, have control over
their work and contribute to decision-making, can act to challenge traditional
expectations of women in the workplace and enhance the extent to which
women workers feel that they benefit from the experience of working in flatter
organizations. The comments from a woman worker in a women's grocery
retail co-operative, which had been formed as a job-creation enterprise from a
failing business, illustrate this point well:

> We answer to ourselves now and if something goes wrong, we'll sort
> it out, whereas before we had someone coming in, an area manager,
> and it didn't matter how hard you worked, it was never hard enough.
> Whereas now we know that everything that we do is down to us and
> we succeed or fail by our own efforts.

There was a further advantage to flatter organizations that was cited
particularly by women workers; this concerned the degree to which less
or non-hierarchical working was flexible in terms of allowing for personal
development and in terms of meeting domestic, family and personal needs.
Flexibility was not mentioned as often by men workers, tending to suggest
that it was less important to them even though they were more likely to be
living in households with young preschool age children than their women
counterparts. But for women workers flexibility was clearly an important
consideration, especially given the extent to which many more women than
men were working part-time or four days per week. This flexibility was

described by a woman worker in a mixed-sex inflatables for the disabled collective in the following way:

> The main advantage is that it is a very flexible way in which to work. You can develop your own ideas and you can also do a little bit of everything, so that although my job is a community development worker, there's scope for me to say, if someone else is working on another project, 'Oh, that sounds really interesting, I'll do that with you.' So your job descriptions are not fixed totally. You might have primary responsibility for a certain area but there's a lot of flexibility around the kind of work that you do . . . so there's an opportunity, because we are quite a small collective as well, for someone like me to actually know a little bit about every area of the collective, if I want to. So I actually end up knowing more about the organization than I would if I were working in a larger organization doing one particular job.

For women workers who had previously worked in more hierarchical settings, the contrasts were stark. As a woman worker in a mixed-sex Playbus project who had been working in her last job as a supply teacher for the local education authority, commented, 'I like the informality of it. Very much in teaching, you're working to a bell or you're working to, you know, there's certain lessons and the structure of it is all there. Here it is very much you can work out what you think is best . . .'

The flexibility to experiment with new patterns of working and thereby challenge traditional notions of how hierarchical power and control in organizations operated was important to several women workers in flatter organizations, particularly in terms of their own development. As a woman worker in a mixed-sex experimental theatre co-operative commented:

> Obviously it does depend on how the co-operative runs but it does have that possibility of allowing you to gain a confidence and a certain amount of self-possession in the way you relate to people and the way you do your job. That is a path that you can follow for yourself, and not be moulded again by a structure which is imposed upon you . . . because the co-operative is such a fluid structure it actually gives quite a lot of leeway to experiment which I think is important.

This flexibility is not without its drawbacks, however, as it makes it much harder to define boundaries, and a number of workers in flatter organizations, both women and men, experienced this as problematic. For example, as one man worker in a mixed-sex scrap recycling collective maintained:

> In a collective, things are not so clear-cut; it's opaque in a way because things are moving around all the time and sometimes you get

confusion . . . I'm not saying it's rosy and wonderful, we do have our arguments and we do disagree with each other and there are a number of blow-ups and disagreements, some of which are bubbling around unsolved.

These points were also made by a man worker in a mixed-sex HIV/AIDS advice and counselling collective and illustrate how organizational flexibility can be experienced as both positive and negative:

When I started as a paid worker, there wasn't a clear structure of, 'You will be like this and you will provide this, this, this and this.' It was much more about just getting in there and finding out about the work, so I did loads of different things. That was one of the appeals, I could do all sorts of things that I wanted to do. I also got a lot of challenges . . . that was what was exciting about the work and in a way, revolutionary. It was very much tied up with a point of view about AIDS. Yes, it is a very painful issue for us individually and as a society, but it also presents many new opportunities for us to change things that are now in need of change . . . it's gone through a lot of permutations since then . . . but at the time it was like we had lots of room to experiment. Lots of room to experiment – *we took on far too much!*

Re-creating Workplace Culture

Several workers mentioned the benefits of the supportive and understanding atmosphere found in many flatter organizations, compared with the lack of such in more hierarchical organizations. In addition to the family analogy drawn upon in the case of the women workers discussed in Chapter 7, several workers, both women and men, also tended to see their workplaces as places where friendships were made, a social network developed, and people could enjoy a more balanced and humane working life. These advantages were not without their gender dimensions however, since women's opportunities for friendship/networking through work tend, traditionally at least, to be more circumscribed than men's. Women workers in flatter organizations were more likely than men to identify benefits in terms of socializing with others and bonding. This point is illustrated by the comments of a black African woman worker in a women's wholefood retail co-operative, who claimed:

Basically for me, because I was a single parent and I was home all the time, I didn't have much of a social life. Not that I have one now! But it was a way of meeting people, because when you are a single parent you tend not to talk to anyone, you can go for days and not talk to an adult. So coming in here, besides working with other women – and most of the women here knew my circumstances so it was quite easy for me to communicate with them – I was able to meet the public, not as walking down the street, as strangers, but getting to know them. And you do get to know an awful lot of people and therefore it's a lot of social contact . . . You wouldn't get that if you worked elsewhere, you'd just treat them as customers or clients and that's the end of it. But here if you go out in the evening, you do meet people who come in here and it carries on beyond the shop . . .

Men workers in flatter organizations did not identify the benefits of bonding and networking *per se*, but did instead point to the benefits of workplace cultures which were less competitive and more 'humane' than most men's workplaces. This was seen as a contrast to most men's experiences of work in more hierarchical organizations, which were evaluated, by extension, as inhuman. As one man worker in a mixed-sex HIV/AIDS advice and counselling collective commented: 'When I look at other people's jobs, and as much as I tear my hair out about this job, [laughs] I do also realize that there is something very real about this job, *there is something very human about it.* There are real gifts to the job as well as hard bits.'

A similar comparison was made by a man worker in a mixed-sex wholefood retail co-operative, who maintained:

One of the syndromes I come up against a lot as a [holistic health] practitioner is 'How do you feel about your work?' I say to people, very often the problems that they have are exacerbated or have their cause in how they're working. They are working in *organizations which have no human values to them*, they are just cogs in a machine, they are just bits and they don't feel they are contributing very much. I think that that shows up in health . . . so there are challenges all round for a small place like this that's run on *much more human lines.*

It may be possible to go further and argue that in valuing more human workplaces like this, men workers in flatter organizations are challenging dominant discourses of what it is to be a masculinized worker. Several men workers suggested that their working lives in flatter organizations were not masculine in any obvious way, and in fact departed from rigid or traditionally discourses of masculinity as displayed and deployed in more hierarchical workplaces. It is important to note that all of the following comments arose unsolicited and unprompted. For example, a man worker in a mixed-sex community transport collective described his attraction to the job and the organization as follows:

I feel that it's a lot to do with being more in touch with the female part of my biology or psyche. I have always been sort of mechanically interested, but alongside that I have always at the same time had a hand in things from writing poetry to art to using pastels. I just sort of like messing about in that . . . right through to the clothes I wear. I have always abhorred suits and that has a lot to do with the collar-and-tie business. Whether liking loose, comfortable clothing is a masculine or feminine trait I've no idea [laughs] but yes, I'm just more comfortable with it and unless there's no choice, I wouldn't go for a job that made me wear a collar-and-tie and all that.

Similar points were made by a man worker in a mixed-sex wholefood retail co-operative, who claimed:

I happen to be male, not a very 'male' male I would say. I'm not a very masculine male in a lot of respects became I think that the female principles are extremely important and not enough men have some of that and somehow they feel it's not very good to have some of that. My life is involved in health care as it is, my own and tai-chi and the principles of all those things, and you can't hold on to all that macho stuff.

For men workers in flatter organizations then, the opportunity to express themselves differently at work was contingent in part on the culture of the organizations for which they worked. Such cultures were perceived as being very different from those in more traditional, hierarchical (masculinized) organizations, as a man worker in a mixed-sex scrap recycling collective explained:

I don't know whether it's because there is a strong female presence here . . . that it works well as a collective. Personally, I think that there has to be at least – I don't know how you would put it – not a strong but a good female input, let's put it that way . . . it's the female and the male side, the caring and the assertive. *It's interesting because you can explore them; I can be sensitive in this sort of group whereas the place I was in before, I would have just attracted ridicule . . .*

Furthermore, it seems that there is a tendency for men workers in flatter organizations to negotiate the more controlling forms that masculinity can take in the workplace; for example, by tempering their own (and by challenging others') expressions of sexism and heterosexism. Several of the men workers claimed to be self-regulating their tendency to dominate and were monitoring their language in attempts to be non-discriminatory. As one man worker in a mixed-sex architects co-operative argued:

I imagine one of your particular concerns is gender, which I never – being a sort of woolly sort of pink, liberal, public school boy – never really had to think about very much except in personal relations.

That was quite interesting and hard and difficult. I mean, it expressed itself originally in my being pulled up over my language of course . . . The women here are very conscious and thought-out and their concerns as women came through as soon as I joined. I was an absolute innocent really! I thought I was terribly nice to everybody, you know, but I just didn't know the half of it. I got really pulled up and I got into great trouble and some of that was because I was a man playing a man's game as the ex-director of a man's firm . . .

By way of contrast, it is worth noting that some women workers in flatter organizations felt that the extent that they could challenge gender power relations was highly limited, due to the ways in which both they and their organizations were marginalized. As a woman worker in a women's sexual abuse advice and counselling collective commented:

To a certain extent, we do subvert, you know, institutionalized sexism in a way – or can do. I mean, the answer really is that we are kept out of power so much that it's very difficult to do that. Only by our mere existence, which is a contradiction, we do it . . . The more models you have, the easier it becomes really.

As was argued in Chapter 8, when women workers in women's (and particularly women-only) flatter organizations present challenges to traditional expectations of the feminized and sexualized woman worker, they are subject to specific forms of discursive and material marginalization, whereas when men workers in flatter organizations rework notions of masculinity as evidenced in workplace relations, as the extracts above indicate, they are condoned or even approved of.

Challenging Gendered Careers

Many men workers in men's and mixed-sex flatter organizations do not appear to be following traditional career paths (for men), and in failing to develop their careers according to traditional expectations of men's working lives, namely as continuous, upward and linear progressions, it can be argued that such men workers are engaging in a form of career abandonment. This involves men workers in flatter organizations adopting patterns of work more closely associated with women workers, such as downwards or sideways job moves, experience of casual or temporary employment, and work in the caring field. As one man worker in a mixed-sex recycled paper co-operative described it:

Probably from about the age of 19 I've always been sort of alternatively-minded in the sense of believing in caring and sharing and stuff like that. Um, I worked as a hospital porter. I'm also a qualified nurse and I've worked on community programmes with the elderly, and children and young people. I've done voluntary work in loads of different things and so it was a *a natural progression into a co-operative business* . . .

In addition, some men workers in flatter organizations perceived the opportunities for occupying managerial or supervisory positions, or the potential for fostering ambitions to hold them, as being highly circumscribed by the structure and culture of the organizations for which they worked. Although according to traditional expectations of men's career aspirations this might have been perceived as negative, on the whole this was felt to be positive by several of the men workers interviewed. As a man worker in a mixed-sex city farm collective argued:

But as far as a career structure in city farm goes, there isn't one, but everybody accepts that. I didn't join because I wanted to get to the top of the tree in city farm. I mean, when you are in a collective you can't get to the top of the tree and it doesn't matter . . . sometimes succeeding is a very personal, individual thing, so you need success, but one thing that you might want to do might be to the detriment of everything else that's going on the farm. I think that the rest of the workers would agree with that, that okay we could go off and do our own individual things but at the end of the day the farm is bigger than, the unit is bigger than, all of us as individuals and that's one thing that all of us have got to bear in mind . . .

A similar point was made by a man worker in a mixed-sex scrap recycling collective:

The other thing that is missing – well, not missing, it's just not apparent – is personal ambition. I was just saying to my wife last night, 'People are not ambitious there in the traditional sense, there's not the rabid ambition, there's not the back stabbing that goes with ambition.' So we're not always wondering, 'Well, what's in it for them? What's their secret agenda?' We have ambitions, ambitions for [name of organization] and within those ambitions we advance as well, because the whole advances.

There appeared therefore to be a sense amongst men workers that flatter organizations necessitated a reworking of traditional goals of achievement and ambition, at least insofar as they pertained to men's working lives or careers. Perhaps surprisingly, the disruption of traditional expectations of men's career paths was most marked in the case of well-educated, professional men in the mid- to late-stages of their working lives, several of whom had left well-paid, high status jobs to found and run flatter organizations. For example, in the case of one man worker in his early fifties, who worked in a mixed-sex wholefood retail co-operative, his working life was outlined as follows:

> The scientific establishment is something I left, I left deliberately. I decided that I was spending too much time learning too much about too little. I was becoming too specialized and so I left to become more general . . . I stopped being a research scientist and I became a science writer . . . I started writing radio programmes on science for the general public . . . But then I made a step away from that because I was becoming a corporate executive and I didn't like the feel of that . . . so I stopped even doing the radio work and I took a break for a year and I became a teaching musician and a practicing musician. My interest in music is in people-music, traditional and old things, but again it was working more and more at a grass-roots level . . . In the space of 10 years I moved from being a deeply committed re-search scientist in one of the finest research establishments in the world, a big organization [in the United States], to being a single, solo performer and teacher, working one-to-one. Meanwhile, in parallel, I got deeply involved in martial arts and in medicine, natural medicine . . . but I was only saying to Sue this morning, had I stayed in the field that I was in – I'm not exaggerating now when I say this – if I'd pursued that, I would have been quite rich by now. I'd be working in the range now at a minimum of \$60–70,000 a year.

The issue of failing to develop or not developing their careers in ways traditionally associated with well-qualified, middle-class men was also touched upon by another man worker in his early fifties who worked in a mixed-sex architects' co-operative:

> When on occasions I've felt that I'm taking on too much responsibil-ity, which is always a danger if you are the oldest member of an otherwise equal team – a danger, not a fact – then I've felt that, you know, 'At your age, what the hell are you scrabbling around down here for?' Note 'down here' and not 'up there' which means on the high path to career and money. You do have to make a rather strong commitment not to do that . . . I don't know, it's quite something but that's what people can't understand because they have allowed them-selves to be brainwashed into thinking that there's only one direction that men anyway are supposed to go in and I mean, there's not much to suggest otherwise out there . . .

Not all men workers in flatter organizations identified with this idea of escaping from or abandoning careers in the traditional sense, however, and not all of them eschewed individual success in terms of high earnings, high status and prospects, in return for some of the other benefits of flatter organizations previously identified. Some men workers even saw the small, flatter organization as a means of bypassing traditional career ladders, and thought they could advance their careers in ways which it would be much harder to do in more hierarchical organizations. As one man worker in a mixed-sex film/video production collective explained:

> What we have set up is a more useful vehicle for us personally, in terms of us becoming producers, than we could have achieved either individually or through going through, say, conventional channels. I don't know, there aren't many people who at 26 have produced high powered, national corporate programming like this. It's a real achievement for me so that then, in terms of where I can take that . . . I certainly feel that I have skills that I can sell and that would be transferable to lots of other situations and at quite a high level . . .

Where does this leave women workers in flatter organizations? For women workers, careers are crucially affected by, amongst other things, their gender and sexuality. Traditionally, women's careers are seen as being of lower status and worth, and women have to engage with these expectations that they will, for example, put their family and personal lives before their careers, which are often considered secondary. As a result some women workers, but no men, made reference to wanting and needing their career worth to be recognized, since so often it was not. As a woman worker in a women's training workshop nursery collective claimed:

> Here I felt that my age didn't really matter, the experience counted and they looked upon me as a person. I really felt that when I came here. I wasn't judged on what my husband did or what my family were or how old I was or whatever. It was just for me and what I could offer. That was important to me.

A similar point was reiterated by a woman worker in a women's computer systems co-operative:

> I suppose I could carry on in the same sort of way for quite a while, although I don't want to because I think that you need to have money, you need to have a reward at the end. I enjoy what I do, I get an awful lot of satisfaction from it but I also need to have a reward that says at the end that I'm being fairly successful. It's more than just having the money to spend. It's a status symbol. *I suppose in a way it says to everyone else that I'm not just sticking things out . . .*

Women workers in flatter organizations therefore appear to exhibit different attitudes towards their career development than many of their men counterparts. Whereas several of the men workers were already in a position of having had high-powered, linear career paths to abandon, women workers were striving to assert their worth in career terms in the first place. This was reflected in an attitude amongst some of women workers in flatter organizations that advancing their careers confirmed their status, and as women this was a much-needed benefit in terms of what they gained from their work. As one woman worker in a mixed-sex inflatables for the disabled collective explained:

> I'm not particularly ambitious but I do want to gradually go up a bit. I don't still want to be on the same level in 15 years' time as I am now, although I don't want to be a manager or a director or anything. I just want to be doing something a little higher up the scale and slightly different. Collectives don't have a promotion structure; you get a salary rise but you don't get promoted to anything because we're all on the same level . . . I suppose there is a bit of pressure because I feel I should move up as well . . .

It may even be possible to suggest that those workers who are least advantaged within the unequally structured UK labour market are most likely to use their experience in flatter organizations to develop their career profiles, whereas those workers who are most advantaged – white, middle-class men – are more likely to enter flatter organizations as a means of escaping from what they perceive as the drawbacks associated with competitive, high-powered, continuous career tracks in male-dominated, hierarchical organizations. The following comments from a black, working-class woman in a mixed-sex dance project collective, illustrate the point:

> It's a stepping stone for me because it's a stepping stone upwards. I don't know what I want to become at the end of the day, but I want to be running my own thing. I don't want to be working for white institutions no more. I want as a black woman to set up my own project in which . . . it will be an all-black project and we will be running it and it will be a successful project and I suppose this is a good run . . .

In terms of the benefits of working in flatter organizations, both women and men workers clearly have some scope for resistance and manoeuvre and, in setting up, running and engaging in waged work in less or non-hierarchical organizations, they disrupt some of the dominant discursive constructions of gendered work, workplace cultures and careers. In this way, women and men workers have scope for 'moving into each other's shoes' as it were, but the extent of experimental repositioning is different for each. In terms of how women and men challenge traditional discourses of themselves as gendered workers, they are clearly in different power positions from which to effect or approach these challenges. As an Asian woman worker in a domestic violence information and advice collective, expressed it:

> Women are more likely to put their necks out than men. I do tend to think that about men and women. Men are more likely to do things for an easy life than women. Women are much more likely to confront things and talk about things than men do. That, I do feel is different about working in a women's organization. I think men are more prone to not rocking the boat really . . . It's the whole thing of what I said to you earlier about whether because you are a woman and you are working for women's rights, then you've got a gut feeling about it whereas obviously, if you are a white, middle-class man then you have got the option of turning an eye away from it because it doesn't actually affect you personally because it never can be you . . .

In short, there are structural and discursive differences in terms of how women and men workers in flatter organizations come to enter into and be positioned into gendered and sexualized relations of power and control, and as a result, differences in terms of how they present challenges to and resist expectations of themselves as gendered and sexualized workers. To some extent, women workers *have* to confront and challenge these power relations, given the disadvantages that women as a whole face in the wider labour market and in organizational life generally. On the other hand, men workers in flatter organizations can *choose* to avoid such issues, although it could be argued that in the case of the mixed-sex organizations it is sometimes by virtue of working alongside politicized women, that men workers are encouraged, if not forced, to challenge dominant constructions of gender and sexuality. However, there is little empirical data to support a possible connection here. Nevertheless, it is possible to maintain that structural and discursive constraints shape the experiences of men and women workers in flatter organizations in different ways, and thereby inform their responses differently as a result. This view is clearly apparent in the gendered ways in which women and men workers in flatter organizations sought to achieve their objectives, and in the ways they constructed images of both themselves and their organizations which allowed them to subvert stereotypes.

Subverting Gender Stereotypes

In some cases it was possible for both women and men workers in flatter organizations to ensure that they were seen by customers, clients and funding bodies in the ways in which they wanted to be seen. For example, 'dressing the part', putting on appropriate gendered/sexualized clothing, hairstyles and make-up at work and so on, was an aspect of work which women and men workers could, to some degree, negotiate as and when they saw fit. Clearly however, this negotiation was gendered; several women workers referred to 'dressing the part' in order to be taken as professional and serious. None of the men workers referred to their negotiation of an appropriate appearance in this way, but for women workers, their clothing, hairstyles and make-up at work was an issue, though it was not always one which they felt themselves to be negatively or passively constrained by. For example, one woman worker in a fashion designers co-operative maintained; 'I do stick the suit on if I'm meeting someone for important contracts but I generally try not to. If we're visiting clients I tend to look tidy, but not overdo it . . . Most people accept that, especially being in fashion, you can get away with being arty-farty so it's not a problem.'

Similarly, a woman worker in a mixed-sex inflatables for the disabled collective, who was wearing a T-shirt and jeans on the day of interview, argued:

> Although none of us wear suits or the sort of traditional working gear – I don't wear my stiletto heels and stuff – our attitude is quite professional. Well, I think if I was going to a meeting that was quite high up, I wouldn't go like this . . . But the other thing is that when you are going out doing events, we've got to do quite a lot of carting around and we've got to take the airbeds out of the van, unroll them and roll them up, lifting people, so you actually get quite dirty and these are actually the most sensible kind of clothes to wear.

To some extent, subverting stereotypes was an integral part of the work of some of the flatter organizations studied, as for example, in the case of the film/video, theatre, dance and publishing organizations, whose products were designed to be visibly consumed. As a woman worker in a mixed-sex touring theatre co-operative commented:

> If you see women in a theatre company going into a hall, putting up lights and rigging up stuff, then people look at you and subconsciously think, 'Oh, there's a woman and she's hammering a nail into a big bit of wood!' We do get people coming up to us and saying, 'Oh, I'll take that big box off you dear, you can't possibly manage that', and over the years we have learnt to say, 'No, it's fine thanks, I can manage . . .' The show we did about women joining the Navy . . . was very popular and there were three women in the cast and one man and they all cross-played, we played different sexes and um, you know, we smoked pipes – not really on stage – but showing these women from about the age of 14 dressing up as men and being taken as men because nobody assumed they weren't. Then you'd finish the show and come out and be taking the set down and people would come up and say things like, 'Oh, women can't do things like that!', and you'd say, 'Well, look, we've just been showing you what they did

two hundred years ago! What are you talking about?' It's only been hammering the point home, using our craft which is our shows, that we hope to overcome that. But it's a long process and some people will never change! [laughs]

Assumptions that workers in flatter organizations, and women workers in particular, are unskilled, inefficient, down-market and unprofessional, can be pre-empted and resisted in various ways by workers. In particular, some of the strategies they adopt involve women workers in being highly competent in their dealings with customers and clients by, for example, presenting an image of the successful expert or entrepreneur as well as appearing caring and conscientious, as the following comments from a woman worker in a women's employment training workshop collective illustrate:

[You have] to give an image that they are not expecting, I think, when you go to visit [clients]. We're both of us quite eloquent at arguing. We had a good presentation pack and we had the right papers. We knew the answers to [his] questions. We didn't try and stall him. We told him who we were, what we did and what we wanted him to do, and then said, 'What would you like us to do for you?' You know, we did a very business-type approach to it and he was just floored . . . So you have to get these negotiations going and once they realize that you're interested and you're serious and your training is of high quality, then you're going to be taken more seriously.

Nevertheless, in order to be taken seriously women workers have to confront contradictory discursive constructions of women as being attractive but not *too* sexual (or sexually 'deviant') while at the same time, being caring and conscientious but not *too* emotional or game-playing/childish. Being too competent and business-like also opens up the possibility that women workers can be seen as unfeminine, sexless and lacking a sense of humour, all of which have been shown to play a part in discursively *and* materially marginalizing women workers in flatter organizations, particularly when they are women-only. These are difficult subject positions to negotiate, and are not ones with which men workers in flatter organizations have to engage. Furthermore, by presenting themselves as serious and competent professionals, men workers in flatter organizations are conforming to, not challenging, gendered expectations of what men's work is like.

Men workers in flatter organizations subvert stereotypes in a different way; they do so by challenging discourses of a masculinity which positions men as competitive, power-hungry and instrumental. They are thus engaging with a different set of discursive constructions from women workers. It could be argued that in subverting stereotypes of white, middle-class men as successful high-achievers, in presenting themselves as having little interest in the motives and rewards that drive such men towards competitive, high-powered careers in hierarchical organizations, men workers in flatter organizations are highly subversive and threatening. For example, this anecdote from a man worker in a mixed-sex architects co-operative showing how unmanly (irrational, lacking in remuneration and so on) his work appeared to be, illustrates the point well:

> [The bank manager] said he would call down sometime. He did call down . . . and he didn't like the sound of us and he didn't like the fact of us and the reasons he gave, interestingly – it was fairly obvious when I thought about it but I'd never heard it before – he said, 'You are a co-operative and one of your rules, I see, is that you can't take away any of the assets that you put up. You get paid and when you leave, what happens?' I said, 'You say good-bye and you leave and the assets of the firm are ploughed back and you keep going. Mr. X leaves but the thing goes on, he's not allowed to take anything with him. In fact, if the whole thing caves in, you're not allowed to sell it off, take it with you or divide it up. You've got to give it to some worthy cause . . .' and he said, 'Why would I want to lend' – we were talking about lending, we had an overdraft – 'Why would I want to lend to someone with no more commitment than that to what he was doing?' – he was talking to me – 'to what he was doing?'
>
> I must say, that absolutely stunned me. It was like saying. 'Why are you in it if you aren't going to make anything out of it in terms of money?' So I told him why I did it, which either he didn't understand or certainly didn't believe, but it was absolutely nothing to do with any of the normal parameters which a normal man outside – let alone a bank manager! – would regard as a decent reason for working in an outfit! It's stupid to do it this way because, in their terms, you don't gain enough materially to justify it, save what your salary gives you. So what you build up is pretty intangible . . . *and I think he felt very threatened.*

Negotiating the Public/Private Divide

Working in a flatter organization can allow workers to reconfigure the traditional boundaries of the public and the private and can offer them a means whereby they can integrate other areas of their lives with their experiences of waged work. It is argued that this has different ramifications for women and men workers, because of the gendered operations of the public/private divide. It is also argued that there are differences in the extent to and ways in which women and men workers in flatter organizations are able to manoeuvre within and across the public/private divide, particularly as far as issues such as sexuality and parenting are concerned. The extent to which there was a gender difference in terms of combining waged work with other aspects of life outside work can be seen in the higher proportion of women workers who had taken extended periods of leave from their jobs and who were able to return to work after having taken time off for reasons that were often, contrary to expectations of women workers, non-family and non-work related. Of the 15 men workers in flatter organizations, 14 of them had been in continuous employment without breaks, compared to 11 of the women workers in women's organizations and only 9 women workers in mixed-sex organizations who had done so. In the case of the women workers who had taken breaks from their jobs, this was for various lengths of time and for a variety of reasons; two women had taken relatively long-term sick leave, three had left and returned after further study and employment elsewhere, one had gone to Spain for three months on personal business and one had taken leave for bereavement. In the case of the single man worker who had had a break, this was six weeks for a long-standing illness. In short, there is evidence here to suggest that women workers in flatter organizations have more scope for mobility, and move more often between waged and unwaged work and other activities than is the case with men workers.

It was clear nonetheless that both women and men workers in flatter organizations experienced a strong sense of overlap or merger between different areas of their working and non-working lives, and their public and private subjectivities. As a man worker in a mixed-sex wholefood retail co-operative expressed it, 'I don't feel that there's any division so that while I'm in this co-op now, it's merged, there's no sharp distinction between this and the rest of my life. It is a part of my life just like a finger is part of my hand.'

This merging of the lives/subjectivities of workers in flatter organizations is illustrated by the extent to which women and men workers often saw their working lives as part of their social and personal lives. A man worker in a mixed-sex recycled paper co-operative, who lived over the shop premises with his ex-wife and two children, commented on the integration of the whole of his life, as follows: 'We actually have a meal upstairs, all together, when we have our co-operative meetings, which we have in the evenings . . . We have a meal together and a laugh and a chat and then we have the meeting afterwards. That's good as well.'

Another woman worker in a mixed-sex language school co-operative also commented on this merging of the traditional boundaries between work and non-work related aspects of her life, as follows:

We do live in each other's pockets and each other's minds sort of thing. But those things have positive sides too because it's just such a lovely atmosphere here, and people, when they walk in, just feel it sort of thing. For example, I had a friend that I met on a course who came up and sat in on one of our academic meetings and she's a summer course organizer for another very big chain school – they're very big in Britain. She said, 'It's just such a different world. I would love to work here because of the enthusiasm, the co-operation, and the motivation, it's just, you know, so evident' . . .

The benefits of being able to bring private troubles into the public sphere of paid work were also seen as particularly important in terms of being able to organize work differently in flatter organizations. A woman worker in a mixed-sex magazine publishing co-operative referred to the care and under-standing extended by workers to one another, as follows:

> If you have a personal problem it's something that you can bring to the co-operative. You don't have to bare your soul or say, 'I've got such-and-such a problem', you know. But you can say, 'Can I have a day off?' It's the compassionate angle I expect I'm referring to really. We're not a particularly paternalistic or maternalistic organization . . . It's not really that. It's just that hopefully it's a conducive and compassionate environment in which to work . . . I think there's a kind of openness here which is quite a good thing. We're more willing to take on board new people and new ideas than perhaps a more conventional set-up.

There was some evidence that in recognizing and responding to the needs of the worker as a whole person, flatter organizations are more benevolent than more hierarchical organizations might be. It is argued that because there is greater scope in flatter organizations for workers to give expression at work to their lives outside work, then flatter organizations can subvert the ways in which public and private are traditionally constituted. This means that there is more scope for sharing problems and experiencing support and understanding than there might be if workers were in more hierarchical organizations and, on the face of it, this does not appear to be gendered in any obvious or predictable way. More in-depth analysis however, reveals that there are gendering pro-cesses operating here. For women workers in flatter organizations, this open-ness often involves expressing their personal feelings concerning relationships, family life and domesticity, with their co-workers. The comments from a black African woman worker in a women's wholefood retail co-operative illustrate the point. 'We're more free to talk about things . . . you feel a bit freer about relationships in a way. We do talk about our housework – how we have got loads of washing to do. We talk about our problems at home. That's basically what we talk about.'

These points were reiterated by a woman worker in a women's computing systems co-operative:

> We can bring our problems in. If I've got a problem at home, I can come in and say to Carol, such-and-such and such-and-such, and she quite understands. She doesn't think I'm getting too involved with my outside work. I think if you were working in an ordinary company you wouldn't be able to come in and say about your problems at home, whereas here you can and the person understands and makes allowances for it.

For this particular woman, the understanding extended by her co-worker was seen as specific to the gender composition of the organization. 'I think if we were six or seven people and we were all women then it would work in the same way, but if there were six or seven of us and we were mostly male, then I don't think it would work like that. I don't know, not having worked in that environment, but I suspect it wouldn't.'

Another woman worker in a women's film/video production co-operative also experienced the women-centred atmosphere in which she worked as more caring and understanding in terms of levels of awareness of women's lives outside paid work, than mixed-sex settings were. The following comments illustrate the point:

> I was just thinking about when I worked in a mixed collective and comparing it to this place. I think the things that are very noticeable are like how when women are more willing and able to talk about emotional aspects, so that here if you are having problems at home, you can bring them to work with you. Because obviously if you have just had a massive row with your husband and you come into work, it's not easy to switch off from it. So like we'll spend time talking about things like that . . . I think that most people wouldn't dispute the fact that men have problems talking about emotions and would see work being separate from that, rather than what you are influencing what you do. If you're having an off-day then it's all right to have an off-day.

Experiencing support and understanding at work is not without its contradictions, however. One woman worker in a mixed-sex language school co-operative felt that the opportunity in flatter organizations to personalize workers' contributions could cause problems:

> The problem with a co-op is that things become too personal in a way that hierarchies don't. Well, they do but you can't do anything about them. You just get fed-up and leave, that's your choice sort of thing, whereas here you have got the chance to say, 'Look, you know, I'm fed-up with you' . . . so it needs stricter guidelines really . . . When we had the time we started trying to build in those things . . . times of leaving and coming in so that people do the same amount of hours, because in a co-op that is very difficult because one person might say, 'I can't get up in the mornings, I'll stay afterwards,' but there's no way of checking . . . Bad feelings! You've got to have everything laid down . . . those structures were imposed by all of us, self-imposed again.

To argue that women workers in flatter organizations necessarily experience greater support and understanding from co-workers, and women co-workers in particular, than they might do in more hierarchical organizations is not to argue that no men workers in flatter organizations have similar experiences. Some men workers also commented upon the greater openness (to emotions, feelings, etc.) that they experienced through their work, but it was unclear whether this arose from the less or non-hierarchical structure of the organization, its gender composition or the content or area of work with which they were involved. As a man worker in a mixed-sex HIV/AIDs advice and counselling collective argued:

> We were very, very smart at how to support each other from the beginning. We were very clear that the working processes of the organization should embody the philosophical aspirations. So it was very, very important that we supported each other well and gave each other time to express our feelings about the work as well as think about the work . . .

Another illustration of this point came from a man worker in a mixed-sex scrap recycling collective. 'It is a safe atmosphere to express your feelings as well. It's a safer atmosphere to be human, especially from a male point of view. You can actually say, "I'm not feeling very happy right now" and it's a caring atmosphere.' However, in both the cases cited above, there is some recognition that this is an unusual way for men to work and organize because men's interactions in the workplace tend to be dominated by impersonal relations. In other words, although there is evidence that men workers in flatter organizations feel that they have greater opportunities to express their feelings at work than they might do if they worked in more hierarchical organizations, nonetheless this is still constituted by gendered expectations of women's and men's experiences of work and organizational life. This can even operate in terms of the expectations women workers have of their men co-workers, as the following comments from the only woman worker in a mixed-sex ethnic restaurant suggest:

> At first I had this funny idea; 'Oh, I just can't work with men!', you know, because you want someone that you can tell your problems to, if you've got problems and things like that. But now I've got used to them and if I've got any problems I just tell them and they help me sort them out, which is good really . . . they can tell with me, you see, because I look miserable sometimes and one of them will ask me what's wrong and I'll explain and he won't say anything, he'll keep it to himself. Because at first I thought that if I was to say anything, they might tell one another and have a talk about it, but they don't. They keep it secret and they sort it out with me.

It is also argued that for men workers, flatter organizations can offer them greater opportunities to avoid the tendency (for men) to elevate paid work over other areas of life; in other words, to find ways of keeping their personal/home lives and work lives in perspective. As one man worker in a mixed-sex animation co-operative described it:

> I've never felt – and this is why I'm never going to be Bruce Halpern or some other major pillar of British society! – I've never felt that work is the primary role in life. There's much more to life than that – I've never worked weekends, for instance. Well, I have worked weekends now and again . . . but we cut that out on the basis that if you are having to work weekends and evenings, you're not doing the job right. Either you get somebody else to work for you or you budget and get people to do it, so we did that.

This refusal to prioritize paid work and careers over life outside work ensures that attention is also given by men workers in flatter organizations to their physical and emotional well-being, relationships with co-workers and friends, and leisure interests. However, the extent to which men workers can negotiate the ways in which paid work dominates all else is circumscribed by, amongst other things, the amount of time and commitment involved in doing their jobs. As one man worker in a mixed-sex radical bookshop explained:

> I have been an active anarchist for a long, long time and the book-shop is part of that in a sense, although to some extent because of the amount of work that it takes up and the time that it takes up, to some extent it precludes what I used to do outside. If you spend 10 or 12 hours a day doing . . . working for a living, you don't necessarily have a lot of energy at the end of that 11-hour day, you know, time to go to meetings or the pub. I rarely go to meetings these days. But then it's a long time since I heard anything new at one!

It is also important to recall that, as was argued in Chapter 7, men workers in flatter organizations do more extra hours above those normally worked and are more likely to have second jobs than women workers. Clearly, this will constrain the extent to which they can balance their working lives with their other commitments outside work.

A further way that the public/private divide is negotiated differently according to gender, is in the differential experiences of women and men workers with regard to combining parenting with work in a flatter organization. It was argued earlier that there was an absence in the sample of women workers with young children and that flatter organizations may be restricted in terms of providing opportunities for women to combine paid work with their child-care commitments. For those women workers in flatter organizations who did have children and other dependants, however, it was felt that there was more recognition of the demands made upon them by their families than there might be if they worked in more male-dominated, hierarchical organizations. This point is illustrated by the comments from a woman worker in a women's computer systems co-operative, who was divorced and living with her 83-year-old mother and six children aged between 6 and 24 at the time of interview. 'The other reason for it being all women was because we all had families to which we were very strongly committed. We wanted to have an understanding working environment if we had to take time off for any reason.' This commitment to parenting, and specifically to mothering, in flatter organizations was also commented upon favourably by a women worker in a women's grocery retail co-operative, who had a son aged 13 and a daughter aged 10 at the time of interview, and also worked with two other women who had children. 'One of us will take all the children if we have got a day off. We'll take all the children or as many as we can or they will go and play in one of the houses nearby or they will come in here where we can keep an eye on them. So that's not a problem...'

A third woman worker in a mixed-sex architectural design co-operative who had a son aged 20 and a daughter aged 14, commented:

> I've got one son who's at university and my daughter's 14 so they're not babies anymore... when she was younger, and she had time off, I used to bring her into the office if I needed to... if there was nothing going on she could have a go on my computer and that kind of thing. I've got an aunt and she's getting very, very forgetful and she lives on her own in a large house. I'd been to the doctor to see when a nurse was going to go over and see her. When I rang, the doctor said, 'Oh, well, we've had a call to go down and visit her' and I thought, 'Oh my God, what's wrong with her now?' Ian, one of the architects here just took me there and said, 'If you need a taxi to come back, just take a taxi...' You wouldn't find that anywhere else! Well, I've never found that anywhere else, just here. People realize that you have got other commitments. It's not just work...

There are also some indications that flatter organizations are supportive places for single and divorced mothers, especially black mothers, to work. This point is illustrated by the comments from two single black mothers, the first of whom was a black African woman worker in a women's wholefood retail co-operative who had two daughters aged 13 and 15 at the time of interview:

> When I came here we made an arrangement that I only worked half days, so that I worked from nine to two o'clock and then I could go and collect my children from school... My youngest had just gone to school, she was just five, and my eldest was seven so they were not independent.

This point was reiterated by a black woman in a domestic violence refuge collective, who had an 18-month-old daughter at the time of interview:

You do get a lot more understanding, but it's because it's women working with women. Like you know as a woman and a mother, you know what's involved. You know how much attention a child needs. You know the needs of a woman, if she's got a child who is at school, then you know that that child is going to finish school at a certain time and it's about arranging somebody to go and pick them up. [Name of organization] allows for that where some places don't. Here you would be actually helped. We have child-care workers who are prepared to take our children if necessary and having that is a big thing which in a sense makes you feel like you are pretty lucky and that people will do things for you . . . I mean there are times when I have brought her into work with me. Luckily I don't have to very often but there are times when I have brought her to work.

Another woman worker in a women's film/video production co-operative who did not have children herself but worked with women who did, commented upon the ways in which the co-operative had attempted to ease the problems of women workers combining paid work with child-care commitments:

If we have evening meetings, we'll pay people's baby-sitters and what have you. We budget for that and we send it to Channel 4 and they just have to accept it. I think that that's good. Most of us couldn't do the work that we're doing if it weren't for those things. If it weren't for being able to have this alternative structure and set-up . . .

Workers with children tended to be concentrated in flatter organizations where several of their co-workers also had child-care commitments. Nonetheless, the organizational level of support for workers with children tended to be highest in women's organizations where the majority of workers had children, as the following comments from a woman worker in a women's employment training workshop collective makes clear:

There's always been a crèche here too which has been for any woman using the centre, so you don't have to be on a course, you can be dropping in and using the centre so that a woman who has got a child and couldn't get child-care facilities, we couldn't take a child on that basis. So it's for users and trainers and workers. It takes about 30 children which is quite large. It's the only free crèche in [name of city] that I know about.

Similar points were made by a woman worker in a women's training workshop nursery collective, who argued:

You get far more family responsibility days here than you would anywhere else . . . and it's very good for everybody. There isn't a problem about bringing in another member of staff if a member of staff has to be home for some reason. There's only two of us here in the nursery who haven't actually got young children. But I have an elderly mother who I may sometime in the not-too-distant, not too much into the future will probably have to take some unpaid leave to care for her for a short time and there wouldn't be any problem about that here. It would be understood that 'Okay, we have to cover for you while you do this' and the place is still there for you if you want it, you know, it wouldn't be frowned upon.

Furthermore, it is possible to see just how far this support to mothers extends by looking at the experiences of women workers who had been pregnant while working for flatter organizations. Many of them described the maternity benefits they had received as much better than they might be entitled to expect in more male-dominated, hierarchical organizations. The comments of one woman worker in a mixed-sex inflatables for the disabled collective, who had a 10-month old son at the time of interview, illustrates the point:

[Name of organization] have been extremely flexible. Like I had extremely generous [maternity leave], which is the other advantage as well of collectives, you don't have to stick to statutory requirements in terms of sick pay or maternity pay or maternity leave. So I had a really generous maternity payment and a really generous maternity leave. I could have had a whole year off and come back to my job as long as my job still existed, which you know is more than you could get from a lot of other employers.

It was not specifically mothering, but parenting as a whole that was supported by some mixed-sex flatter organizations, as the comments from another woman worker in a mixed-sex language school co-operative, who was living with her (woman) partner and an 8-year-old boy at the time of interview, makes clear:

SO: Are there commitments to having things like maternity leave built into the structures?

Oh, yes! And paternity leave and partner leave, not being 'istic' at all. Any leave to do with families is built in as well. That's part of the programme that we have developed over the last few years, to improve our own situation and to make things very much more clearer so that it's not a personal issue if somebody gets pregnant or whatever, or somebody's partner gets pregnant.

Just how far some women workers in flatter organizations were able to manoeuvre and negotiate with respect to taking leave for family responsibilities can be illustrated in the case of a woman worker in a sexual abuse advice and counselling collective, who commented:

> We had this huge voting session and masses of discussion about the value of women's work, and valuing ourselves, and conditions which actually looked at women's needs. So that we had maternity leave, which was not paternity leave but was for women who were close to other women who were having babies as well, so that they could take time off. So that I was able to take time off when my sister had a baby . . .

It appears therefore that women workers in flatter organizations are able to create opportunities for provision for parents and co-parents that are unheard of in more hierarchical organizations. Even so, this does not necessarily solve all of the difficulties that some workers experienced in combining the more private aspects of their family lives with the public aspects of their work lives, as the comments of a woman worker in a mixed-sex experimental theatre co-operative, who had two sons aged 8 and 4 at the time of interview, and who lived in the same building that the co-operative had its offices, makes clear:

> I'm living [on the premises] so that if the phone goes at eleven o'clock at night and there's a problem to be dealt with, then those of us who live there deal with it. So physically we're just going to remove ourselves . . . I have a yearning after all this time to actually get that split [between home and work] back, and I think that's probably because of the children . . . They are getting to an age now where they really need more space and more time. But of course when they were little, it was very useful. It was very useful, I can't deny it. When you have got a newborn baby and work is quite literally down the stairs then, you know, the advantages of it are very obvious. Again that's one of the good things about the co-operative ethic, it should allow women a much greater freedom for how they organize their working day to enable them to be able to carry on working and also to be able to balance the family . . . I found a great deal of support from other members of the co-op. It's been fairly good for the children to grow up with other adults around who are just as capable at getting a juice or changing a nappy as I am and although I didn't expect it, people do a great deal . . . and certainly because our work involves going out and performing, there have been times when both Greg and myself have gone out working and have left the children for a week with other members of the co-op. That has also been very good because of the working and living situation here being so close . . .

What all these points do suggest is that for those women workers who do have children and other dependent relatives to care for, the support of co-workers in flatter organizations is often essential. This means that women workers' commitments at work and outside of it are able to be integrated in a variety of ways which allow them greater freedom to combine their care of dependants with their paid work commitments. For men workers in flatter organizations, on the other hand, the extent to which such organizations enable men workers to reconfigure aspects of fathering and paid work, takes a different form. Amongst several of the men workers interviewed there was a recognition that the demands made upon men working in hierarchical organizations generally often resulted in a neglect of family relationships, and men workers in flatter organizations took steps to challenge this tendency. As a man worker in a mixed-sex city farm collective with a daughter aged 6 months at the time of interview, explained:

> [The neglect of family life] is a danger, but I think that it is different here. I think that in hierarchical organizations men do that especially, because they get more kudos. It is a lot of the time not actually needed, it's one of those things that seem to have got built into the whole working ethos in hierarchical organizations, that you're out to impress the whole time. I think that if a lot of people sat down and thought about it, it's a waste of time. It's really, really stupid. It's getting like the Japanese, you know, they see their wife and family for about five minutes in the morning and so God only knows how they manage to have any children. It's beyond me and it's a waste of time. There's more to life than working. Like Bernard, one of our workers has just come in and said, 'Oh, my daughter's got flu. I'm going to have to go home and look after her', and you know, I can't think of any hierarchical organization where you could go in and see your manager and say, 'Look, I've got to go home, my daughter's got flu.' They'd just say, 'What are you talking about? You're meant to be working. We're paying you for this work!' That's the great thing about working in a collective . . .

Working in flatter organizations which allow men workers greater freedom to devote time and energy to their family relationships was therefore seen as extremely important by several of the men workers, and a challenge to the ways in which men usually worked. Men workers appeared to feel that they had greater freedom in this respect than they would have if they worked in more hierarchical organizations. Their views are illustrated by a man worker in a mixed-sex wholefood retail co-operative, who commented:

> that's what I feel a lot of work does, it separates. Instead of bringing people together, it separates them, it breaks up families . . . if my wife

had children and she wanted to continue what she does, she couldn't do that because the organization won't let her. They just don't make provision for that, whereas . . . the conditions of employment here, we've got it written in. There's paternity leave and maternity leave and so on, written into our constitution. It's not easy but it's the way we feel it should be. Yes, so basically we have fair and equitable paternity and maternity leave, written in.

Similar views were expressed by a man worker in a mixed-sex animation co-operative, who had an 18-month-old son at the time of interview:

We do have quite good control over how we practice our business. You know, it does obviously interact with our personal lives, which is quite important. You have to be able to work with the two. It would be hopeless, certainly with a young child, to do some of the things we do now, in a traditional workplace. It would be impossible.

SO: Can you think of any examples?

Well, we had paternity leave which would just be unheard of. I don't know, maybe a couple of companies operate it. But you know, people go, 'Cor blimey! That's a bit of a luxury, isn't it?' You're overlooking the whole relationship at home by saying, 'Uh . . . er . . . can't do that'. You know, I mean, if you're happy at home you're more happy at work and the whole thing interacts, the whole business! [laughs]

The same point was made by a man worker in a mixed-sex city farm collective, indicating that men workers in flatter organizations attached importance to the need to balance their home and work lives in a way that men in more hierarchical organizations were traditionally unable to do:

There's far more understanding of things like that. It's like, my wife had a baby six months ago and I was going to all these antenatal classes and I was the only bloke there who actually got paternity leave, and I had two weeks' paternity leave. The others were all working in hierarchical organizations and were incredibly jealous . . . They would have had to take it off as holiday or not at all . . . but it's like this machismo thing – 'I've got to grin and bear this!' – and it's all part of this getting a bigger ego, and I think it's pointless! [laughs] There's more to life than working . . . I want to be able to have time off and go and enjoy a walk in the countryside and being with my wife and baby and that type of thing.

However, flatter organizational support for men worker's involvement with families and child-care was not without its contradictions, as the following comments from a single man without children, who worked in a mixed-sex graphic design co-operative, made clear:

> Certainly in principle I think that it's important and I do actually quite like it when Alan's daughter comes in and draws. On the other hand, it can be a disruption at times when you want to get on with things and she's whining about something and Alan can't really concentrate. None of us wants to take her on because we're busy at that moment, so it works both ways, but theoretically I think it's important.

For some men workers in flatter organizations, the issue of finding the right balance between their home/family lives and their working lives went further than the granting of paternity leave and the acknowledgment of their roles as fathers. The issue of balancing multiple commitments became, for some men workers, one of the features that constructed their work identities, particularly their masculinity. As the comments of the only man worker in a mixed-sex wholefood retail co-operative illustrate:

> I wouldn't mind having more males [working] here if they were people that were what I consider balanced people who don't deliberately reject – or by neglect reject – the balancing principles that, for example, put families first.

> *SO*: Is that quite important? Since a lot of men's work isn't like that at all, is it?

> No, it's quite the opposite. You're a successful executive and that means you're away from home most of the time, you know, you earn a tremendous amount of money, you've got high blood cholesterol, you don't feed yourself very well, you hardly know your kids . . . You have to have a balance between that. I am not saying I am balanced, but I believe in that. I believe in that kind of balance. It's that that has kept me working here.

The discussion so far suggests that there is support for the argument that workers in flatter organizations challenge organizational processes and practices which deny the importance of women's and men's private lives, but that such challenges by workers are nonetheless gendered. However, it is not always the sexism but the heterosexism of male-dominated, hierarchical organizations that is an important issue for lesbian and gay workers. It could be suggested that flatter organizations allow lesbian and gay workers a 'safer haven' in which to express their sexualities. This point was raised by a woman worker in a women's sexual abuse advice and counselling collective, who explained:

I think once I'd moved to [name of city] and started to focus more on women's issues and joined rape crisis line, I started to realize that I could be openly a lesbian in workplaces. So now I feel very differently. I feel I could choose where I worked and then it was much more an issue to be myself, whereas now I would feel, 'I might tell them, I might not' because I know it's all right, whereas then I feel I very much had to defend my position the whole time. So that was a very big factor in why I ended up going for this job. There are certain jobs that I feel it would be impossible to apply for openly as a lesbian, like teaching in schools. You're very unlikely to get employed . . .

It was also felt by some workers that there was greater recognition in flatter organizations of the needs of lesbian and gay workers than there would be of their needs in more hierarchical organizations. As the comments of a lesbian worker in a women's employment training workshop collective make clear:

As a lesbian, if my partner is sick and my partner's child is sick then I get automatic leave or I get recognition for that. I have a much easier time here. I was out at my last place of work, they were very sympathetic to a point, but not to that extent. Within my department it was fine, but I was working for a university and I couldn't imagine going to them and saying, 'My partner's son is ill. I have to go home.' That wasn't possible, whereas it's very possible here . . . So that, for instance, if it is happening, if I do have homophobic comments made to me, I don't ignore them, I do challenge them, whereas maybe in a different environment I would ignore them or I wouldn't feel safe to challenge them because I wouldn't feel safe to challenge them because I wouldn't feel that I would get back up.

It appears therefore that flatter organizations can offer lesbian and gay workers a safer environment in which to be open than many male-dominated, hierarchical organizations. Whereas women-only organizations are seen as most conducive in this respect by lesbian workers, it is not the case that all flatter organizations are free of sexism, racism and homophobia, and the conclusion that all flatter organizations are progressive in these respects has to be treated with caution. That there is only limited grounds for optimism about the benefits for women workers of working in flatter organizations is clear, given the earlier argument about how material and discursive constraints operate on a gendered basis to marginalize women workers and their organizations. How all these fieldwork findings might be analysed more comprehensively is the subject of the conclusions to be presented and discussed in Chapter 10.

Chapter 10

Conclusions

The aim of this book has been to explore how far an analysis which takes gender and sexuality as a central focus of work and organizational life is useful for making sense of the material and discursive relations which structure and inform the experiences of a particular group of workers whom, it may be argued, are least likely to be adversely affected by gendered and sexualized power relations. Such workers have been selected for their concentration in particular organizations within the social economy, namely, those which have adopted a less or non-hierarchical structure. In short, the focus has been upon what have been termed flatter organizations such as worker co-operatives and collectively run project organizations. The book concludes that gender and sexuality are necessary for the comprehensive analysis of workers' experiences within such organizations. Findings from the empirical data presented in Part II support both the first line of argument; namely, that women and men workers in flatter organizations are limited in the extent to which they can overcome power relations predicated upon gendering and sexualizing processes, *and* the second line of argument, namely that there is also some scope for resistance and manoeuvre on the part of workers in such organizations, albeit that this is nonetheless informed by gender power relations. These conclusions will be discussed in more detail shortly.

The emphasis upon gender and sexuality in this book is in spite of a historical legacy in the literature on the social economy and on flatter, less or non-hierarchical organizations which has tended to play down the significance of gender and sexuality in such settings and has concentrated instead upon organizational and economic factors (Coates, 1976; Cornforth et al., 1988; Eccles, 1981; Lockett, 1978; Logan and Gregory, 1981; Oakeshott, 1978; Stanton, 1989; Thomas and Thornley, 1989). Such studies have tended to focus solely upon the social class and occupational positions of workers within such organizations and their location within certain sectors of the economy, variously known as the third, non-profit, voluntary sector, or more recently, the social economy (Cornforth and Hooker, 1989; Paton, 1991; Taylor, 1986; Thomas and Thomas, 1989). This tendency to focus upon economic and organizational factors alone is also true for ethnographic and case-study research which concentrates upon single-sex, flatter organizations such as women's co-operatives (Tynan, 1980b; Wajcman, 1983). My research has attempted to

avoid replicating this concentration upon occupational and class-based analyses of workers' experiences within flatter organizations. This has meant that
occupation and social class diminish in terms of acting as a framework for
analysis, and that the analysis instead addresses the issue of how gender and
sexuality structures and informs workers' experiences. In particular, this book
has focused upon settings in which these dynamics may be thought to have
little or no impact, since organizations with a less or non-hierarchical structure
might be considered to be the most likely to have enabled workers to overcome some of the inequalities typically associated with gender and sexuality.
Paid work in flatter organizations is, therefore, a critical case for analysis of the
extent to which gendering and sexualizing processes and practices permeate
all organizations, whether hierarchical *or* less or non-hierarchical.[1]

It has been argued that certain organizations within the social economy
offer women in particular the chance to carve out *alternative spaces* for themselves (Cadman et al., 1981; Goffee and Scase, 1985). These alternative spaces
are conceptualized in these writings as an alternative not only to the gender
power relations of hierarchical organizations but also to those of marriage
and the family. This way of conceptualizing women's work experiences
tends to draw upon one of the traditional perspectives within research on
gender and work, namely that women's paid work situations are largely determined by women's position within the family, and that women's paid work
simply reflects and reinforces their roles as housewives and mothers. At
its extreme, there has been a tendency within this perspective on women's
working lives to posit marriage/motherhood and career as either/or choices
for women. Those women who have escaped or rejected the traditional wife/
mother role are seen as being emancipated career women, entering the labour
market on the same terms as men. This book questions the validity of using
such a perspective in relation to the women workers under consideration here,
and argues that the experiences of both women and men workers in flatter
organizations is far more complex than this simple binarism of marriage/
motherhood and paid work/career, would suggest. Although there is a need to
move beyond such binarism, however, it is necessary to return to the two lines
of argument set up at the beginning of the book in order to move the discussion forward.

The Two Lines of Argument

The first line of argument focused upon the material and discursive constraints
which inform the experiences of women and men workers in flatter organizations in gender-specific ways. This has meant exploring the ways in which
gendering processes and practices, and the structures and discourses which
uphold and inscribe them, play a part in limiting the extent to which women
workers can enter into and engage in paid work in flatter organizations
on equal terms with their men counterparts. In particular, the first line of

argument explored both the material and discursive constraints associated with gendered work in such organizations, and examined the ways in which marginalization (of workers and their organizations) operated in gendered (and sexualized) ways, with problematic effects for women workers in women-only organizations in particular.

The second line of argument on the other hand, suggested that flatter organizations offer women and men workers some scope to challenge and resist inequalities associated with gender and sexuality. This argument involved exploring the strategic manoeuvres that workers in flatter organizations are able to engage in and how these too differ according to gender. In particular, this second line of argument explored what it is that women and men workers in flatter organizations achieve in terms of the benefits that accrue to them; for example, how they are able to challenge traditional gendered careers and gender stereotypes of workers and how they negotiate the public/private divide in ways which benefit both women and men. In short, by studying women and men workers in single-sex and mixed-sex flatter organizations, the intention of the book has been to analyse the ways in which workers in such organizations are both circumscribed by material and discursive constraints, *and* the ways in which it is possible for them to challenge and resist such constraints. There is support for both of these apparently contrasting lines of argument, but it is also claimed that the analysis is more complex and subtle than envisaged when the two lines of argument were originally set up in this way. In order to explore this further, the conclusions of the first argument will be discussed.

The Constraints of Work in Flatter Organizations

At first sight it may appear difficult to argue that women workers in flatter organizations are materially disadvantaged when compared to their men counterparts and that flatter organizations offer limited scope to workers to overcome these inequalities in earnings, employment status and turnover/tenure. Nevertheless, this appeared to be the case for the sample of women and men workers examined here. Furthermore, it is difficult to separate the extent to which these disadvantages arose because of the differences which women and men workers brought with them to work, from the extent to which they arose because of the ways in which the state, the labour market, and the social economy is structured. For example, the finding that women workers' earnings were consistently lower on average than their men counterparts can be partly explained by the greater tendency of men workers in flatter organizations to be both graduates and full-time workers. However, there were other factors, such as the gendering of the state benefits system in ways which structurally disadvantaged women workers who sought to 'top up' their wages (often even lower than average because of the non-instrumental value-base of the organizations which comprise the social economy) with benefits.

Conclusions

Another complicated pattern arises in the differences in women and men's turnover and tenure; whereas more men workers were in permanent jobs in the sense that they had no plans to leave, women workers were characterized by having a lower turnover rate than their men counterparts. This may reflect women workers' reduced opportunities within the labour market; they stayed in flatter organizations for longer on average than men because their job mobility was more restricted. But at the same time, women workers were more likely to feel that their jobs were insecure and precarious (hence their greater likelihood of making plans to leave). This also reflects women workers' concentration in more casualized, temporary jobs. So although their jobs may not appear to them to be as long-term on average as the men's, it may be that there is a tendency for women workers to continue for longer in them (when possible) because of the lack of other suitable alternatives. Several women workers in flatter organizations, for example, felt that having been their own bosses, they could not envisage working in male-dominated, hierarchical organizations in the near future. These considerations would help explain women workers' greater longevity of employment in flatter organizations (their lower turnover *vis-à-vis* men) with what on the face of it appears a contradiction, namely, their greater likelihood of stating an intention to leave in the next 6 to 12 months (their reduced tenure *vis-à-vis* men).

The absence of many women workers with child-care commitments, particularly women with preschool age children in the sample tends to support the view that combining parenting and work in a flatter organization takes a different form for women than men. It can be argued that this reflects the unequal structuring of the labour market and maternity and paternity as constructed both in material and discursive terms. Hence, a possible explanation for the absence in the sample of many women workers with young children lies in the difficulties women in particular face in combining paid work outside the home with the demands of caring for young children, since women tend to assume greater responsibility for child-care than men, who tend to play a support role rather than take prime responsibility (Brannen and Moss, 1991). Furthermore, although the findings indicated that more men workers in flatter organizations experience difficulties in combining their paid work with their other commitments and more of them have children living with them, it could be argued that this difficulty in juggling their multiple commitments might be the result of more men workers having second jobs, rather than because of the difficulties in combining domestic and child-care commitments with paid work. In the majority of cases, it appeared that the men workers undertook second jobs in order to expand their recreational interests, rather than as an additional source of income. This reflects the structuring of men's employment generally in that they tend to have full-time, continuous employment and take responsibility for economic provisioning within the family home as well as having a greater range of recreational interests outside the home and, arguably, more leisure time (Finch and Mason, 1993; Goodnow and Bowes, 1994; Morris, 1990).

Given that fewer women workers than men in the sample had child-care commitments, it may seem odd that many more women workers than men were nonetheless working in part-time or four day per week jobs in flatter organizations. The conventional view that part-time jobs allow women workers the freedom of choice to fit their paid work around their domestic and family commitments does not appear to apply to women workers in flatter organizations in any simple way (Hakim, 1991; McRae, 1991). There must therefore be other reasons why women workers' jobs in flatter organizations tend to be structured on a part-time or four day per week basis. It is possible to argue that such structuring meets the requirements of organizational start-up and survival in this sector of the social economy, irrespective of whether those workers who then fill those jobs are wives and/or mothers. When jobs are created in flatter organizations in the social economy then, even when there is an expectation that most or all of the workers who then fill those jobs will be women, it seems that it is wider economic factors concerning the securing of grants, loans and sales, for example, that create pressures for those jobs to be structured on a part-time or four day per week basis, rather than any overt political commitment to recognizing women's domestic and family commitments, though this may be present as a contributory factor. This argument therefore problematizes the claim that part-time jobs are more likely to be filled by women workers primarily because women attach great importance to having flexible hours of work which fit around their domestic and family responsibilities (Hakim, 1991).

Flexibility of employment, in terms of hours worked, overtime and the after-hours commitment expected of different workers, is also problematic in flatter organizations. There was a greater tendency for women workers in the sample to undertake less well-remunerated, additional work over and above their contracted hours, although the extent to which they did this in terms of actual number of extra hours they worked were no greater on average than the men workers' extra hours. However, this can be analysed in terms of women workers' greater tendency to express commitments towards their paid work which were emotional, relational and familial in form and it is argued that there are gender-specific orientations which underpin women workers' greater tendency towards self or collective exploitation in flatter organizations (MacFarlane, 1987). There is a long established tradition within feminist research on work and organizations to analyse the culture of workplaces in which women predominate (like shops, factories and offices) in terms of the *cult of femininity* found there (Barker and Downing, 1980; Pollert, 1981; Westwood, 1984). In each case, these writers see this cult of femininity as arising in both its collusive and oppositional forms, from women workers' lives as housewives and mothers outside the labour market. It is argued here that aspects of this cult of femininity can be found in alternative, less or non-hierarchical organizations and even amongst women who are not them-selves wives and/or mothers. Such familial orientations can be seen as collusive in that they support and encourage relations based upon women's assumed greater nurturing and caring roles in families, even when women do not actually perform the roles of wives and mothers. They also contribute to the greater tendency for women workers in flatter organizations to materially engage in their own self or collective exploitation in terms of doing more after-hours work for less remuneration than their men counterparts. This analysis also draws upon feminist post-structuralist views of gender power relations in organizations and the labour market as emanating not from a single material source – the labour of housewives/mothers – but as arising from discourses which position subjects within power relations which are fluid and unstable, and which have no fixed set of meanings which can be read unambiguously from material conditions (Acker, 1990; Nicholson, 1990). In the case here, flatter organizations become women workers' 'babies', needing constant nur-turing and care from their 'mothers'.

However, this is not to overstate the case. The extent to which women workers' greater emotional, relational and familial orientations underpins their self or collective exploitation is difficult to specify, since the relationship between the material and the discursive is impossible to trace empirically. However, it would seem odd if there were no connections at all between the assumed greater nurturing and caring roles of women as wives/mothers, wo-men's adoption of emotional, relational and familial orientations towards their paid work and their greater involvement in less well-remunerated, after-hours work for their flatter organization. The exact specification of such connections are difficult to substantiate very fully on the basis of the empirical findings presented here and are offered by way of a tentative rather than a firm conclusion. There are a number of related points that can be made. To argue that familial orientations towards their paid work are characteristic of women workers in flatter organizations is not the same as arguing that such women willingly undertake additional work simply because of the ideas they have picked up in the family and elsewhere about their proper roles as nurturers and carers. Several women workers in mixed-sex flatter organizations clearly resented having to clean and tidy up after their men co-workers. The gender power relations which women workers enter into when they take up paid work often involves the exploitation of their 'nurturing' labour, with all the familial and sexualized undertones that involves (Adkins, 1995; Delphy and Leonard, 1992). In other words, rather than willingly carrying out this less well-remunerated, additional work for their organizations, undertaking extra work under these conditions is often an unwritten employment specification for women workers in flatter organizations, as elsewhere. Thus it can be argued that it is the discursive and material constructions of gendered and sexualized power relations in the labour market itself, and not simply women workers as active agents or subjects, that account for women worker's tendency to give more freely of their labour than their men counterparts. That this argument appears to hold true for flatter organizations supports the contention that such power relations pervade even those settings where they might be thought to have least purchase – namely, in the less or non-hierarchical organizations of the social economy.

The Marginalization of Flatter Organizations

The findings on the marginalization of both the workers themselves and their flatter organizations support the view that such marginalization takes gender-specific forms related to the gender and assumed sexuality of workers *and* the gender-composition of the organization. This claim offers an important additional dimension to conventional views that the marginalization of flatter organizations is due almost solely to their small size, lack of capital, location in certain sectors of the economy, or assumptions concerning their fringe, alternative or amateur approaches to setting up and running effective social economy or non-profit organizations (Cornforth et al., 1988; Mellor et al., 1988; Landry et al., 1985; Thornley, 1981). It is argued instead that in addition to all this, women workers in flatter organizations (and women's flatter organizations in particular) experience several forms of exclusion and marginalization not shared by their men counterparts. Most of the men workers and the mixed-sex organizations appear to engage with stereotypes (of both themselves and their organizations) as being radical, left-wing and hippie, and were to a greater or lesser extent seeking to counteract that. But women workers dealt with this and more. It is argued that first, women workers are more likely to experience a sense of estrangement from the real world, which they see not simply as being hard-nosed and commercial but also as being sexist/heterosexist, and of which they are not part. Second, they are not accepted as fully competent adult workers due to assumptions being made about their lack of maturity and expertise; women workers in flatter organizations are thus more likely to suffer from a lack of credibility, and thereby experience more trivialization and patronization than their men co-workers and men counterparts. Third, conventions concerning the oddity of workers in flatter organizations tend to be appropriated in gender-specific ways so that forms of sexual joking operate to ridicule women workers in such organizations.

Fourth and perhaps most important, women workers and their flatter organizations are not marginalized solely by their location in the social economy nor by their location outside dominant discourses of gender, hierarchy and male domination, since neither of these conditions by themselves or in combination offer sufficient explanation. Women's flatter organizations are marginalized by being positioned in complex relations to discourses of feminism, separatism and lesbianism. In this way, when women work in flatter organizations their assumed lesbianism is articulated through gendered power relations in ways which position both them and their organizations as simultaneously threatening *and* needing to be marginalized, materially restricted and

Conclusions

disempowered, in spite of their small size, lack of capital and location in the social economy. Clearly it is not necessary to establish women worker's sexuality in any real sense for these processes to operate; it is sufficient for flatter organizations to be inscribed as lesbian for the women workers in those organizations, whether lesbians themselves or not, to experience the material consequences. As a result they can suffer serious loss of sales, grants and contracts, whether or not they self-identify as lesbian or support feminism, separatism or lesbianism at all. This analysis therefore goes beyond conventional views of power, gender and sexuality in organizational life which for the most part have concentrated upon hierarchies, even sometimes in small to medium-sized firms (Acker, 1990; Burrell, 1984; Filby, 1992; Hearn and Parkin, 1987; Hearn et al., 1989). Furthermore, it is highly significant for feminist analyses of work that sexuality can be shown to attach at the level of the organization, as well as at the level of individual bodies or lifestyles, an argument often unacknowledged both in the feminist literature which 'adds on' lesbians in the workplace (Hall, 1989; Schneider, 1988; Squirell, 1989; Taylor, N. 1986) and in the feminist literature on women's co-operative and collective organizations in the social economy (Brown, 1990, 1992; Fried, 1994; Gould, 1980; Mansbridge, 1980; Martin, 1990; Rothschild, 1990; Wajcman, 1983). Even in some of the most groundbreaking feminist work on gender and power in co-operative organizations, the articulation of sexuality at the organizational level is left relatively untouched and unanalysed and only gender is given attention (Hacker, 1988, 1989). This book on the other hand, argues that in the case of women's flatter organizations, and in the case of those in particular that are women-only, not only gender but also sexuality is deeply implicated both in terms of the discursive marginalization *and* the material survival and success of such organizations.

Feminist analyses have long argued that hierarchically structured organizations are gendered, and whereas it has been established that women, by virtue of their gender, have less influence than men in terms of obtaining capital in the form of loans and grants, this has not been problematized with reference to the sexualization of women workers. Some women managers in hierarchically structured women's organizations in the social economy and women proprietors of hierarchical, private share-holding businesses have been highly successful, particularly when they conform to heterosexualized discourses of power (Bowman and Norton, 1986; Hertz, 1986). So it is not simply gender that is at stake in the tendency towards the social and economic marginalization of women's flatter organizations. What this analysis has introduced is a specifically sexualized category – *the lesbianized organization* – which acts as further evidence of the way in which sexuality acts as a central platform in the reproduction of gendered power relations in organizations. Furthermore, that this is the case in that supposedly safer, supportive environment that women's flatter organizations are held to offer (Trevithick, 1987; Undercurrents, 1981) suggests that when women workers organize in ways which challenge male-dominated hierarchy, their marginalization must

182

necessarily take a lesbianized form because hierarchical power and control relations are not only gendered but are also heterosexualized in ways which seek to position imputed lesbians and lesbianism as beyond the pale. Women workers in women's flatter organizations, whether they explicitly seek to or not, not only present a challenge to male-dominated hierarchy as such, but also threaten heterosexualized power and control relations. It is not surprising, therefore, that they should routinely experience forms of lesbianization which seek to treat them as suspect, stigmatized and illegitimate, nor that they should be materially restricted as a consequence.

It is possible to take the argument further and suggest that it is doubtful whether the discourses surrounding men's homosexuality attach to mixed-sex and men's flatter organizations in the same way, if at all. Organizations, whether hierarchical or less/non-hierarchical, are sites of men's power and control and thus in mixed-sex and men's organizations, dominant discourses articulate with heterosexuality or an affable (rather than threatening) homosociability (Hearn et al., 1989; Pringle, 1989). Men's flatter organizations may experience homosexualization only if they explicitly offer services and products for and by the gay community, but not otherwise. Given the power attributed to the pink pound and the gay male vote, however, it is unlikely that material support for such organizations will be curtailed in ways which correspond to the experiences of their women counterparts. In summary, it is not simply the case that male-dominated hierarchical organizations are constituted by gendered and sexualized processes and practices, whilst flatter organizations are not. Gender and sexuality are interrelated with the production and reproduction of material and discursive relations of power and control in both hierarchical and less or non-hierarchical organizations, albeit in ways which are deeply embedded, complex and contradictory. As a result, it is not valid to present women's flatter organizations simply as safe space for women's resistance to gendered and heterosexualized hierarchy (Cadman et al., 1981; Goffee and Scase, 1985). Clearly such organizations are also sites for contested discourses which rest upon a hitherto neglected element of power relations involving the routine sexualization of both women workers in flatter organizations *and* those organizations themselves.[2]

What consequences does all this have for theories of gender, sexuality, work and organization? First, this extends the analysis of sexuality beyond that of the psychic or private domain in which it is often seen as located, even by some feminist theorists (Walby, 1990). Second, it suggests that most feminist analyses which locate women's domestic and family roles as central to the understanding of their lives of paid employment are also incomplete because they underplay both heterosexuality and lesbianism (Bradley, 1989; Crompton and Sanderson, 1990; Rees, 1992; Yeandle, 1984). Third, whereas the view of the public organization as infused by sexuality has been the subject of scrutiny by some feminist theorists, this has only been insofar as heterosexualized power relations in hierarchical organizations and occupational hierarchies are implicated (Acker, 1990; Adkins, 1995; Cockburn, 1983, 1985; Pringle, 1989).

Conclusions

Fourth, sexual identity has rarely been explored in the context of research on gender and work, and where power relations in organizations have been problematized with reference to lesbianism, this has been largely at the level of adding on the experiences of individual lesbians in public sector hierarchies and corporate companies (Hall, 1989; Schneider, 1988; Squirell, 1989; Taylor, N. 1986). The lesbianization of women workers either in the social economy generally, or in flatter organizations in particular, and how this connects with gender power relations more widely has not been touched upon, although this has been addressed with respect to social movement organizations (Roseneil, 1995). Before going any further however, it is necessary to address some of the conclusions reached with respect to the second line of argument, and it is to this matter that the next section is directed.

Flatter Organizations as Sites of Agency and Resistance

The second line of argument suggested that material and discursive constraints can be challenged and resisted by workers in flatter organizations, albeit in gender-specific ways. Women and men workers in such organizations are not passive or static, but are able to reflect upon the ways in which they are treated differently because of their gender, sexuality and the gender composition of their organizations. As a result, they may actively engage in strategic forms of oppositional resistance to male-dominated, familial power and control relations (Pollert, 1981; Pringle, 1989; Westwood, 1984). Any view of workers as powerless to resist the forces that constrain them fails to acknowledge the capacity for workers to negotiate and manoeuvre within those constraints. When agents/subjects enter into discourses of power, they can destabilize and undermine both the ideas and the conditions of their lives (Foucault, 1979). For example, workplace cultures in hierarchical organizations and the high-powered linear career tracks of white, middle-class men are not static and fixed but are highly unstable. This allows room for workers to effect fissures in these dominant discursive and material positionings, thus allowing them the opportunity to challenge the meanings given to work and careers. Unlike some Foucauldian theoretical work which, as has been pointed out by feminists, looks at the experimental subject positioning of non-sexed subjects, this second line of argument is not gender-neutral (Hartsock, 1990; McNay, 1992; Nicholson, 1990). Men workers in flatter organizations are not seen as destabilizing or challenging in the same way as women workers because they are not subject to the same constraints in social economy organizations or in the labour market more generally, that women workers are. Since women workers face different constraints concerning their gender and sexuality from their men counterparts, resistance takes on a different meaning and emphasis for women than for men.

The findings related to what workers achieve in terms of working in flatter organizations appear to show that both women and men reaped benefits that they would not necessarily find in more hierarchical organizations. Both women and men workers have some scope to 'move into each other's shoes' as it were, and in so doing, they challenge conventional gender power relations. But the extent to which women and men workers were able to manoeuvre in this way was clearly different. Whereas Cornforth et al. (1988), Stanton (1989) and Thomas and Thornley (1989) have already clearly established some of these benefits in relation to flatter organizations, they have not problematized them with reference to gender. This book does so, and goes further to argue that although men workers in flatter organizations are challenging dominant discourses of men's work by means of what has been termed here *career abandonment*, women workers tend to use such organizations as stepping stones to other jobs – an interesting reversal of gendered expectations of paid work. In reaching these conclusions, this book has shown how men workers are able to enjoy some of the benefits traditionally associated with women's work (for example, supposedly having less pressurized, less competitive working lives) whereas women workers are able to enjoy the benefits traditionally associated with men's work (for example, taking control, having responsibility and making decisions). Both women and men workers cited the value of having a more supportive, understanding and humane working environment, though for men workers this was seen more in terms of balancing the ethos of high-powered, male-dominated and hierarchical workplaces; for women workers it was seen more in terms of greater flexibility and tolerance.

There is also some evidence that there are differences in terms of how women and men workers in flatter organizations come to enter into relations of advantage and disadvantage, and how such relations are negotiated. To some extent, women workers in flatter organizations have no choice but to confront gender power relations in order to survive; for example, assumptions that they are in an assistant role to a man boss (in fact a co-worker), and that being professional and efficient means having men in control. Men workers on the other hand, can avoid many of the issues relating to the gendering of work because they are advantaged by such relations, and not only survive but also progress by conforming to gender expectations of themselves as men workers.[3] It is possible to argue that men workers in flatter organizations, perhaps more so than elsewhere, by virtue of taking on board a specifically feminist critique of the unequal benefits which accrue to women and men workers in the labour market, come to challenge gender power relations in work and organizational life. However, there is only scant evidence that men workers in flatter organizations are acting from pro-feminist, as opposed to pragmatic considerations, in this respect. Finally, it should be noted that the extent to which women workers can present a challenge to gendered and sexualized power relations is fraught with contradictions. Even if it is possible to negotiate and experiment with some of the discursive and material conditions of gender and sexuality, there are intractable difficulties for women workers, related to the problems of marginalization, trivialization and exclusion previously discussed. Flatter organizations have been positioned as marginal and peripheral (to the economy as a whole if not the social economy specifically), and it is argued that this is more so the case when such organizations are women-only and/or orientated towards women's issues. As has been suggested already, marginalization revolves around discourses of women workers as less credible *and* more threatening than their men counterparts. It is therefore important to acknowledge the ways in which discourses of gender and sexuality are differentially challenged by women and men workers in flatter organizations.

This can partly be achieved by exploring the ways in which women and men workers in flatter organizations can circumvent the public/private divide. This merging or blurring of the public/private has been seen as characteristic of flatter organizations *per se*, particularly those which are all-women or in which women predominate (Tynan, 1980b; Wajcman, 1983). Women workers are seen as bringing aspects of their outside lives into work, and fitting their lives of paid work around their other interests and commitments. Those women workers in flatter organizations, for example, who had taken extended breaks from their jobs had done so for reasons very often associated with their own development (travel abroad and/or periods of further study) as much as for reasons of illness or child-care commitments. Their organizations had enabled them to do this in ways which suited their own timetables (to an extent) and allowed them to combine their work with other non-domestic activities and pursuits.

For both women and men workers in flatter organizations there are several further ways in which the public/private divide is negotiated, if not circumvented altogether. One way is by means of seeking a more rounded life, in which the paid work and the home/social lives of workers interconnect. This supports the conclusions of Cornforth et al. (1988) and Thomas and Thornley (1989) but takes this further by problematizing it with reference to gender. Women workers in women's flatter organizations connect this integration of home and work to the women-centredness of their organization. Many of the women workers, particularly those who were single or divorced mothers, felt that it was easier to get support and understanding for the demands made upon them by their domestic commitments, than it might be in more hierarchical organizations. The narrow devotion to paid work above all else, which is held to typify expectations of men's work, can also be negotiated by men workers giving priority to other concerns, particularly with regard to their opportunities to be more open and feeling about their roles as fathers/carers, and so on. It was also acknowledged by men workers that this is not typical of their experiences in more hierarchical organizations or at work generally. One further way in which workers can take advantage of provisions that are almost unheard of in more hierarchical organizations is to create their own entitlements to maternity and paternity leave, and to go beyond the statutory entitlements. In the case of at least one flatter organization, there was a right to 'naternity' (as opposed to *maternity*) leave, which allowed women to take time off when other women to whom they are close give birth. As far as the breaking down or circumventing of the public/private divide is concerned, what all this suggests is that workers in flatter organizations are not passive victims of structural and discursive inequalities; they are able to experience certain benefits and secure certain achievements in ways which do not figure at all in more hierarchical organizations, albeit not in an ungendered or gender-free context.

Conclusions

The last section of the book will attempt to pull together some of the loose threads of the two lines of argument presented here. Throughout this book, gender and sexuality have been used as theoretical prisms through which to refract and make sense of the experiences of a group of workers who share a common organizational rather than occupational position. Taking the organization as the critical site for analysis and comparing women workers' experiences with those of their men counterparts has allowed relatively neglected aspects of the literature on gender, sexuality, work and organization to come to light. This includes placing emphasis upon the discourses surrounding gender and sexuality and the ways in which they are challenged or resisted by workers, as well as focusing upon socio-structural constraints at both the material and the discursive level. Running throughout the book has been an emphasis on how the discursive and the material reflect and reinforce one another and structure women and men workers' experiences in different ways.

This book has also shown that a critical feminist approach to the study of the differential experiences of workers in flatter organizations can yield fruitful empirical data with which to explore two apparently contrasting lines of argument. Throughout much of the book, these two lines of argument have been presented as contrasting, whereas it is possible to synthesize these two approaches to the study of gender, sexuality, work and organization.[4] There has been a tendency to compartmentalize research on gender, work and organization as located either within the socio-structural or the agency-orientated tradition of research and theory. There has also been a particular tendency in the literature on gender and work to see gender and sexuality as located primarily in the private sphere of the home/family and only spilling over from there into the public sphere of paid work and organization, rather than being in any way central. However, the somewhat false polarization of structure and agency, home/family and work/organization, is problematic when the experiences of workers in flatter organizations are analysed.

To begin with, it is worth noting that some of the experiences of workers in flatter organizations do not lend themselves solely to either a socio-structural or agency-orientated analytical approach. For example, men workers' conformity to views of them as masculine (efficient, skilled and professional, producing quality goods and services, and so on), *and* their career abandonment (leaving behind well-paid, high-powered jobs in hierarchical, private or public sector organizations to work in flatter organizations in the social economy) does not fit into any neat slot within a socio-structural versus agency framework. Indeed, during the process of analysing the data, it was difficult to place certain themes within any one single camp; in other words, there was and is a need to find ways of overcoming the somewhat artificial separation of the data on the experiences of women and men workers in flatter organizations into a socio-structural versus agency framework. How this might be achieved is the subject of this final section of the book.

Before attempting this task, a number of provisos need to be noted. Creating a synthesis can involve throwing out some ideas which may be useful, despite the post-structuralist claim that theoretical pluralism is desirable be-cause power/knowledge is fragile and uncertain. Employing a range of appar-ently contrasting theoretical perspectives may not be the problem factor, since sociology, like other disciplines, is not a unified paradigm or an established body of proven knowledge. A further proviso concerns the process of syn-thesis itself – a process which can simplify and damage social experience by attempting to connect and even lump together disparate elements of that experience. Nevertheless, bearing in mind these provisos, an attempt will be made to argue for a means of synthesis, without merely seeking to paper over the cracks of the structure and agency dichotomy.

In order to do this it is useful to look more closely at two dimensions of the arguments developed earlier – namely, family and sexuality. Feminists have tended to argue that women's absorption into the patriarchal, nuclear family is politically reactionary (Delphy and Leonard, 1992; Gittins, 1993). Many feminists identify marriage and the family as the key source of women's oppression and would argue that familialism in all its manifest forms repres-ents a deference to the construction of women-as-maternal which feminism in part seeks to challenge. But familialism is not so coherent or unitary a discourse as this suggests, and family can have a range of meanings, some of which may be positive for women; for example, the family organization as a place for gaining support or nurture, a place to be feeling and so on. Sexuality can be turned around in similar ways; whereas anti-lesbianism is seen as a central platform in the production and reproduction of hierarchical gender power relations, lesbianism can also represent a positive celebration of women's sexuality (Jeffreys, 1990, 1993). Flatter organizations may provide particularly supportive environments in which to express lesbianism, albeit it should be recognized that they offer safer, as opposed to safe, environments.

Discursive practices concerning familialism and lesbianism are thus clas-sic grounds for contestation. By focusing upon those organizations in which there are real expectations that gender inequalities can be overcome, it has been possible to demonstrate the pervasiveness of the gendered and sexualized aspects of work and organization. Work in flatter organizations is not organized simply through the class and gender relations of occupational segregation, familialism and lesbianism (as discursive and materially con-structed in specific ways) which play crucial parts in constituting the experi-ences of workers in such organizations. However, the theoretical analysis of gender, work and organization is often incomplete because they are the very areas that are relatively underexplored as important dynamics. This is a problem that reveals itself in several feminist theories of gender and the labour market (Crompton and Sanderson, 1990; Rees, 1992; Walby, 1990) and is highlighted by Pringle's (1989) claim that family/sexuality and paid work have been treated as separate dynamics in the construction of gender power relations. In this way, the analysis, for example, that Hacker (1989) has made of gender construction and reinforcement in the Mondragon co-operatives, persuasive as it is, is only part of the story since she leaves both 'family' and sexuality largely untouched and unanalysed. Although it is clear that gender, sexuality and 'family' are distinct, it is also clear that they are related. This book has argued that gender, familialism and lesbianism in particular are interrelated with the production and reproduction of discursive practices and material conditions in flatter, less or non-hierarchical organizations. This book has thus attempted to move beyond hierarchy to explore the gendering and sexualizing of those workers and organizations where perhaps it is assumed that such processes may have least purchase on bodies/organizations – namely, in the less or non-hierarchical parts of the social economy typified by worker co-operatives and collectively-run project enterprises. It is argued that this book has also attempted to go beyond existing research in arguing that in the case of women workers in flatter organizations, not only is hierarchy problematized, but familial and heterosexualized power and control relations are also problematized in ways hitherto unexplored by existing research on gender, sexuality, work and organization.

How does such a concentration upon the dynamics of 'family' and lesbianism as constituted in flatter organizations help provide a way of overcoming the binarism of the two lines of argument set up earlier? Familialism and sexuality have tended to be ignored or posited as external to the material relations of production and reproduction by many sociologists, including some feminists (Hartmann, 1981; Himmelweit, 1983). Excluding them from the economic and structural and locating them in the cultural or discursive defines them in a limited way, whereas it is clear from the analysis presented here that familialism and sexuality are neither wholly socio-structural nor discursive, nor external to the dynamics of work, organizations and the labour market, nor simply private components of individuals' lives. They are pivotal in terms of providing a more comprehensive way of theorizing the relationship between the socio-structural and agency-orientated aspects of the lives of women and men workers in flatter organizations. There is much to be gained from attempting to employ familialism and sexuality in this way. If they are neglected, there are several serious implications. First, by seeing familialism and sexuality as not part of work, organizations and the labour market, then feminists can end up supporting a limited approach to the analysis of these areas. Second, this ultimately relegates both familialism and sexuality to non-work, and to the extra-organizational, which serves to bolster the view that there are two distinct spheres (the public and the private) which is a distinction that feminists have fought. To counterbalance this is not to include familialism and sexuality in all studies of gender, work and organization (though this may be a useful project in itself), rather it is to incorporate specific aspects of familialism and sexuality as central to the constitution of gender power relations in specific settings – to highlight, as here, how aspects of 'family' and lesbianism operate in flatter, less or non-hierarchical organizations, in ways which disadvantage women workers *vis-à-vis* their men counterparts.

In this way it is possible that seeing familialism and sexuality as an integral part of work and organization will provide a link between constructions of gender power relations in waged and non-waged work. Familialism and sexuality are integral to work and organizations, and this is no less (though differentially) true of flatter organizations as it is of hierarchical ones. This argument has been neglected in the literature on gender and work, and in the literature on the social economy, because of the reliance on theories which give primacy to other dynamics, very often the relentless 'inner logic' of capitalist relations. When analysis is undertaken at the socio-structural and agency-orientated levels, and when these are not treated as discrete but are seen as interwoven, as in the case of 'family' and lesbianism as they are constituted in flatter organizations, then it becomes possible to explore the complex interconnections between them. In short, to demonstrate that gender inequalities are not located primarily in one site – such as the hierarchical organization – but pervade even what might be thought of as that most unlikely of settings – the flatter, less or non-hierarchical organizations of the social economy.

Notes

1 Critical case analysis has typically been used to study the extreme or deviant and the examination of these unusual settings – in this case less or non-hierarchical organizations – in order to test the limits of applicability of theories of gender, sexuality and work, has indeed proved extremely useful.
2 It would be interesting to explore how such lesbianizing processes operate in related spheres of organization beyond women's flatter organizations in the social economy, and the extent to which a disembodied lesbianizing of women in particular occupations, organizations and workplace settings acts to systematically deprive women of access to material resources, power and control. There is clearly much potential here for further research.
3 Men workers in flatter organizations can and do choose to subvert masculinity in terms of presenting a challenge to men's traditional (instrumental/careerist) patterns; they can foster working, personal and family lives which, for example, are more typical of women workers (when they are seen as non-career orientated) and are more commonly associated with feminist aspirations in the workplace (for balance and co-operative working relations, for example). But in challenging the down-market and inefficient

image of flatter organizations, men workers conform to traditional expectations of men as efficient, serious and professional. There are contradictions,
therefore, in the forms that men's resistance takes, and in many cases such
subversions are more of an option than a necessity.

4 Attempts to synthesize structure and agency are not without precedent.
Giddens (1984, 1990) has argued that socio-structural approaches may be
used to elaborate and develop strategy or agency-orientated approaches,
not to stand in opposition to them. Giddens does not see structure and
agency as mutually exclusive but as *polarities*, each of which is unstable on
its own. He conceptualizes actors as capable, self-monitoring and know-
ledgeable. However, critics of Giddens have argued that the dichotomy of
structure and agency is needed because the dichotomy itself is real; social
structures and agents are radically different things. Giddens has also been
criticized for attempting to construct an overambitious and totalizing grand
theory and for collapsing structure into agency, leading to an exaggerated
view of the knowledgeability, capability and power of agents (Craib, 1992).

Appendix 1

Introductory Letter and Interview Guide

Date as postmarked

Dear

Further to our phone conversation, I am writing with details of the research I'm undertaking on paid workers in co-operative and collective organizations. (For collectives only: My research focuses upon voluntary and non-statutory organizations in which there is a commitment to team or collective working, or at least a flatter, organizational structure.)

I am currently a postgraduate student with the Open University and the aim of the research is to explore paid workers' motivation for and their perceptions of entry into and experiences of working within co-operative and collective organizations.

For the main fieldwork stage of the research, I am attempting to interview a cross-section of paid workers in different regions and in various sectors of the economy. This would involve a short-answer questionnaire and semi-structured, taped interview lasting about an hour. With your agreement and co-operation, I should like to conduct such an interview with one of either you or your co-workers in the near future. I can of course give assurances that the interview transcripts will remain confidential and anonymous throughout, and that I will not be repeating anything said in the interview to outside parties. However, I would hope to use anonymous quotes from the interview to illustrate points or themes once I reach the writing up stage.

I enclose a photocopy of the interview guide taken from my research proposal. If you feel you could offer assistance in this research undertaking, perhaps I could phone back at a later date to arrange a convenient date and time for interview?

Thanking you in advance for your help,

Sarah Oerton

The Interview Guide

(To be sent to interviewees with the introductory letter)

The fieldwork for this research will consist of a number of semi-structured interviews with paid workers in mixed gender and all-women co-operatives and collectives. The interviews will last about an hour and be tape-recorded. It is anticipated that they should take the form of a freestyle conversation around certain topics which are listed below, rather than follow a set of rigid questions. In other words, the questions explored in the interview should arise in the course of the interview itself. Certain topics however form the main focus and are as follows:

1. Can you describe the organization you work for and how you came to work here?

2. What alternative types of employment did you consider and what affected your decision to work here?

3. Why did you choose a co-operative/collective work setting?

4. Are the types of employment you have had in the past and the types of industry/organizations you have worked for very similar or very different to the job you have now?

5. Are there any common aims or objectives for which you see yourself working?

6. What form does your commitment to your work take?

7. Do you see your organizational culture and the type of work you do as being affected by gender?

8. What are the main rewards you get from working here?

9. What are the disadvantages or constraints upon the work you can do?

10. What directions and opportunities exist for the future?

Appendix 2

The Questionnaire: Paid Workers in
Co-operative and Collective Organizations

This is a self-completion questionnaire designed to provide some biographical data to supplement the taped interviews. All answers will be treated in confidence. It is not necessary to record your name or answer any questions you don't want to.

First, I'd like to ask you some questions about work.

1. What is the name of the co-operative or collective organization you work for?

2. When was the organization founded?

3. Were you involved in setting up the organization?
   YES
   NO

4. Did you start working here as a paid or unpaid worker?
   PAID
   UNPAID

5. How long have you worked here?
   a) as a paid worker   years   months
   b) as an unpaid worker   years   months

6. What is your job title or occupation?

7. What duties does that mainly involve?

8. Is your job full-time or part-time?
   FULL-TIME
   PART-TIME
   OTHER (e.g. four-day week) Please specify.

9. How many hours per week on average do you normally work?
   — HOURS PER WEEK

10. How many people work here besides yourself?
    — PAID WORKERS
    — UNPAID WORKERS

11. How many of the other workers, besides yourself, are full or part-time?
    — FULL-TIME
    — PART-TME
    — OTHER (e.g. four-day week)

12. Are the workers currently in the co-operative or collective:
    ALL WOMEN
    ALL MEN
    MIXED

13. Since when has the organization been:
    ALL WOMEN
    ALL MEN
    MIXED

14. Have you been working continuously since working here, i.e. no breaks for long-standing illness, maternity leave, travel, paid/unpaid leave, etc. (but not counting holidays)?
    YES
    NO

15. If you have had a break in your present job, could you indicate what this was for and how long it lasted?

16. Do you ever work extra hours?
    OFTEN
    SOMETIMES
    NEVER

17. If you work extra hours are these paid or unpaid?
    PAID
    UNPAID
    OTHER (e.g. time off in lieu)

18. Were you in paid employment prior to working here?
    YES
    NO

19. If no, were you:
    FULL-TIME STUDENT/TRAINEE
    UNEMPLOYED AND SIGNING ON
    UNEMPLOYED AND NOT SIGNING ON
    CHILD-REARING/HOUSE KEEPING
    OTHER (e.g. long-standing illness, travel etc.)

20. What was your last occupation?
    JOB TITLE/OCCUPATION
    ORGANIZATION/INDUSTRY
    or:
    DIDN'T HAVE ONE

Appendix 2

21. How long were you in your last job?
    — YEARS   — MONTHS

22. Why did you leave that job?

23. Are you currently doing any other paid work?
    YES
    NO

24. What other paid work are you doing?

25. On the whole, do you enjoy your job?
    MOSTLY
    SOMETIMES
    NOT VERY MUCH

26. How long do you think you will go on working here?
    LESS THAN 1–6 MONTHS
    LESS THAN 12 MONTHS
    MORE THAN 12 MONTHS
    NO PLANS TO LEAVE
    DON'T KNOW

27. How would you describe the pay you get in your job?
    EXCELLENT
    GOOD
    FAIR
    POOR
    VERY POOR

28. Could you indicate which bracket your take-home pay comes into?

Weekly	Annual
Less than £40	Less than £2000
£41–80	£2001–4000
£81–120	£4001–6000
£121–180	£6001–9000
£181–240	£9001–12,000
Over £240	Over £12,000

Finally, I would like to ask you some questions about yourself.

29. What is your age now?

30. At what age did you complete full-time education?

31. What are the highest educational qualifications you have obtained?
    'CSE'/'O' LEVEL or equivalent
    'A' LEVEL or equivalent
    DEGREE or equivalent professional
    OTHER (please specify)

32. What is your marital status?
SINGLE
MARRIED
SEPARATED/DIVORCED
WIDOWED
NOT MARRIED BUT LIVING WITH PARTNER

33. How many other people, including children, live with you?
Sex   Relationship to you   Age
1.
2.
3.
4.
5.
6.
To sum up, you share your house with — other people.

34. How easy or difficult do you find it to combine your job with your other commitments (e.g. child-care, household chores)?
VERY EASY
QUITE EASY
QUITE DIFFICULT
VERY DIFFICULT

35. Do you ever meet your co-workers socially, out of work hours?
ONCE A WEEK OR MORE OFTEN
ONCE A MONTH OR MORE OFTEN
ONCE A YEAR OR MORE OFTEN
NEVER

36. If you had to say you were middle or working-class, which would you say?
MIDDLE
WORKING
DON'T KNOW/OTHER

37. Which ethnic/racial group would you say you belonged to?
WHITE
AFRO-CARIBBEAN
AFRICAN
ASIAN
OTHER (please specify)

References

ACKER, J. (1990) Hierarchies, jobs, bodies: A theory of gendered organizations, *Gender and Society*, **4**, (2) June, pp. 139–58.

ACKER, S. (1989) (Ed.) *Teachers, Gender and Careers*, London: Falmer Press.

ADKINS, L. (1995) *Gendered Work: Sexuality, Family and the Labour Market*, Buckingham: Open University Press.

ALLATT, P., KELL, T., BRYMAN, A. and BYTHEWAY, B. (1987) *Women and the Life-Cycle: Transitions and Turning Points*, London: Macmillan Press.

ANTHIAS, F. (1983) Sexual divisions and ethnic adaption: The case of the Greek Cypriot women, in PHIZACKLEA, A. (Ed.) *One Way Ticket: Migration and Female Labour*, London: Routledge and Kegan Paul.

ASHBRIDGE MANAGEMENT COLLEGE (1988) *Management for the Future*, Ashbridge Management Research Group/Foundation for Management Education, quoted in BROWN, H. (1992) *Women Organizing*, London: Routledge.

ASTIN, H. S. (1984) The meaning of work in women's lives: A socio-psychological model of career choice in work behaviour, *The Counselling Psychologist*, **12**, pp. 446–83.

BAGGULEY, P. and WALBY, S. (1988) *Women and Local Labour Markets: A Comparative Analysis of Five Counties*, Lancaster Regionalism Group Working Paper, University of Lancaster.

BARKER, J. and DOWNING, H. (1980) Word processing and the transformation of the patriarchal relations of control in the office, *Capital and Class*, Special Issue **10**, Spring, pp. 64–99.

BARRETT, M. (1980) *Women's Oppression Today: Problems in Marxist Feminist Analysis*, London: Verso.

BARRETT, M. and MCINTOSH, M. (1979) Christine Delphy: Towards a materialist feminism? *Feminist Review*, **1**, pp. 51–72.

BARRETT, M. and MCINTOSH, M. (1980) The 'family wage': Some problems for socialists and feminists, *Capital and Class*, **11**, pp. 51–72.

BARRON, R. D. and NORRIS, G. M. (1976) Sexual divisions and the dual labour market, in BARKER, D. L. and ALLEN, S. (Eds) *Dependence and Exploitation in Work and Marriage*, London: Longmans.

BEECHEY, V. (1977) Some notes on female wage labour in capitalist production, *Capital and Class*, **3**, Autumn, pp. 45–66.

BEECHEY, V. (1978) Women and production: A critical analysis of some socio-logical theories of women's work, in KUHN, A. and WOLPE, A. M. (Eds) *Feminism and Materialism: Women and Modes of Production*, London: Routledge.

BEECHEY, V. (1983) What's so special about women's employment? A review of some recent studies of women's paid work, *Feminist Review*, **15**, pp. 23–45.

BENSTON, M. (1969) The political economy of women's liberation in *Monthly Review*, **21** (4). Reprinted in TANNER, L. B. (Ed.) *Voices from Women's Liberation*, New York: Signet.

BLAND, L., BRUNSON, C., HOBSON, D. and WINSHIP, J. (1978) Women 'inside and outside': The relations of production, in Women's Studies Group, Centre for Contemporary Cultural Studies, University of Birmingham, *Women Take Issue: Aspects of Women's Subordination*, London: Hutchinson.

BOURNE, P. G. and WICKLER, N. J. (1978) Commitment and the culture mandate: Women in medicine, *Social Problems*, **25**, pp. 430–40.

BOWLES, G. and DUELLI KLEIN, R. (1983) *Thories of Women's Studies*, London: Routledge and Kegan Paul.

BOWMAN, M. and NORTON, M. (1986) *Raising Money For Women*, London: Bedford Square Press.

BRADLEY, H. (1989) *Men's Work, Women's Work: A Sociological History of the Sexual Division of Labour in Employment*, Cambridge: Polity Press.

BRADLEY, K. and GELB, A. (1983) *Co-operation at Work: The Mondragon Experience*, London: Heinemann Educational.

BRANNEN, J. and MOSS, P. (1991) *Managing Mothers: Dual Earner Households After Maternity Leave*, London: Unwin Hyman Ltd.

BREWIS, J. and GREY, C. (1994) Re-eroticizing the organization: An exegesis and a critique, *Gender, Work and Organization*, **1**, (2) April, pp. 67–82.

BRISTOL COUNCIL FOR VOLUNTARY SERVICE (1989 sixth edition) *The Guide to Bristol's Community Groups*, reference booklet suplied by BCVS, The Southville Centre, Southville, Bristol.

BROWN, H. (1990) Women's centres: Relationships between values and action, *Journal of Management Studies*, **27**, (6), pp. 619–35.

BROWN, H. (1992) *Women Organising*, London: Routledge.

BRUEGAL, I. (1979) Women as a reserve army of labour: A note on recent British experience, *Feminist Review*, **3**, pp. 12–23.

BUCHANAN, D., BODDY, D. and McCALMAN, J. (1988) Getting in, getting on, getting out and getting back, in BRYMAN, A. (Ed.) *Doing Research in Organizations*, London: Routledge.

BURRELL, G. (1984) Sex and organization analysis, *Organizational Studies*, **5**, (2), pp. 97–118.

CADMAN, E., CHESTER, G. and PIVOT, A. (1981) *Rolling Our Own: Women as*

Printers, Publishers and Distributors, Minority Press, Group Series No. 4, London: Minority Press.

CARTER, N. (1987) *Control, Consciousness and Change: A Study of the Development Process of a Worker's Co-operative*, unpublished PhD thesis, University of Bath.

1991 Census Report of Great Britain (1993) Office of Population, Census and Surveys, London: HMSO.

COATES, K. (Ed.) (1976) *The New Worker's Co-operatives*, Nottingham: Spokesman Books for the Institute of Worker's Control.

COCKBURN, C. (1983) *Brothers, Male Dominance and Technological Change*, London: Pluto Press.

COCKBURN, C. (1985) *Machinery of Dominance: Women, Men and Technical Know-how*, London: Pluto Press.

COCKBURN, C. (1986) The relaxation of technology: What implications for the theories of sex and class? in CROMPTON, R. and MANN, M. *Gender and Stratification*, Cambridge: Polity Press.

COCKBURN, C. (1988) The gendering of jobs: Workplace relations and the reproduction of sex segregation, in WALBY, S. (Ed.) *Gender Segregation at Work*, Milton Keynes: Open University Press.

COLLINSON, D. L., KNIGHTS, D. and COLLINSON, M. (1990) *Managing to Discriminate*, London: Routledge.

CORNFORTH, C. (1981) *The Garment Co-operative: An Experiment in Industrial Democracy and Business Creation*, Co-operatives Research Unit Case Study No. 5, Milton Keynes: The Open University.

CORNFORTH, C. (1983) Some factors affecting the success or failure of worker co-operatives: A review of empirical research in the United Kingdom, *Economic and Industrial Democracy An International Journal*, **4**, pp. 163–90.

CORNFORTH, .C. and HOOKER, C. (1989) Conceptions of management in the social economy, paper presented to the Conference on Management, Organisation and the Social Economy, 8–9 March, Milton Keynes: The Open University.

CORNFORTH, C., THOMAS, A., LEWIS, J. and SPEAR, R. (1988) *Developing Successful Workers's Co-operatives*, London: Sage Publications.

COSER, L. A. (1974) *Greedy Institutions: Patterns of Undivided Commitment*, New York: Free Press.

COYLE, A. (1984) *Redundant Women*, London: The Women's Press.

COYLE, A. and SKINNER, J. (1988) *Women and Work: Positive Action for Change*, Basingstoke: Macmillan Education.

CRAIB, I. (1992) *Anthony Giddens*, London: Routledge.

CROMIE, S. and HAYES, J. (1988) Towards a typology of female entrepreneurs, *The Sociological Review*, **36**, (1) February, pp. 87–113.

CROMPTON, R. and SANDERSON, K. (1990) *Gendered Jobs and Social Change*, London: Unwin Hyman.

CROWLEY, H. and HIMMELWEIT, S. (1992) *Knowing Women: Feminism and Knowledge*, Milton Keynes: Polity Press in association with Blackwell Publishers Ltd and The Open University.

DALE, A. and GLOVER, J. (1990) *Analysis of Women's Employment Patterns in the UK, France and the USA: The Value of Survey-Based Comparisons*, Department of Employment Research Paper 75, UK.

DALLA COSTA, M. and JAMES, S. (1972) *The Power of Women and the Subversion of the Community*, Bristol: Falling Wall Press.

DELPHY, C. (1977) The main enemy: A materialist analysis of women's oppression, *Explorations of Feminism*, **3**, London: Women's Research and Resources Centre.

DELPHY, C. (1980a) A materialist feminism is possible, *Feminist Review*, **4**, pp. 79–105.

DELPHY, C. (1980b) Patriarchy, feminism and their intellectuals, DELPHY, C. (1984) *Close to Home: A Materialist Analysis of Women's Oppression*, translated and edited by Leonard, D., London: Hutchinson.

DELPHY, C. and LEONARD, D. (1992) *Familiar Exploitation: A New Analysis of Marriage in Contemporary Western Societies*, Cambridge: Polity Press.

DEPARTMENT of EMPLOYMENT (1988) *Employment for the 1990s*, White Paper, London: HMSO.

DEPARTMENT of EMPLOYMENT (1991) Employment statistics, *Employment Gazette*, **99**, (6) May.

DEX, S. (1984) *Women's Work Histories; An Analysis of the Women and Employment Survey*, Research paper 46, London: Department of Employment.

DEX, S. (1985) *The Sexual Division of Work*, Brighton: Wheatsheaf Books.

DEX, S. (1988) *Women's Attitudes Towards Work*, Basingstoke: Macmillan Press.

DIAMOND, I. and QUINBY, L. (Eds) (1988) *Feminism and Foucault: Reflections and Resistance*, Boston, MA: Northeastern University Press.

DOERINGER, P. B. and PIORE, M. J. (1971) *Internal Labour Markets and Manpower Analysis*, Lexington, MA: Lexington Books.

EASTLEA, B. (1983) *Fathering the Unthinkable: Masculinity, Scientists and the Nuclear Arms Race*, London: Pluto Press.

ECCLES, T. (1981) *Under New Management*, London: Pan Books.

EHRLICH, C. (1981) The unhappy marriage of marxism and feminism: Can it be saved? in SARGEANT, L. (Ed.) *Women in Revolution: The Unhappy Marriage of Marxism and Feminism*, London: Pluto Press.

ELSHTAIN, J. B. (1981) *Public Man, Private Woman: Women in Social and Political Thought*, Princeton, NJ: Princeton University Press.

EMERSON, T. (1983) *The Story of Neighbourhood Textiles*, Co-operatives Research Unit Case Study No. 6, Milton Keynes: The Open University.

EQUAL OPPORTUNITIES COMMISSION (1988) *Women and Men in Britain; A Statistical Profile*, London: HMSO.

ESSEX, S., COLLENDER, C., REES, T. and WINCKLER, V. (1986) *New Styles of Training for Women: An Evaluation of South Glamorgan Women's Workshop*, Manchester: Equal Opportunities Commission, HMSO.

European Foundation for the Improvement of Living and Working Conditions Annual Report (1991) Luxembourg: Office for Publications of the European Community.

EVERYWOMAN (1990) *The Everywoman Directory of Women's Co-operatives and Other Enterprises*, London: Everywoman.

FERGUSON, M. and WICKE, J. (1994) *Feminism and postmodernism*, Durham, NC: Duke University Press.

FILBY, M. (1992) The figures, the personality and the bums: Service work and sexuality, *Work, Employment and Society*, **6**, (1) March, pp. 23–42.

FINCH, J. and MASON, J. (1993) *Negotiating Family Responsibilities*, London: Routledge.

FLEDBERG, R. and GLENN, E. (1979) Male versus female: Job versus gender models in the sociology of work, *Social Problems*, **26**, (5) June, pp. 524–38.

FOUCAULT, M. (1979) *The History of Sexuality: An Introduction*, translated by Hurley, R., Harmondsworth: Penguin.

FOUCAULT, M. (1985) *The Use of Pleasure*, translated by Hurley, R., Harmondsworth: Penguin.

FOUCAULT, M. (1986) *The Care of the Self*, translated by Hurley, R., Harmondsworth: Penguin.

FRANKENBERG, R. (1966) *Communities in Britain: Social Life in Town and Country*, Harmondsworth: Penguin.

FREEMAN, J. (1974) The tyranny of structurelessness, *Berkeley Journal of Sociology*, **17**, pp. 151–64.

FREEMAN, J. (1979) Resource mobilization and strategy: A model for analyzing social movement organization actions, in ZALD, M. N. and McCARTHY, J. D. (Eds) *The Dynamics of Social Movements*, Cambridge, MA: Winthrop.

FRIED, A. (1994) 'It's hard to change what we want to change': Rape crisis centers as organizations, *Gender and Society*, **8**, (4) December, pp. 562–83.

GARDINER, J. (1976) Domestic labour in capitalist society, in BARKER, D. L. and ALLEN, S. *Dependence and Exploitation in Work and Marriage*, London: Longmans.

GIDDENS, A. (1984) *The Construction of Society: Outline of the Theory of Structuration*, Cambridge: Polity Press.

GIDDENS, A. (1990) *The Consequences of Modernity*, Cambridge: Polity Press.

GITTINS, D. (1993) *The Family in Question: Changing Households and Familiar Ideologies*, Basingstoke: Macmillan Press.

GLENDINNING, C. and MILLAR, J. (1987) *Women and Poverty in Britain*, Brighton: Wheatsheaf Books, Ltd.

GOFFEE, R. and SCASE, R. (1985) *Women in Charge: The Experiences of Female Entrepreneurs*, London: Allen and Unwin.

GOODNOW, J. J. and BOWES, J. M. (1994) *Men, Women and Household Work*, Oxford: Oxford University Press.

GOULD, M. (1980) When women create an organization: The ideological imperatives of feminism, in DUNKERLEY, D. and SALAMAN, G. *The International Yearbook of Organizational Studies 1979*, London: Routledge and Kegan Paul, pp. 237–51.

GREED, C. (1991) *Surveying Sisters: Women in a Traditional Male Profession*, London: Routledge.

GUTEK, B. A. (1985) *Sex and the Workplace: Impact of Sexual Behavior and Harassment on Women, Men and Organizations*, San Francisco, CA: Jossey Bass.

GUTEK, B. A. and LARWOOD, L. (1987) *Women's Career Development*, Newbury Park, CA: Sage Publications.

HACKER, S. (1988) Gender and technology at the Mondragon system of producer co-operatives, *Economic and Industrial Democracy: An International Journal*, **9**, (2) May, pp. 225–43.

HACKER, S. (1989) *Pleasure, Power and Technology: Some Tales of Gender, Engineering and the Co-operative Workplace*, London: Unwin Hyman.

HADJIFOTIOU, N. (1983) *Women and Harassment at Work*, London: Pluto Press.

HADLEY, R. and HATCH, S. (1980) *Research on the Voluntary Sector: Some Proposals for Exploring Alternative Problems of Welfare Provision*, a Report to the SSRC Sociology and Social Administrative Committee, London: Social Science Research Council.

HAKIM, C. (1979) *Occupational Segregation*, Research Paper No. 9, December, London: Department of Employment.

HAKIM, C. (1981) Job segregation: Trends in the 1970s, *Employment Gazette*, December, pp. 521–9.

HAKIM, C. (1991) Grateful slaves and self-made women: Fact and fantasy in women's work orientation, *European Sociological Review*, Oxford: Oxford University Press, **7**, (2) Sept, pp. 101–21.

HALL, M. (1989) Private experience in the public domain: Lesbians in organizations, HEARN, J. et al. (Eds) (1992) *The Sexuality of Organization*, London: Sage Publications, Ltd.

HANDY, C. (1988) *Understanding Voluntary Organizations*, Harmondsworth: Penguin.

HARDING, S. (1981) What is the material basis of capitalism and patriarchy? in SARGEANT, L. (Ed.) *Women in Revolution: The Unhappy Marriage of Marxism and Feminism*, London: Pluto Press.

HARTMANN, H. (1979) Capitalism, patriarchy and job segregation by sex, in EISENSTEIN, Z. (Ed.) *Capitalist Patriarchy and the Case for Socialist Feminism*, New York: Monthly Review Press.

HARTMANN, H. (1981) The unhappy marriage of marxism and feminism:

Towards a more progressive union, in Sargeant, L. (Ed.) *Women in Revolution: The Unhappy Marriage of Marxism and Feminism*, London: Pluto Press.

Hartsock, N. (1990) Foucault to power: A theory of women? in Nicholson, L. (Ed.) (1990) *Feminism/Postmodernism*, London: Routledge.

Hatch, S. (1980) *Outside the State: Voluntary Organisations in Three English Towns*, London: Croom Helm.

Hearn, J. (1977) Towards the concept of a non-career, *Sociological Review*, **25**, (2), pp. 273–88.

Hearn, J. (1981) Crisis, careers and careers guidance, *British Journal of Guidance and Counselling*, **9**, (1), pp. 12–23.

Hearn, J. and Parkin, W. (1987) *'Sex' at 'Work': The Power and Paradox of Organizational Sexuality*, Brighton: Wheatsheaf Books.

Hearn, J., Sheppard, D. L., Tancred-Sheriff, P. and Burrell, G. (Eds) (1989) *The Sexuality of Organization*, London: Sage Publications, Ltd.

Hertz, L. (1986) *The Business Amazons*, London: Andre Deutsch.

Himmelweit, S. (1983) Production rules OK – Waged work and the family, in Segal, L. (Ed.) *What's to Be Done About the Family?*, Harmondsworth: Penguin in association with the Socialist Society.

Holland, J. (1980) *Women and Work: A Review of Explanations for the Maintenance and Reproduction of Sexual Divisions*, Bedford Ways Paper 6, London: University of London.

Howarth, R. (1988) *Women's Link Up: Report of the Fifth National Conference*, Leeds: Industrial Common Ownership Movement.

Humphries, J. (1977) Class struggle and the persistence of the working-class family, *Cambridge Journal of Economics*, **1**, (1), pp. 241–58.

Industrial Common Ownership Movement (1983) *The Co-operative Way*, Leeds: ICOM Publications.

Industrial Common Ownership Movement (1991) *Women's Link-Up Newsletter Issue No. 1*, August.

Jackall, R. and Crain, J. (1984) The shape of the small worker co-operative movement, in Jackall, R. and Levin, H. M. (Eds) *Work Co-operatives in America*, San Francisco, CA: University of California Press.

Jeffreys, S. (1990) *Anticlimax: A Feminist Perspective on the Sexual Revolution*, London: The Women's Press.

Jeffreys, S. (1993) *The Lesbian Heresy*, London: The Women's Press.

Jeffries, K. and Thomas, A. (1987) Measuring the performance of worker co-operatives, in Hopper, T. and Cooper, D. (Eds) *Critical Accounts*, Macmillan: London.

Jensen, J., Hagen, E. and Reddy, C. (1988) *Feminization of the Labour Force: Paradoxes and Promises*, Cambridge: Polity Press.

Johnson, N. (1981) *Voluntary Social Services*, Oxford: Blackwell and M. Robinson.

Kanter, R. M. (1975) Women and the structure of organizations: Explorations in theory and behaviour, in Millman, M. and Kanter, R. M. *Another*

Voice: Feminist Perspectives on Social Life and Social Science, New York: Anchor Press/Doubleday.

KNIGHTS, D. and WILLMOTT, H. (Eds) (1986) *Gender and the Labour Process*, Aldershot: Gower Publishing.

Labour Force Survey 1990 and 1991, a survey carried out by OPCS, the General Register for Scotland and the Department of Economic Development in Northern Ireland, on behalf of the Department of Employment and the European Community (1992) OPCS Series LFS no. 9, London: HMSO.

LAND, H. (1982) The family wage, in EVANS, M. *The Woman Question: Readings on the Subordination of Women*, London: Fontana.

LANDRY, C., MORLEY, D., SOUTHWOOD, R. and WRIGHT, P. (1985) *What a Way to Run a Railroad: An Analysis of Radical Failure*, London: Comedia Publishing Group.

LANE, J. E. (1981) *The Motivation of Full-Time Workers in Voluntary Agencies*, unpublished MSc thesis, Cranfield Institute of Technology.

LAWRENCE, B. (1987) The fifth dimension – Gender and general practice, in SPENCER, A. and PODMORE, D. (Eds) *In a Man's World: Essays on Women in Male-Dominated Professions*, London: Tavistocks Pub.

LEGGE, K. (1987) The fifth dimension – gender and general practice in SPENCER, A. and PODMORE, D. (Eds) *In a Man's World: Essays on Women in Male-Dominated Professions*, London: Tavistock Pub.

LEWIS, J. (1984) *Women in England 1870–1950*, Brighton: Wheatsheaf Books.

LEWIS, J. and PIACHARD, D. (1987) Women and poverty in the C20, in GLENDINNING, C. and MILLAR, J. *Women and Poverty in Britain*, Brighton: Wheatsheaf Books, Ltd.

LOCKETT, M. (1978) *Fakenham Enterprises Limited*, Co-operatives Research Unit Monograph No. 1, Milton Keynes: The Open University.

LOGAN, C. and GREGORY, D. (1981) *Co-operatives and Job Creation in Wales; A Feasability Study*, Wales, TUC.

MACFARLANE, R. (1987) *Collective Management Under Growth: A Case Study of Suma Wholefoods*, Co-operatives Research Unit Case Study No. 8, Milton Keynes: The Open University.

MACKINNON, C. A. (1979) *Sexual Harassment of Working Women: A Case of Sex Discrimination*, New Haven, CT: Yale University Press.

MACKINNON, C. A. (1982) Feminism, marxism, method and the state: An agenda for theory, *Signs: Journal of Women in Culture and Society*, **7**, (3), pp. 515–44.

MACKINNON, C. A. (1983) Feminism, marxism, method and the state: Towards feminist jurisprudence, *Signs: Journal of Women in Culture and Society*, **8**, (4), pp. 635–5.

MACKINNON, C. A. (1987) *Feminism Unmodified: Discourses on Life and Law*, Cambridge, MA: Harvard University Press.

MACNALLY, F. (1979) *Women For Hire: A Study of the Female Office Worker*, London: Macmillan.

References

McNay, L. (1992) *Foucault and Feminism: Power, Gender and the Self*, Cambridge: Polity Press in association with Blackwell Publishers.

McRae, S. (1991) *Maternity Rights in Britain: The Experience of Women and Employers*, London: Policy Studies Institute.

Mansbridge, J. J. (1980) *Beyond Adversary Democracy*, New York: Basic Books Inc.

Marshall, J. (1984) *Women Managers: Travellers in a Male World*, Chichester: Wiley.

Martin, J. (1989) *Some Techniques for Collective Working*, Co-operatives Research Unit, Milton Keynes: The Open University.

Martin, J. and Roberts, C. (1984) *Women and Employment: A Lifetime Perspective*, the Report of the 1980 Department of Employment/Office of Population, Censuses and Surveys, Women and Employment Survey, London: HMSO.

Martin, J. and Wallace, J. (1984) *Working Women in Recession: Employment, Redundancy and Unemployment*, Oxford: Oxford University Press.

Martin, P. Y. (1990) Rethinking feminist organizations, *Gender and Society*, **4**, (2) June, pp. 182–206.

Mellor, M., Hannah, J. and Stirling, J. (1988) *Worker Co-operatives in Theory and Practice*, Milton Keynes: Open University Press.

Mincer, J. (1960) Labor force participation of married women: A study of labor supply, in National Bureau of Economic Research, *Aspects of Labour Economics*, Princeton, NJ: Princeton University Press.

Mincer, J. (1966) Labour force participation and unemployment: A review of recent evidence, in Gordon, R. and Gordon, M. (Eds) *Prosperity and Unemployment*, New York: John Wiley.

Mitchell, J. (1974) *Psychoanalysis and Feminism*, London: Allen Lane.

Morris, L. (1990) *The Workings of the Household*, Cambridge: Polity Press.

Munroe, C. (1989) *Finance for Worker Co-ops*, Co-operatives Research Unit Monograph No. 8, Milton Keynes: The Open University.

Musgrove, B. and Wheeler Bennett, J. (1972) *Women at Work*, London: Peter Owen, Ltd.

Myrdal, A. and Klein, V. (1956) *Women's Two Roles: Home and Work*, London: Routledge and Kegan Paul.

Nicholson, L. (Ed.) (1990) *Feminism/Postmodernism*, London: Routledge.

Nieva, V. F. and Gutek, B. A. (1981) *Women and Work: A Psychological Perspective*, New York: Praeger.

Oakeshott, R. (1978) *The Case for Worker's Co-operatives*, London: Routledge and Kegan Paul.

O'Connor, R. and Kelly, P. (1980) *A Study of Industrial Workers' Co-operatives*, Dublin: The Economic and Social Research Institute.

Oerton, S. (1993) A safer place in which to work? The disclosure of lesbianism in the feminist research process, paper presented to the British Sociological Association Conference on Research Imaginations, University of Essex, 5–8 April.

OERTON, S. (1994) Exploring women workers' motives for employment in co-operative and collective organizations, *Journal of Gender Studies*, **3**, (3) November, pp. 289–97.

OERTON, S. (1996) Sexualizing the organization, lesbianizing the women: Gender, sexuality and flat organizations, *Gender, Work and Organization*, **3**, (1) January, pp. 26–37.

OLESEN, V. L. and KATSURANSIS, F. (1978) Urban nomads: Women in temporary clerical services, in STROMBERG, A. H. and HARKNESS, S. (Eds) *Women Working*, Palo Alto, CA: Mayfield.

OLIVER, N. (1987) *The Evolution of Recycles Limited 1977–1983*, Co-operatives Research Unit Case Study No. 9, Milton Keynes: The Open University.

OPEN UNIVERSITY CO-OPERATIVE RESEARCH UNIT (1989) *Directory of Co-ops in the UK, 1988*, Milton Keynes: Open University.

PARSONS, T. and BALES, R. F. (1956) *Family Socialisation and Interaction Process*, London: Routledge.

PATON, R. (1979) *Fairblow Dynamics*, Co-operatives Research Unit Monograph No. 2, Milton Keynes: The Open University.

PATON, R. (1980) *Some Problems of Co-operative Organization*, Co-operatives Research Unit Monograph No. 3, Milton Keynes: The Open University.

PATON, R. (1991) The social economy: Value-based organizations in the wider society in BATSLEER, J., CORNFORTH, C. and PATON, R. *Issues in Voluntary and Non-Profit Management*, Wokingham Addison-Wesley Publishing Company in association with The Open University.

PAVALKO, R. M. (1971) *Sociology of Occupations and Professions*, Itasca, IL: F. E. Peacock Inc.

PIORE, M. J. (1975) Notes for a theory of labour market stratification, in EDWARDS, R. L., REICH, M. and GORDON, D. M. (Eds) *Labour Market Segmentation*, Lexington, MA: D. C. Heath.

PLUMPTON, B. (1988) *Oakleaf: The Story of a Radical Bookshop*, Co-operatives Research Unit Case Study No. 11, Milton Keynes: The Open University.

POLLERT, A. (1981) *Girls, Wives, Factory Lives*, London: Macmillan.

PRINGLE, R. (1989) *Secretaries Talk: Sexuality, Power and Work*, London: Verso.

PURCELL, K. (1986) Work, employment and unemployment, in BURGESS, R. (Ed.) *Key Variables in Social Investigation*, London: Routledge and Kegon Paul.

RAMAZANOGLU, C. (1989) *Feminism and the Contradictions of Oppression*, London: Routledge.

REES, T. (1992) *Women and the Labour Market*, London: Routledge.

RHOADES, R. (1980) *Milkwood Co-operative Ltd.*, Co-operatives Research Unit Case Study No. 4, Milton Keynes: The Open University.

RICH, A. (1980) Compulsory heterosexuality and lesbian existence, *Signs: Journal of Women in Culture and Society*, **5**, (4), pp. 631–60.

References

RIGGE, M. and YOUNG, M. (1983) *Revolution From Within: Co-operatives and Co-operation in British Industry*, London: Weinfield and Nicholdson.

ROBERTS, I. and HOLYROYD, G. (1990) Small firms and family forms, paper presented at the British Sociological Association Conference, April, Guildford: University of Surrey.

ROSENEIL, S. (1995) *Disarming Patriarchy: Feminism and Political Action at Greenham*, Buckingham: Open University Press.

ROTHSCHILD-WHITT, J. (1979) The collectivist organization: An alternative to rational-bureaucratic models, *American Sociological Review*, August, **44**, pp. 509–27.

ROTHSCHILD, J. (1990) Feminist values and the democratic management of work organizations, paper presented to the 12th World Congress of Sociology, International Sociological Association, Madrid, Spain, July.

ROTHSCHILD, J. and WHITT, J. A. (1986) *The Co-operative Workplace: Potentials and Dilemmas of Organizational Democracy and Participation*, Cambridge: Cambridge University Press.

RUBERY, J. (1980) Structured labour markets, worker organization and low pay, in AMSDEN, A. H. (Ed.) *The Economics of Women and Work*, Harmondsworth: Penguin.

SARGEANT, L. (Ed.) (1981) *Women in Revolution: The Unhappy Marriage of Marxism and Feminism*, London: Pluto Press.

SCASE, R. and GOFFEE, R. (1980) *The Real World of the Small Business Owner*, London: Croom Helm.

SCHNEIDER, B. (1988) Invisible and independent: Lesbians' experiences in the workplace, in STROMBERG, A. H. and HARKNESS, S. *Women Working: Theories and Facts in Perspective*, Mountain View, CA: Mayfield Pub. Co.

SECCOMBE, W. (1974) The housewife and her labour under capitalism, *New Left Review*, **83**, pp. 3–24.

SHARPE, S. (1984) *Double Identity: The Lives of Working Mothers*, Harmondsworth: Penguin.

SPENCER, A. and PODMORE, D. (1987) *In a Man's World: Essays on Women in Male-Dominated Professions*, London: Tavistock Publications.

SPENDER, D. (1980) *Man-made Language*, London: Routledge and Kegan Paul.

SPENDER, D. (1982) *Invisible Women*, London: Writers and Readers Publishing Co-operative.

SQUIRELL, G. (1989) In passing . . . teachers and sexual orientation, in ACKER, S. (Ed.) *Teachers, Gender and Careers*, London: Falmer Press.

STANTON, A. (1983) *Collective Working in the Personal Social Services: A Study with Nine Agencies*, unpublished MSc thesis, Cranfield Institute of Technology.

STANTON, A. (1989) *Invitation to Self-Management*, Ruislip: Dab Hand Press.

STROMBERG, A. H. and HARKNESS, S. (1988) *Women Working: Theories and Facts in Perspective*, Mountain View, CA: Mayfield Publishing Company.

TANCRED-SHERIFF, P. (1989) Gender, sexuality and the labour process, in HEARN, J., et al. (Ed.) *The Sexuality of Organization*, London: Sage Publications, Ltd.

TAYLOR, A. (1986) *Worker Co-operatives and the Social Economy*, Leeds: ICOM Publications.

TAYLOR, N. (Ed.) (1986) *All in a Day's Work: A Report on Anti-Lesbian Discrimination in Employment and Unemployment*, London: Lesbian Employment Rights.

THOMAS, A. (1985) *Clothing Co-ops*, Co-operatives Research Unit Occasional Paper No. 5, Milton Keynes: The Open University.

THOMAS, A. (1990) UK worker co-operatives, 1989: Towards the 10,000 jobs mark? in *Yearbook of Co-operative Enterprises*, pp. 175–84, Milton Keynes: The Open University.

THOMAS, A.M. and KITZINGER, C. (1994) 'It's Just Something That Happens: the invisibility of sexual harassment in the workplace' in *Gender, Work and Organization*, **1**, 3, July 1994, pp. 151–61.

THOMAS, M. and THOMAS, A. (1989) Participative or collective working: A characteristic of social economy organisations?, paper presented to the Conference on Management, Organisation and the Social Economy, 8–9 March, Milton Keynes: Open University.

THOMAS, A. and THORNLEY, J. (Eds) (1989) *Co-ops to the Rescue*, London: ICOM Co-Publications.

THORNLEY, J. (1981) *Worker's Co-operatives: Jobs and Dreams*, London: Heineman Educational Books.

TREVITHICK, P. (1987) *Local Resource Centres for Women*, Bristol: Bristol Womankind.

TYNAN, E. (1980a) *Unit 58*, Co-operatives Research Unit Case Study No. 1, Milton Keynes: The Open University.

TYNAN, E. (1980b) *Little Women*, Co-operatives Research Unit Case Study No. 2, Milton Keynes: The Open University.

TYNAN, E. (1980c) *Sunderlandia*, Co-operatives Research Unit Case Study No. 3, Milton Keynes: The Open University.

TYNAN, E. and THOMAS, A. (1981) *Careers of Activists in Workers Co-operatives*, Working Paper, Co-operatives Research Unit, Milton Keynes: The Open University.

TYNAN, E. and THOMAS, A. (1984) *KME: Working in a Large Co-operative*, Co-operatives Research Unit Monograph No. 6, Milton Keynes: The Open University.

UNDERCURRENTS (1981) *Women in Co-ops*, Special Issue No. **44**, June–July.

VANCE, C. (1989) Social construction theory: Problems in the history of sexuality, in ALTMAN, D., et al. (Eds) *Homosexuality, Which Homosexuality? Essays from the International Scientific Conference on Gay and Lesbian Studies*, Amsterdam: Schorer/London GMP Publishers.

WAJCMAN, J. (1983) *Women in Control: Dilemmas of a Worker's Co-operative*, Milton Keynes: Open University Press.

WALBY, S. (1986a) Gender, class and stratification: Towards a new approach, in CROMPTON, R. and MANN, M. (Eds) *Gender and Stratification*, Cambridge: Polity Press.

WALBY, S. (1986b) *Patriarchy at Work*, Cambridge: Polity Press.

WALBY, S. (1988) Gender politics and social theory, *Sociology*, **22**, (2) May, pp. 215–32.

WALBY, S. (1990) *Theorising Patriarchy*, Oxford: Basil Blackwell.

WALES CO-OPERATIVE CENTRE (1988) *Wales Co-operatives Centre Co-operatives Directory, 1988*, reference booklet supplied by the Wales Co-operatives Development and Training Centre Ltd, Cardiff.

WALLSGROVE, R. (1990) 'Working collectively', *Off Our Backs*, **xx**, (20) February, pp. 20–21.

WEST, J. (Ed.) (1982) *Women, Work and the Labour Market*, London: Routledge and Kegan Paul.

WESTWOOD, S. (1984) *All Day, Every Day: Factory and Family in the Making of Women's Lives*, London: Pluto Press.

WILLIS, P. (1977) *Learning to Labour: How Working-Class Kids Get Working-Class Jobs*, London: Saxon House.

WISE, S. and STANLEY, L. (1987) *Georgie Porgie: Sexual Harassment in Everyday Life*, London: Pandora Press.

WOOLHAM, J. (1987) *Wholegrain Foods and the Bean Shop: Organisational Problems in Small Co-operatives*, Co-operatives Research Unit Case Study No. 10, Milton Keynes: The Open University.

YEANDLE, S. (1984) *Women's Working Lives: Patterns and Strategies*, London: Tavistock Publications.

YOUNG, I. (1981) Beyond the unhappy marriage: A critique of dual systems theory in SARGENT, L. (Ed.) *Women in Revolution: The Unhappy Marriage of Marxism and Feminism*, London: Pluto Press.

ZARETSKY, E. (1976) *Capitalism, the Family and Personal Life*, London: Pluto Press.

Index

Acker, J. 73
Adkins, L. 72–3
age, of interviewees 98
agency–oriented approaches 11, 51
  relationship with socio-structural
    approach 187–8
  to workers in flatter organizations
    10–11, 12, 85–6, 177, 184–7
  see also resistance; women workers
all-women organizations 6, 95
  see also women-only organizations

Barker, J. 57
Barrett, M. 42, 44, 45–6
Barron, R.D. 41
Beechey, V. 42
benefits 104–5
Bland, L. 42
Bowman, M. 24
Bradley, H. 45
burn-out, in women's flatter organizations
  107
businesses, research on women's 20–3

capitalism
  in marxist feminist analyses of women's
    work 40–3
  and patriarchy in feminist analyses of
    work 46–8, 62
careers
  career breaks 162
  career profiles of flatter organization
    workers 28–30, 53
  flatter organizations as challenge to
    gendered career paths 153–8
  tenure and turnover in flatter
    organizations 107–8
  women's work profiles 52–3

child-care commitments 112–13, 167–72,
  178–9
  see also motherhood
class, see social class
clerical workers, culture of resistance 57–8
Cockburn, C. 74–5
collective organizations
  failings and marginalization of 16–17,
    18–19, 25–6
  features of 15–16
  tenure and turnover in 29–30
  women-only collectives 5–6
collective-exploitation 84, 115–18, 179, 180
collectivist-democracy, see flatter
    organizations
Collinson, D.L. 48, 49
control
  familialism as means of 59–60
  by workers in flatter organizations 146,
    147–8
co-operatives
  benefits of 28
  failings and marginalization of 18–19,
    25–6, 123
  features of 15, 17–18
  informal hierarchies and inequalities in
    27, 76
  research on gender issues in 23–4, 26–9
  tenure and turnover in 28–9
  women in 5, 20, 21, 24, 52, 76
Cornforth, C. 17, 29
Coyle, A. 37
Crain, J. 5
Cromie, S. 22

decision making, by workers in flatter
    organizations 146, 147–8
Delphy, C. 44–6, 77

flexibility, of flatter organizations 148–50, 179
Foucault, M. 69–70
  feminist use of Foucauldian analysis 71
Freeman, J. 17
funding, *see* finances and funding

gay men
  expression of sexuality in flatter organizations 173–4
  research on experiences at work 66–7
  see also homosexualization
gender
  challenges to and subversion of stereotypes of 152–3, 158–61
  feminist analyses of sexuality and 70–3
  feminist approaches to inequalities in paid work 43–9
  Foucauldian analysis of sexuality and 69–71
  gendered processes in flatter organizations 8, 9, 10, 76–7, 84–5, 158, 176–80
  gendering of technologies 74, 75
  marxist feminist approaches to inequalities in paid work 40–3
  neglected in research on voluntary sector 19
  occupational segregation by 33–4, 39, 41–2, 46, 47
  and research on flatter organizations 7, 23–9, 87
  and sexuality in organizations 73–7
  in stereotypes of flatter organizations 125–6
gender differences
  in commitment, familialism and self-exploitation 26, 51–2, 115, 117–22, 166, 179, 180
  in earnings 102–6, 115, 177
  in family and work commitments 110–13
  in full and part-time work 34–6, 105–6, 179
  in perceived benefits of flatter organizations 147–9
  in presentation of self and organizations 129–30, 159
  in resistance 145, 184–6
  in turnover and tenure 106–10, 178
gender/job model 37–9, 77
Goffee, R. 20–2

Hacker, S. 75–6
Hakim, C. 35–6
Hall, M. 67–8
Hartmann, H. 46–7
Hayes, J. 22
Hearn, J. 62, 63, 64–5
Hertz, L. 52
heterosexuality
  discourses in flatter organizations of 137–8
  discourses in hierarchical organizations of 65, 66, 68
  as feature of power relations at work 64, 73
hierarchical organizations
  discourses of heterosexuality in 65, 66, 68
  familialism in 59
  gender and sexuality in 73
hierarchy
  flatter organizations as challenge to power of 146–9, 182–3
  informal in co-operatives 27
homosexualization 138–40, 183
  see also gay men; lesbianization
housework, *see* domestic roles
Howarth, R. 20

income, *see* earnings
interviews 88, 92–3
  interviewee profiles 96–9

Jackall, R. 5
job-creation and saving 18, 94–5

labour market
  influence on women's employment position 39, 102
  marxist feminist theory of dual labour market 41–2
  patterns of women's participation in 32
  reserve army of labour 42–3
  role of sexuality in 72
  see also occupational segregation by gender
Landry, C. 17
Lane, J.E. 19
Legge, K. 54
Lesbian Rights Support Group 68
lesbianism
  agency and structural aspects of 188, 189

Index

voluntary sector 3, 19, 24

wages, *see* earnings
Wajcman, J. 25, 26, 52
Walby, S. 39, 47–9
Wallsgrove, R. 25
welfare benefits 104–5
Westwood, S. 55
Whitt, J. Allen 16
Wicke, J. 71
women entrepreneurs, research on 20–3
women workers
  as active agents 10–11, 48–9, 51, 86
    occupational choices 35–6, 53, 54, 55, 156–7
    resistance to sexualization and familialism 64, 66, 72–3
    subversion of gender stereotypes 158–60
    temporary workers 57, 58
    women's work cultures 55–6, 57
  career breaks 161–2
  commitment, self-exploitation and familialism at work 51–2, 84, 115, 118–22, 179, 180
  disadvantaged position in flatter organizations 84–5, 102
  earnings 33, 102–6
  employment/family dichotomy 21–3, 38–9, 176
  family and work commitments 32–3, 110–13, 166–71
  feminist approaches to women's work 43
    concept of family wage 44
    domestic mode of production 44–6
    interaction of capitalism and patriarchy 46–8
  marginalization of 25–6, 181–3
    heterosexual discourse and sexualization 48, 63, 66, 137
    as lacking competence and maturity 132–3
    lesbianization 138, 140–4, 181–3
    as peripheral to real world 130–1
    ridiculed as odd 136
    as secondary workers 134
  marxist feminist approaches to women's work
    domestic labour debate 40

dual labour market 41–2
  reserve army of labour 42–3
occupational segregation 33–4, 39, 41–2, 46, 47
part-time employment 34–6, 105–6, 179
participation in co-operatives 5, 20, 21, 24, 52, 76
participation in voluntary sector 24
patterns of employment 32
sociological approaches to women's work 36–7
socio-structural theories of women's work 9–10, 51
support from co-workers 163–5
tenure and turnover in flatter organizations 106–7, 108, 109, 178
workplace cultures of 55–6, 150–1, 179
women-only organizations
  development of 5–6
  ridiculing and marginalization of 25, 136–7
  see also all-women organizations
women's flatter organizations
  marginalization of 25–6, 181–3
    heterosexual discourse 137
    as lacking competence and maturity 132
    notions of 'deviant' sexuality 138, 140–4
    problems of funding 142–3, 144, 182
    ridiculing of 133–4, 136–7
    stereotypes of feminism 140–4
  self-exploitation 116, 117
  support from co-workers 163–5
  tenure and turnover in 106–7
  understanding of family commitments 168–9
  women's centres 6
  see also all-women organizations; women-only organizations
worker co-operatives, *see* co-operatives
workers
  as active agents, *see* resistance
  political goals of 95–6
  profiles of interviewees 96–9
  see also men workers; women workers
workplace cultures 55–7, 150–3, 179

Yeandle, S. 53